Southern Living

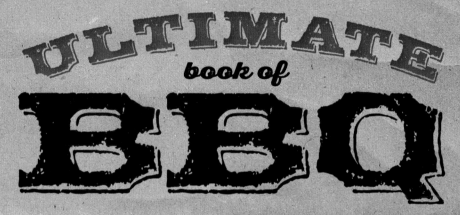

ULTIMATE
book of
BBQ

with **PITMASTER**
CHRISTOPHER PRIETO

text by
ASHLEY STRICKLAND FREEMAN

Oxmoor
House®

CONTENTS

For a long time, we Southerners were rigidly parochial in our barbecue preferences, insisting that "real barbecue" was whatever local style we ate growing up. In recent years, though, aided by television shows, books, and the Internet, we're becoming increasingly well-versed in the abundant and diverse varieties found across the South. We enjoy sampling a wide assortment of sauces, meats, and side dishes, and deciding for ourselves the ones we like best.

This book brings those various recipes together into a single volume that surveys the many different ways that Southerners cook and enjoy barbecue today. It starts with the basics—the history, the cuts of meat, the equipment. And then it's time to get cooking.

For master-level guidance on all things meat, *Southern Living* turned to Christopher Prieto, champion pitmaster and proprietor of PRIME Barbecue near Raleigh, North Carolina. Raised in Houston, Prieto learned early on the beef-centric flavors of Texas-style barbecue. After honing his skills on the Kansas City Barbecue Society circuit, Prieto set up shop midway between the whole-hog and pork shoulder regions of North Carolina.

Prieto draws upon this cross-regional experience to give step-by-step instructions for cooking old standbys like beef brisket and pork butt, as well as more esoteric cuts like beef ribs and spatchcock turkey. His insights are supplemented by tips from some of the South's most noted pitmasters, like Tim Byres of Smoke in Dallas, Justin and Jonathan Fox of Atlanta's Fox Bros. Bar-B-Q, and Carey Bringle of Nashville's Peg Leg Porker.

Low-and-slow may be the traditional barbecue mode, but Southerners love to grill hot and fast, too, and this book provides an array of ideas for grilling beef, chops, fish, and chicken. There are insider tips on how to keep vegetables from sticking to the grill, inventive ways to use backyard grills, and even recipes for grilling pizzas.

We tend to associate barbecue with summer, for that's the peak season for outdoor dining. But the bold flavors of barbecue can—and should—be enjoyed any time. Several soups and chilis offer a touch of smoke for cooler days, and hearty cuts like beef chuck rolls and dishes like grilled balsamic Brussels sprouts are perfect year-round. There's even a selection of "rainy day" recipes for the stove-top or slow cooker.

No meal would be complete without plenty of side dishes, and the editors have selected the best *Southern Living* has to offer. Some are barbecue icons—collard greens, hush puppies, baked beans. Others, like grilled watermelon with prosciutto, have a more contemporary flair. And, of course, there are recipes for the full range of regional sauces, from the fiery eastern North Carolina vinegar sauce to the tangy Alabama white sauce, plus six varieties of coleslaw.

Taken together, it's a comprehensive survey of the techniques and styles of contemporary Southern barbecue. Whether you're looking to entertain with pit-cooked pork shoulders or grill a few steaks for a casual family meal, there is much to choose from within these pages. So get that fire going. It's time to eat.

**ROBERT MOSS,
CHARLESTON, SOUTH CAROLINA
JANUARY 2015**

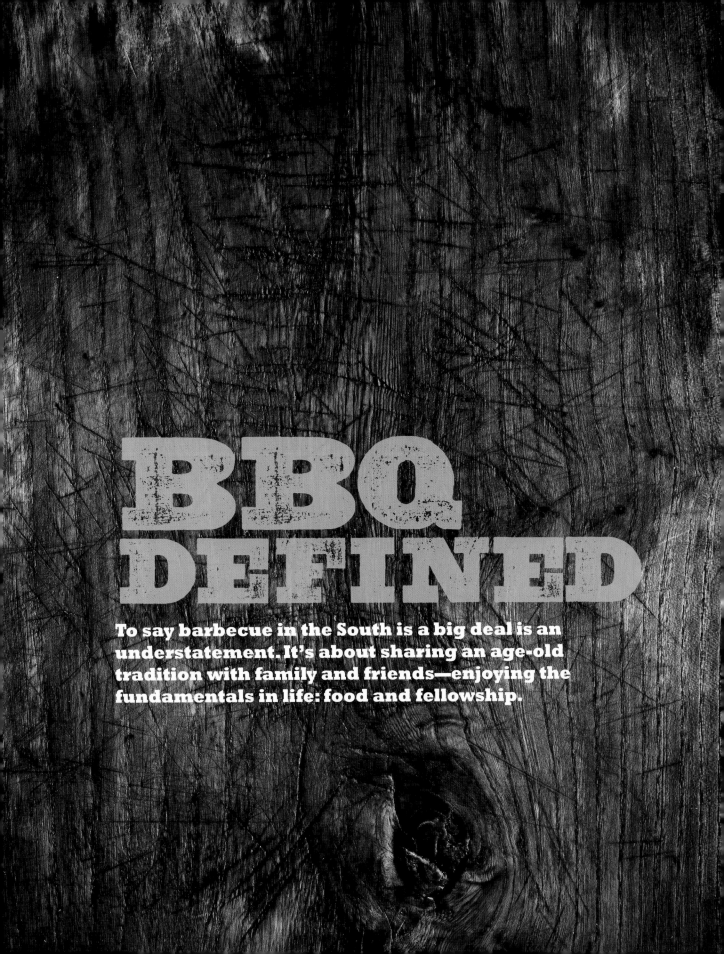

BBQ DEFINED

To say barbecue in the South is a big deal is an understatement. It's about sharing an age-old tradition with family and friends—enjoying the fundamentals in life: food and fellowship.

BBQ THEN & NOW

Regions throughout the country take real pride in their barbecue, and it is a culinary delight that is quintessentially American.

While few will argue that achieving delicious barbecue takes deft seasoning and just the right amount of smoke, to a Southerner, it requires a little bit more—it also takes care, dedication, and attention.

Southerners love to debate the finer points of sauce and style, but barbecue brings people together far more than it pushes them apart. On any given day at the local barbecue joint, you'll see high-powered executives in tailored suits sitting elbow to elbow with stay-at-home moms or construction workers. In backyards and at community gatherings, you'll find toddlers, teenagers, and old-timers sipping sweet tea side by side and enjoying pulled pork, sliced brisket, and pork ribs—maybe all three.

Ask 10 different Southerners where the best barbecue can be found and you're bound to get 10 different answers—and each of them is likely to name a barbecue joint they've been visiting for years. Ask a pitmaster for his recipe for barbecue and he'll have an answer, too: It's top-secret. Many barbecue operations are family affairs, and often recipes go to the grave.

But while most Southerners agree that bona fide barbecue requires cooking meat low and slow over a fire, they often disagree about what type of meat or sauce makes the best. There are even skirmishes about favorite sides and drinks. Everyone has an opinion, and everyone is more than happy to share it.

A BRIEF BBQ HISTORY

Cooking meat over a fire is nothing new; it's basically been around since fire was discovered. And smoking is an age-old way to extend the life of meat when refrigeration isn't an option. Our modern-day barbecue blends these two ancient methods, with adaptations from different cultural and regional influences. Who settled a particular area of the country, the way they cooked and seasoned their meat, and what products were available affected what kind of barbecue became the specialty of each region of the South.

A lot of fanciful explanations have been offered to explain where the term "barbecue" came from. Many have claimed it's the French phrase *barbe à queue*, which means head-to-tail cooking, like whole-hog barbecue in North Carolina. Others say it's from the Bar BQ Ranch in Texas, where they branded "BQ" on the cattle. The dictionary-makers, though, point to the Taíno people of the Caribbean, whose word *baribicu*—referring to the frame of sticks over which they dried and cooked meat—became *barbacoa* in Spanish and barbecue in English.

SOUTHERN ORIGINS

All over the South, you'll find a patchwork of barbecue styles, with countless variations in meat and sauce. The many nuances to this American favorite changed over time as the result of a range of different influences.

The barbecue technique that took root in Virginia and the Carolinas evolved from a process the British borrowed from Native Americans: drying or cooking meat on a grill of green sticks over a smoldering fire. They combined the methods they learned with those they brought from England, basting the meat with butter or vinegar to keep it moist during cooking. During the 19th century, salt and black or

red pepper were the typical seasonings in the sauce—and you can still find this formula today, especially with Carolina-style whole-hog barbecue, which is doused in a vinegary-pepper sauce.

As Americans moved westward, they took with them their traditions of pit-cooking meat outdoors, carrying barbecue across the Appalachians into Kentucky and Tennessee, and then across the Mississippi into Texas and beyond. Immigrants from other cultures added their tastes and recipes to each region, too, resulting in myriad flavors and styles. The Piedmont of North Carolina was inhabited by a large German population, a fact to which historians point to explain the popularity of German-style coleslaw (it's vinegar-based as opposed to mayonnaise-based) as a barbecue side.

In central South Carolina, German immigrants have been credited with introducing mustard, crown-ing their pulled pork with a tangy, bright yellow sauce. Germans also settled a large part of Texas, as did Czechs, and they introduced traditions of meat smoking to the area. The first bar-becue restaurants in Texas sprang up in meat markets, where butchers sold smoked meats to cotton pick-ers on sheets of butcher paper, along with crack-ers and pickles. In Kentucky, mutton (lamb) was prolific, so it was the meat of choice, and a spicy stew called burgoo was always served along with it.

As commercial food manufacturing and distribution developed, it shaped America's regional barbecue styles. In the Piedmont of North Carolina, pitmasters began cook-ing pork shoulder instead of the whole hog during the early 20th century as those smaller cuts became commercially available. Around the same time, tomato-based sauces began to make their appearance thanks to manufac-tured products such as ketchup. In the 1960s, the rise of a national meat-packing industry with standardized cuts prompted most Texas meat markets to switch from buying and butchering forequarters of beef to cooking pre-packaged cuts, with brisket becoming the cut of choice.

BBQ TASTES TODAY

Today, boundaries have blurred somewhat between the barbecue regions. Tennessee barbecue is just as varied as its geography, with smoked shoulder and sweet, tomato-based sauce in the Appalachian Mountains and eastern Carolina-style whole-hog and slaw in the west. In whis-key country, you'll find the potent libation lurking in barbecue sauce, while Memphis is home to smoked shoulder and dry-rubbed ribs. Wet ribs with tomato-based sauce are prominent in Kansas City, as is beef brisket, a result of the city's history as a cattle stockyards. In Alabama, a range of sauces, from vinegar- to ketchup-based types to the distinctive white barbecue sauce, are on menus. You'll also find pork shoulder and ribs. And in South Carolina, don't assume it's just about mustard-based sauces—you can find everything from thin tomato-based sauce near the North Carolina border to spicy vinegar-based varieties in the northeast-ern part of the state.

BBQ&A

WHAT IS IT?

In the South, barbecue is a noun, and that noun does not include what you cook the meat on.

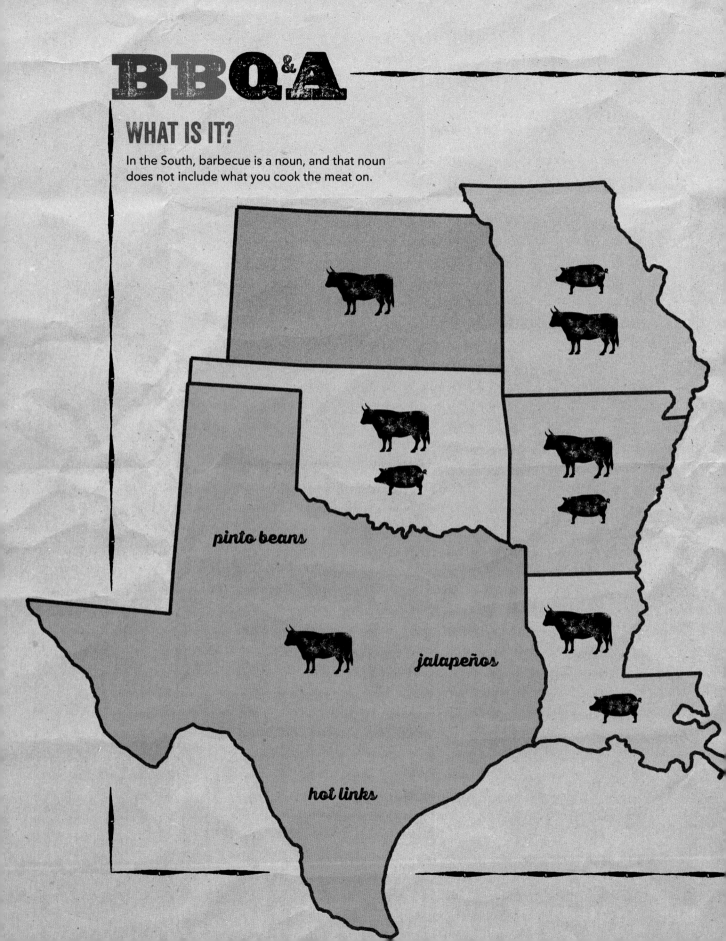

pinto beans

jalapeños

hot links

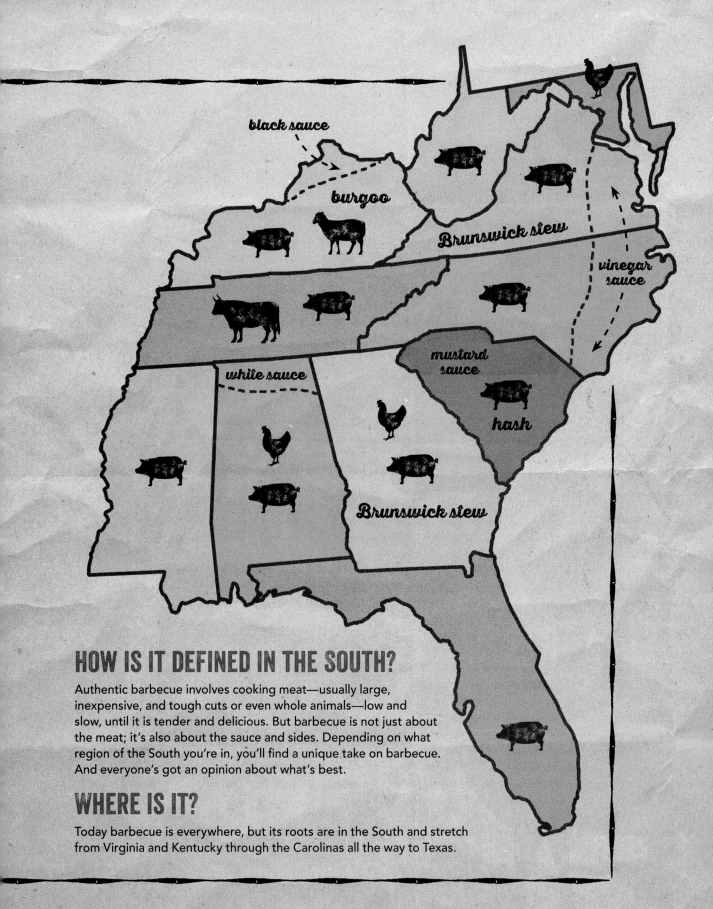

black sauce

burgoo

Brunswick stew

vinegar
sauce

mustard
sauce

hash

white sauce

Brunswick stew

HOW IS IT DEFINED IN THE SOUTH?

Authentic barbecue involves cooking meat—usually large, inexpensive, and tough cuts or even whole animals—low and slow, until it is tender and delicious. But barbecue is not just about the meat; it's also about the sauce and sides. Depending on what region of the South you're in, you'll find a unique take on barbecue. And everyone's got an opinion about what's best.

WHERE IS IT?

Today barbecue is everywhere, but its roots are in the South and stretch from Virginia and Kentucky through the Carolinas all the way to Texas.

WHAT ARE THE BEST MEATS?

Regional favorites came to be because certain animals were more readily available than others. While you'll most likely find pork in almost every barbecue joint, some meats take precedence in certain regions.

FINGER-LICKIN' CHICKEN

While many pitmasters add chicken to their menus, smoked chicken is especially popular in Maryland, northern Alabama, and Georgia.

PIG OUT

Pork is probably the most popular meat for traditional barbecue. In eastern North Carolina, whole-hog barbecue is the way to go. Whole hogs are cooked low and slow over wood. Then everything is chopped and pulled by hand—sometimes even including the skin. Elsewhere, pork shoulder or hams are more common.

WHERE'S THE BEEF?

In Texas and the Midwest, it's all about the beef, where cattle are free to roam over acres and acres of land. Brisket, beef ribs, and hot links are the barbecue of choice at joints in these parts.

EVERYTHING ELSE

Mutton is a favorite in the mountain region of Kentucky, and slow cooking this often-tough meat makes it super tender. In central Texas—while it pales in comparison to the popularity of beef—don't be surprised to find goat barbecue. (You also can find goat in certain areas of Mississippi.) Turkey, lamb, and even duck can be found if you look hard enough.

WHAT'S IN A SAUCE?

This essential element of barbecue has been the cause for many barbecue feuds. Barbecue sauce usually has at least one of the following bases: vinegar, tomato/ketchup, or mustard. Some sauces can even include two or more of these, but typically one flavor stands out.

A range of sweeteners, from sugar to molasses to honey, can be added in as well. The result is a rainbow of sauces to choose from, and every region has its favorite. In many parts of Texas, barbecue fans insist that the proper sauce is no sauce at all.

RED TOMATO-BASED SAUCE

You'll find this sauce all over, but every region tends to add its own twist. In Texas, you'll taste the influences of Mexico in a spicy pepper-enhanced version. In Memphis, the sauce is sweetened with brown sugar or molasses for sticky and sweet ribs.

WHITE MAYONNAISE-BASED SAUCE

Normally found in northern Alabama, this tangy sauce combines flavors of mayonnaise, vinegar, and black pepper, and is delicious served on smoked chicken. The consistency depends on the creator—it can range from thin to thick.

BLACK WORCESTERSHIRE-BASED SAUCE

This sauce is probably the rarest of the regional sauces and is available in western Kentucky. It's made from a blend of vinegar and Worcestershire sauce and is served with lamb and mutton.

YELLOW MUSTARD-BASED SAUCE

This is how they like it in central South Carolina, generally well-sweetened with brown sugar and/or honey.

CLEAR VINEGAR-BASED SAUCE

This sauce is indigenous to eastern North Carolina and Virginia, where a mixture of cider vinegar and crushed red pepper is typically doused on whole-hog barbecue.

YOUR SIDE OR MINE?

Some Southern regions also are pretty opinionated about what's served with their barbecue. While baked beans, coleslaw, hush puppies, potato salad, French fries, corn on the cob, and slices of white bread are standard, certain areas of the barbecue belt offer up their own tasty options.

HOT LINKS *(pictured counterclockwise from top)*

In Texas, a barbecue plate is naked without a few of these accompaniments.

HASH

Popular in South Carolina, this stew-type dish generally made with fresh pork shoulder is often served over rice.

BURGOO

Similar to Brunswick stew, this spicy Kentucky dish often includes pork or chicken along with a range of veggies, and in many parts mutton gives it a distinctively rich, gamey flavor.

BRUNSWICK STEW

Though its origin is hotly debated, Brunswick stew is a must alongside pulled pork and ribs in Georgia, Virginia, and parts of the Carolinas and Tennessee. It's a tomato-based stew with chunks of vegetables and pork, beef, and/or chicken.

DRINKS

Like the meat, sauce, and sides, what you use to wash down your barbecue depends upon where you hang your hat. Coca-Cola and sweet tea, for example, are the drinks of choice throughout the South. In Texas Hill Country, a bottle of Big Red is preferred, while other parts of Texas serve locally brewed beer. In North Carolina, it's Cheerwine, the cherry-flavored soft drink that's been a staple there since it was created in 1917.

BONA FIDE BBQ

In much of the South, pork is considered the quintessential barbecue meat, but don't be afraid to smoke up beef, chicken, turkey, lamb, seafood, and even vegetables.

PORK

When it comes to barbecue, Southerners can't seem to get enough of pork. But when pitmasters are choosing what cut of the hog to use, they often have specific preferences.

PICKIN' PARTS OF THE PIG

A pig pickin' is a common party in the South, especially in the Carolinas and the Lowcountry. These parties center around an entire hog that is slow-cooked over a fire for hours. When it's pulled off the fire, guests can pick the tender meat right off the pig.

Whole-hog cooking also is found at many restaurants throughout the South, although it's becoming a lost art. Barbecue joints outside of eastern North Carolina may smoke pork shoulders instead of the whole animal. Check out the meats to the right, and on the following pages, to see how you can create authentic pulled, chopped, or sliced pork at home, or fire up the grill for hot and fast pork chops and other cuts made for quick cooking.

tip from the **PITS**

I like loin back ribs because they are the most tender. I'm sure you've heard the saying "high on the hog." Loin back ribs are higher on the animal so they are more tender.

SKIP STEELE, PAPPY'S SMOKEHOUSE, ST. LOUIS

❶ PORK SHOULDER

This is the ideal cut for authentic, slow-cooked barbecue pork. That's because the hog's shoulder is naturally full of connective tissues, so when cooked at high temperatures, the meat becomes tough. But when you cook it low and slow, the tissues melt away and baste the meat in its own juices, leaving you with a barbecue that's moist and flavorful. Whole pork shoulder can be difficult to find at the grocery store, so opt for a smaller Boston butt, which comes from the upper part of the front leg, above the shoulder blade, and has lots of fat and marbling.

❷ PICNIC HAM

Don't let the name fool you—this cut is not a ham you'd slice for sandwiches or serve for a holiday meal. Also known as just "picnic," this cut includes the lower portion of the hog's foreleg and contains more fat than the shoulder, which results in very rich meat. The picnic is best cooked low and slow, and is often reserved for pulled pork, grinding, or braising.

❸ PORK SPARERIBS

These large and highly flavorful ribs are cut from the bottom of the hog's rib cage and often include the brisket—bony meat hanging from the bottom of the slab. Spareribs require a longer cooking time than smaller baby back ribs, and are generally more flavorful because the meat has more fat and marbling. They are best when cooked low and slow, and when basted and wrapped during the final hours of cooking.

❹ ST. LOUIS CUT RIBS

This cut of rib is also known as Kansas City cut and just means that the extra rib tips from a traditional rack of spareribs have been removed and what remains is a flat rectangular slab. St. Louis cut rib bones are straight and flat, so they are ideal for browning on the stove-top.

❺ COUNTRY-STYLE SPARERIBS

These ribs are the meatiest of all, with a higher meat-to-bone ratio. But, they're not really ribs at all. They are cut from the front part of the baby back ribs near the shoulder, and they're best prepared like pork chops or braised in the oven or slow cooker.

BBQ&A

Pulled, chopped, or sliced?

Stumble upon a local barbecue joint and there's a good chance you can guess what type of barbecue will be served based on what area of the South you're in. In North Carolina, the pork will probably be finely chopped. In South Carolina, Georgia, and Alabama (as well as many other Southern spots), you'll find pulled barbecue. To achieve the long, succulent strands of meat, pitmasters either pull the meat by hand (wearing heat-resistant gloves, of course) or with two forks. You'll occasionally find sliced pork, too, but slicing is often reserved for beef brisket, especially in Texas.

Once you've decided among pulled, chopped, or sliced, you might want to consider whether you want moist inside meat or drier, smokier, and crunchier outside meat, called the bark. Many barbecue joints let you choose—and you can't go wrong either way.

❻ BABY BACK RIBS

The meatiest and tenderest of the ribs, baby back ribs are perfect as appetizers because they're also the shortest and smallest. They are cut from underneath the loin muscle and tend to have a more curved shape than spareribs. The meat is lean and mild, so these ribs should be cooked low and slow, then basted and wrapped for the most delicious results.

❼ PORK CHOPS

There are many different types of pork chops to choose from, and they are all delicious. You can cook them quickly on the grill, or indoors on the stovetop when the weather is less than ideal, or you can slowly smoke them for extra flavor.

LOIN CHOPS Also known as porterhouse chops, these have a T-bone in them and include the firm meat of the pork loin on one side of the bone and the tender meat of the tenderloin on the other.

RIB CHOPS These are pork chops that have been cut from a rib roast and are either boneless or bone-in with a baby back rib attached. They are very lean and are ideal for brining, stuffing, or quick-grilling.

❽ PORK LOIN *(pictured)*

This tender cut of pork runs the entire length of the hog alongside the ribs and is available as pork loin chops or a pork loin roast. Boneless loins are ideal for stuffing, but to avoid drying out, they should not be cooked to an internal temperature of higher than 140°.

❾ PORK TENDERLOIN

The tenderest cut of pork you can buy (and generally the priciest), the pork tenderloin shouldn't be confused with a pork loin roast. The tenderloin is a long, narrow, tapered muscle that lies below the loin starting just behind the last rib. It's about the size of the forearm of a 10-year-old human and weighs about 2 pounds. It's extremely tender and delicious grilled or roasted, and cut into medallions.

tip from the PITS

Look for ribs that have not been enhanced. Ribs packed in cloudy water typically means that they've been enhanced with a nitrate or sodium solution. Also buy the heaviest ribs with the most meat—about 2½ lb.—but stay away from wide-boned ribs because that indicates they are likely sow's ribs and you're paying for more bone than meat.

**SKIP STEELE,
PAPPY'S SMOKEHOUSE,
ST. LOUIS**

BEEF

Beef—certainly not overshadowed by pork— also includes several cuts ideal for low-and-slow cooking and hot-and-fast grilling. Many connoisseurs, especially those from Texas, would bet that some beef cuts (namely brisket) are even better than pork when prepared by the right pitmaster.

With acres of land dedicated to raising steer, Texans and Oklahomans are partial to beef barbecue. For slow-cooking, brisket is the prized cut. For hot-and-fast grilling, the options are endless. Grilling is one of the best ways to cook beef; it sears in the juices and enhances flavor. Beef barbecue originated mostly in Texas, via its Caribbean, German, and Czech settlers.

tip from the **PITS**

The best way to master the brisket is practice. It's not going to happen right away. If it does, rethink the business you are in! Brisket has such a small window of perfection—it's either under cooked (tough and dry) or over cooked (dry and crumbly) so it takes practice to find that right spot.

JUSTIN AND JONATHAN FOX, FOX BROS. BAR-B-Q, ATLANTA

① BRISKET

This boneless cut of beef is one of the toughest, making it ideal for long smoking over low heat. This cut is found near the breast or lower chest and is full of connective tissue and covered in a thick fat cap that adds superb flavor as it slow-cooks. Whether sliced or chopped, it's delicious served on a bun or a plate accompanied with hot links.

② CHUCK

This bulky shoulder region of the steer is where many roasts and steaks are cut. You'll find chuck roast (a great pot roast) and flat-iron steak here. Ground chuck is great for burgers with its blend of flavorful fat and meat.

③ ROUND

The hindquarters yield lean and often tough cuts of beef, so you'll want to cook these cuts low and slow. Ground round is a leaner option for burgers.

④ BEEF SPARERIBS

Located where the best meat is found, beef spareribs offer a wonderful balance of muscle and fat for great flavor. The spareribs are the curved back ribs near the spine and should be cooked low and slow.

⑤ BEEF SHORT RIBS

Beef short ribs are meatier and can be found on the sides of the steer in the short plate and into the chuck. The bones can be as long as 4 or 5 inches and are wonderful braised or cooked low and slow, followed by a quick turn on the grill.

⑥ LOIN

If you want a delicious steak, with or without the hefty price tag, this is the part of the steer from which to buy. Here is where you'll find tri-tip, tenderloin, New York strips, T-bones, porterhouse steaks, and hanger steak. Ground sirloin is the leanest option for ground beef.

⑦ TENDERLOIN

Whether whole or cut into filet mignon steaks, this cut is prized for its tenderness. It's incredibly lean, so quick-grill the steaks or pay close attention to the meat thermometer when cooking the entire tenderloin. For rare, cook to 140°; anything above 170° is well done and not recommended.

BBQ&A

Prime, Choice, or Select?

It is mandatory for the Food Safety and Inspection Service (FSIS) arm of the USDA to regulate and inspect beef for freshness. However, grading for quality is voluntary, and must be requested and paid for by meat producers and/or processors. So why pay to have beef graded? USDA grades are based on uniform Federal standards, which means all must meet the same grade criteria. USDA Prime, the highest grade beef, is produced from young, well-fed cattle and has abundant marbling. Prime roasts and steaks are excellent to broil, roast, or grill. USDA Choice is high quality, but has less marbling than Prime. Choice roasts and steaks from the loin and rib will be very tender, juicy, and flavorful and are also suited for dry-heat cooking. USDA Select is uniform in quality and leaner than higher grades. It is tender, but because it has less marbling, it may lack some of the flavor of the higher grades. Only tender cuts should be cooked with dry heat—others are best braised.

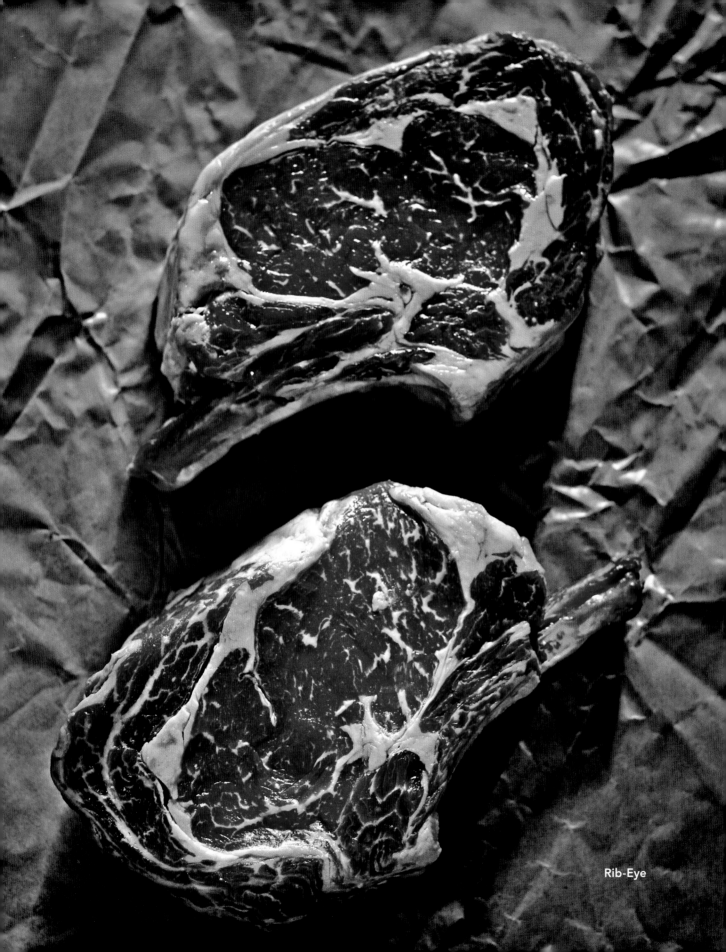

Rib-Eye

❽ STEAKS

No matter your price range, it's easy to find a delicious, steak-house-worthy steak you can enjoy without leaving your own house.

RIB-EYE This wonderfully marbled steak offers the utmost in flavor, with abundant fat that melts away as it grills. To help prevent flare-ups on the grill, trim the rim of fat around the edges of the steak.

NEW YORK STRIP Cut from the loin and also called shell steak or just strip steak, this cut is slightly firmer than a rib-eye but still offers superb flavor.

FILET MIGNON Cut from the tenderloin, filets are very lean and the most tender cut available. They also come with the heftiest price tag but are well worthy of a special occasion. For the best results, sear them quickly on a blazing hot grill.

PORTERHOUSE This steak offers the best of both worlds, with a center bone connecting a New York strip and a filet mignon. To avoid overcooking the filet portion of the steak, start out over a fire-hot side of the grill and finish on a cooler side.

T-BONE Just like a porterhouse, this steak has both the New York strip and the filet mignon, but the tenderloin is not as big due to the steak being cut farther forward on the steer.

TOP SIRLOIN This large, flat-cut steak is ideal for marinating and quick-grilling or threading onto kabobs. For the most flavor, look for sirloin steaks with a good amount of marbling, and be sure to grill them to medium rare at the most; otherwise, they could end up tough.

TRI-TIP Considered the "poor man's tenderloin," this roast is cut from the sirloin region of the steer and can be cooked like a roast or grilled like a steak. If you decide to grill it, be careful not to overcook it. It's one of those cuts that you want to grill quickly or cook low and slow for ultimate tenderness.

FLANK This flavor-rich flat steak is super for marinating and should be quickly seared. To avoid a chewy texture, cut the steak against the grain into thin slices.

SKIRT Even more flavorful and juicy than flank steak, this coarsely grained steak is found on the plate side of the steer on top of the rib bones. It's great quickly grilled and thinly sliced against the grain, or used for fajitas.

HANGER Also from the plate side of the steer, this steak is actually part of the diaphragm and hangs between the rib and the loin. Before this cut became popular among chefs, it flew under the radar and butchers often kept it for themselves. Prepare it as you would a flank or skirt steak.

FLAT-IRON Cut from the shoulder, this top blade steak is surprisingly tender. Cook it hot and fast for the ultimate texture, and remove the thin line of gristle in the center if necessary.

MUTTON & LAMB

Whether you're cooking mature sheep (mutton) or tender young lamb, both are great alternatives to beef or pork. Mutton is the preferred meat for barbecue in parts of Kentucky due to the abundance of sheep there in the late 1800s. While the sheep population is much lower there today, mutton is still a favorite on many Kentucky menus. Lamb also is an excellent "other red meat." Because it's a smaller animal, there are fewer cuts to work with for grilling, but that doesn't make them any less delicious than their pork and beef counterparts.

❶ GROUND LAMB

This ground meat is excellent for burgers if you're looking for something a little different. Cook it as you would ground beef.

❷ SHOULDER

Mutton and lamb shoulder should both be cooked low and slow, much like pork shoulder. The long cooking process tenderizes the tough meat, which can then be chopped for sandwiches or other dishes.

❸ LEG

Lamb legs can be grilled, roasted, or smoked whole to achieve delicious results. They're available with the bone in or out; if you opt for boneless leg of lamb, be sure to tie it to ensure even cooking.

❹ LAMB LOIN CHOPS *(pictured)*

Whether left as an entire rack or separated into individual chops, lamb chops are ideal for quick-grilling or roasting. If separated into chops, they are best when thick-cut. The tender lamb loin is encased in a thick layer of fat that protects the meat as it cooks. It can be trimmed away and Frenched for a fancier presentation, if desired.

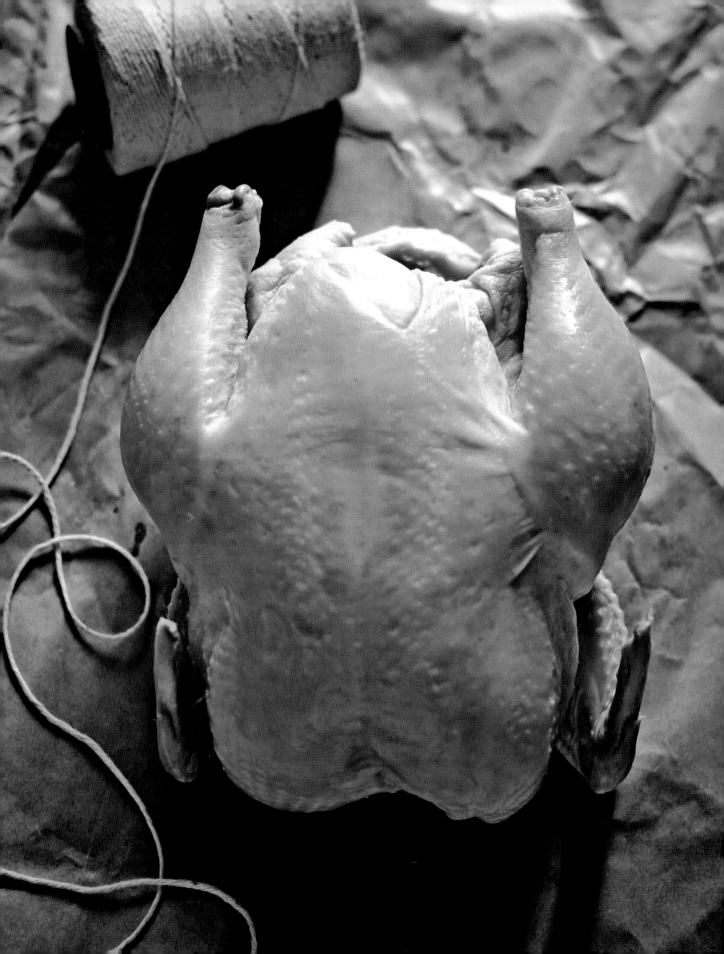

CHICKEN, TURKEY & OTHER POULTRY

This favorite white meat is almost as common as pork on barbecue restaurant menus. You can order it pulled like pork, or opt for a slow-smoked half or quarter. In northern Alabama, you'll find white, mayonnaise-based barbecue sauce to accompany smoked chicken. Turkey, duck, and Cornish hens are also flavorful choices for the grill. Whether you cook poultry low and slow or hot and fast depends on the parts of the bird you're using.

❶ WHOLE CHICKEN AND TURKEY

If smoked chicken or turkey is what you're going for, it's best to cook the entire bird all at once for several hours over indirect heat.

❷ BREASTS AND WINGS

You can grill the breasts and wings still attached or separated, but a quick-grill method is the easiest option. For the ultimate in juiciness, buy bone-in breasts. The bone helps retain the moisture for slow-smoking or quick-grilling. Boneless, skinless chicken breasts, however, are great for versatility and speed of cooking.

❸ THIGHS AND LEGS

As with breasts and wings, you can purchase thighs and legs as chicken quarters, or separated into individual pieces. The dark meat has higher fat content that yields more flavor. These versatile pieces can be slow-cooked over indirect heat or quick-grilled.

FUELING THE FIRE

We like to think that man invented fire, and then man cooked his first barbecue.

BARBECUE LIKE A PRO

The beauty of cooking barbecue is that you don't need fancy, expensive equipment to get great results. All you need is patience and a few key tools of the trade.

While many professional pitmasters use large open pits to smoke their barbecue, you can easily make pulled pork, ribs, brisket, and other favorites at home on the grill.

The first step is to determine what type of cooking you'll be doing. Authentic barbecue has to be cooked low and slow over hardwood or fruitwood. Steaks, chicken breasts, and other thin meats are best when quick-grilled. Whether you have a charcoal grill or a gas grill, you can still achieve delicious results and make barbecue like a pro in no time.

GAS & PROPANE GRILLS

Gas grills are easy to use, and they maintain a consistent temperature for long periods of time. To turn them on, open the propane valve, turn the knobs on, and use the starter to light the grill. Allow the grill to preheat with the burners on high for 10 to 15 minutes before grilling. If you are in the market for a gas grill, explore your options: If you are just starting out, go with a smaller model. If you feed larger groups, opt for a bigger grill.

CHARCOAL GRILLS

While they tend to be more hands-on, charcoal grills typically cost less than gas. They also impart a great smoky flavor, and can offer years of backyard grilling and smoking. A chimney starter is a must for lighting charcoal easily.

You will need to consider which type of charcoal to use. There are benefits to both charcoal briquettes and lump charcoal.

CHARCOAL BRIQUETTES

Charcoal briquettes are probably what you think of when you hear the word charcoal. These are compressed nuggets of sawdust, coal, and cornstarch, and they create even heat and are ideal for new grillers. Briquettes burn steadily for long periods of time and produce a great smoking setup. Be careful, though, when purchasing briquettes; some brands are soaked with lighter fluid, and if it's not burned off completely, it could impart a chemical-like taste to food.

LUMP CHARCOAL

A favorite of pitmasters, lump charcoal is created when large wood logs are burned slowly in a pit to remove the natural water and resin, leaving behind large chunks of charcoal. This charcoal is easy to light and allows for a range of heat when smoking and grilling. It also infuses your food with a delicious smoky flavor.

USING A SMOKER

If you want to take backyard barbecue to the next level, consider investing in a traditional smoker. There are many models to choose from to fit your barbecue needs.

STANDARD WATER SMOKER

A bullet-shaped smoker is great for beginners and takes up little space. Starting as low as $200, this type of smoker is perfect for the occasional backyard griller. Most come with a water pan designed to help regulate temperature and keep the meat moist during the cooking process. The charcoal and wood sit in the bottom of the smoker below the water pan, and the food is cooked on top where the vents are located.

BARREL SMOKER

Also known as an offset smoker, barrel smokers are particularly popular among Texans. The design keeps the charcoal and wood off to the side from the main barrel and features a vent to adjust the temperature. The shape also helps regulate the amount of smoke inside the barrel, and large drain valves allow for easy cleanup.

PIT SMOKER

If you love to smoke food, you may want to consider a large, heavy-duty pit smoker. These smokers have a slight advantage over small smokers: They keep a regulated temperature for longer periods of time. And because they hold more heat, you have to tend to the fire less often. Even better, they last forever with the proper care.

GAS SMOKER

If you are accustomed to gas grills, a gas smoker offers some of the same conveniences. These smokers often have stainless steel construction, a firebox, and an attached gas grill for all-in-one cooking.

SMOKING IN A CHARCOAL GRILL

You don't need a smoker to achieve great barbecue flavor. All you need is your backyard charcoal grill. Here's how to light your fire.

START CHARCOAL: With a chimney starter: Pour charcoal in chimney starter, stuff newspaper in the bottom, and light the paper. (Place the chimney in the grill while heating.) With an electric starter: Place the starter in the grill and top with charcoal. Plug in the starter and allow charcoal to stand about 5 minutes to heat. Allow the charcoal to burn until it is ashy; pile the charcoal onto one side of the grill.

COVER GRILL: Keep the lid closed and allow grill to preheat about 10 minutes. Check temperature of the grill; it should read between 225° and 250° for optimal smoking. Adjust the air vents to achieve a higher or lower temperature. To increase the heat, open vents to allow more air to circulate and fuel the fire. To decrease heat, close the vents slightly, but not completely.

ADD CHIPS: Once the grill reaches the desired temperature, place a handful or two of wet wood chips directly on top of the coals. (The chips should have soaked for at least 30 minutes.) Replace the grill grate and place the meat in the center of the grate, not directly over the pile of coals.

CLOSE THE LID: After about 5 minutes, check the thermometer to ensure the grill has maintained the correct temperature. Once it does, hands off. Keep an eye on the temperature, but keep the lid closed to allow the smoke to stay in. Every hour or so, add a handful of chips and three or four unlit charcoal briquettes.

THE MINION METHOD

When it comes to starting his smoker, our award-winning pitmaster Christopher Prieto prefers what is known as the Minion Method, which was created by Jim Minion for the Weber Smokey Mountain cooker. "One of the advantages this method has over others is there's less chance that the cooker will run hotter than you want," Prieto explains. "It's easier to start with a few hot coals and bring the temperature up to 225° to 250° than it is to start with a red-hot cooker and bring the temperature down."

The Minion Method is simple and sets up the charcoal so it achieves a longer, more consistent burn. If prepared correctly, your fire should burn between 6 and 10 hours at 225° to 275°, and will eliminate the need to add more fuel, making it ideal for meats that require long, low-and-slow cooking.

Some pitmasters create a donut-shape with the unlit charcoal chamber, then fill the hole with the lit charcoal, so the charcoal slowly burns from the inside out. There is one disadvantage to using the Minion Method: cooking over unlit charcoal. Since the Minion Method goes against the idea that charcoal briquettes should be completely lit and white before cooked over, those with sensitive palates could detect an off flavor. However, numerous winning teams on the barbecue circuit use this method without any negative effects to the quality of their barbecue.

1. FILL the smoker's charcoal chamber with unlit charcoal briquettes.

2. SPREAD several chunks of wood beneath the unlit charcoal.

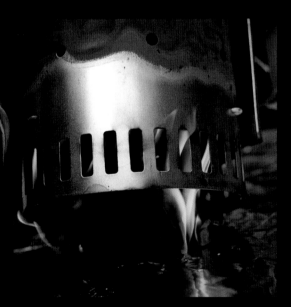

3. FILL the chimney starter about halfway with charcoal and light it.

4. AFTER 7 to 10 minutes, and once the charcoal at the top of the chimney is ash white, pour it over the unlit charcoal in the charcoal chamber. That's it.

WOODS FOR SMOKING

There are so many great options of wood for smoking, and every type has a unique flavor profile that will infuse the meat as it cooks. Stick to hardwoods (as opposed to soft woods like cedar, pine, or spruce), as soft woods contain resin and tar that can produce an unpleasant aroma and lend an off-taste to the meat. Stay away from pressure-treated woods, too; they can potentially contain harmful chemicals and toxins that you don't want to breathe in.

When choosing the type of hardwood, consider how long the meat will smoke; if it takes less time to cook, you may opt for a stronger-flavored wood to impart a smoky taste. You need to also consider whether to use wood chips or chunks.

WOOD CHIPS

Chips are best for meats that require less smoke time (two hours or less), such as steak or chicken. Since they are smaller, they burn faster.

WOOD CHUNKS

Chunks are ideal for hefty cuts of meat that require long cooking times, such as pork shoulder or brisket.

ALDER

This type of wood can infuse fish and chicken with a slightly sweet flavor.

FRUITWOODS

Delicate fruitwoods like apple, cherry, and peach are wonderful with pork, poultry, and fish.

HICKORY

Probably the most widely used, hickory is a versatile wood that is wonderful with most meat and fish. Its earthy, rich flavor strikes the perfect chord, particularly with pork.

MAPLE

Medium in smokiness, maple works well with pork, poultry, and vegetables and provides a sweet flavor.

MESQUITE

This is the strongest-flavored wood of all and is popular with Texas barbecue. It lends the utmost in smoky flavor, but can make foods bitter if used in excess. It's best for beef and robust meats.

OAK

Oak is another all-purpose wood that is milder than hickory. It's a go-to wood for pork and poultry, but can also stand up to beef.

PECAN

This Southern favorite is slightly less intense than hickory and is great for all types of meat.

WALNUT

A step below mesquite, walnut produces a strong flavor that is ideal for beef.

INDIRECT GRILLING

Large and tough cuts of meat require longer cooking times, so indirect grilling is the way to go. For this low-and-slow cooking method, the fire is built on one or both sides of the meat instead of directly underneath it, which allows the heat to circulate around the food and cook it evenly for tender, juicy barbecue. If large cuts of meat are cooked using a direct grilling method, the outside will burn before the inside cooks. This gentle method also works well for whole chickens, fish, and smaller cuts of meat to impart smoke and add a boost of extra flavor.

USING A CHARCOAL GRILL

There are several ways to set up an indirect cooking environment using a charcoal grill. You may want to use a drip pan (pictured) to catch any grease that may accumulate in order to prevent flare-ups. Choose any one of these three versions for indirect grilling:

VERSION 1

Place a drip pan in the center of the grill on the charcoal grate. Arrange hot coals on both sides of the charcoal grate. Place the grill grate on top of the setup, and grill the meat over the drip pan.

VERSION 2

Place a drip pan on one side of the grill on the charcoal grate. Arrange hot coals on the other side of the charcoal grate. Place the grill grate on top of the setup, and grill the meat over the side with the drip pan.

VERSION 3

Place a drip pan in the center of the grill on the charcoal grate. Arrange hot coals completely surrounding the pan on the charcoal grate. Place the grill grate on top of the setup, and grill the meat over the drip pan.

DIRECT GRILLING

Similar to broiling, hot-and-fast grilling directly over the heat source is ideal for tender and thin cuts of meat. It's great for searing to lock in moisture and to achieve attractive grill marks. Burgers, steaks, chicken breasts, pork chops, and fish fillets should be cooked using this method.

USING A CHARCOAL GRILL

Spread hot coals in an even layer on the charcoal grate. Replace the grill grate, and cover with the grill lid. Preheat 10 minutes, and adjust the temperature if needed by opening or closing the air vents. To increase the heat, open the vents; to decrease the heat, close the vents slightly. Place the food on the grill grate, and cook according to the recipe instructions.

USING A GAS GRILL

Light all the burners on high, close the grill lid, and preheat the grill for 10 minutes. Place the food on the grill grate, and cook according to the recipe instructions.

COMBINATION GRILLING

Sometimes using both direct and indirect grilling can greatly benefit the end result. Whether with steaks or larger cuts of meat, you can start by searing the meat over direct heat, and then transferring them to indirect heat to finish cooking. Combining the two methods also gives you more control over cooking the meat to perfection. For example, you can sear steaks or chicken over direct heat and then move them over indirect heat to finish.

tip from the PITS

Keeping your smoker or grill clean will help lengthen its life and also provide you with a smooth and flavorful cook.

Make sure to clean the ash out of your smoker 24 hours after you cook in it, and scrape the grates while they're still hot. Spread heavy-duty aluminum foil inside the bottom to prevent fat from cooking to the surface. And degrease, replace parts, and repaint those areas that need it quarterly.

CHRISTOPHER PRIETO, PRIME BARBECUE, WENDELL, NORTH CAROLINA

LOW & SLOW

Large and tough cuts of meat require longer cooking times, so low and slow is the way to go. Here award-winning North Carolina pitmaster Christopher Prieto teaches step-by-step techniques for eight popular cuts of beef, pork, and poultry.

BEEF BRISKET

Pitmaster Christopher Prieto gets real and talks brisket—one of the prime cuts of beef, and most popular for Texas barbecue.

I consider beef brisket the king of barbecue. This cut of meat comes from the chest of the cow behind the front legs and consists of two muscles: the deep pectoral muscle commonly referred to as the flat, and the supraspinatus muscle known as the point. The point, which is the fatty end of the brisket, has a rib-eye-like texture, while the flat, which runs along the entire brisket, has leaner meat like a sirloin. Whole packers include both the flat and point.

WHOLE PACKER VS. FLAT

I cook only whole packer briskets and never just flats, even though they are easier to find in stores. The point on a brisket is essential to

the cooking process because it contains a lot of marbled fat, which keeps the meat tender and moist. It's also the part of the brisket that you can re-season, add back to the smoker when the flat is fully cooked, and continue to smoke for a barbecue delicacy, burnt ends.

QUALITY IS KEY

Quality is essential to a delicious end product—I recommend CAB (certified angus beef) grades or higher. Check with your local grocer to see if they carry CAB grade meat, or order directly from a butcher. Finally, and most important, check the meat's sell-by date. You want to buy the freshest brisket possible.

what to look for	*Chris' top tips*	*best served with*
◆ A 12- to 14-lb. brisket that is longer than it is wide, and with the grain as close to lengthwise as possible	◆ Charcoal briquettes are essential to this recipe. I prefer competition briquettes.	◆ **SAUCE:** A smoky or peppery barbecue sauce cut with brisket drippings
◆ A brisket with even thickness and a solid flat	◆ Maintain a constant temperature of 250° in your smoker.	◆ **SIDES:** Pinto beans Dill pickles Sliced white onion Plain white sliced bread
◆ A layer of soft, white fat, and even marbling	◆ Rest the brisket for at least 2 hours before slicing.	

1. TRIM FAT. Remove any large or hard patches of fat from the flat (the meat that runs along the entire brisket) so the rub will adhere to the meat and create a nice bark during cooking.

2. REMOVE HARD FAT. Next, remove the hard fat heel that sits between the point and the flat. This fat should be removed because it will not render during cooking.

3. TRIM AND SHAPE. Continue trimming excess fat from the brisket, as well as any fat that appears discolored. Trim from both sides of the brisket, and square off the edges. This will help ensure an even cook.

4. CHECK THE FATCAP. Finally, check the fatcap side for any hard or large patches of fat. Trim the fatcap to ¼-inch of fat throughout. (Here I was required to trim a thicker strip of fat running the length of the brisket.)

5. FINAL PRODUCT. The finished brisket should be nice and square, with even fat and marbling throughout. Tip: If you plan to remove the point from the flat to re-smoke burnt ends later, cut a guide that "separates" the point from the flat before it goes on the smoker.

6. APPLY RUB. Brush or rub the entire brisket with Worcestershire sauce so the seasoning will stick. Once the brisket is moist, apply a heavy coating of Beef Rub (page 326) and let the brisket stand for a minimum of 4 hours before placing it on the smoker.

7. SMOKE IT. Place the brisket, fat side down, on the top food grate and close the smoker. Smoke 5 hours or until a meat thermometer inserted into the center of the brisket where the point and flat meet registers 165°.

8. CHECK THE BARK. Once the meat reaches 165°, the brisket should have a rich, dark mahogany color, and the brisket will no longer take on any smoke during the cooking process.

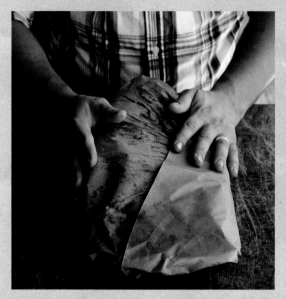

9. REMOVE AND WRAP. At this point, remove the brisket from the smoker, and wrap it tightly in wax-free butcher paper. Return it to the smoker and cook for 3 to 5 more hours, checking temperature hourly until a meat thermometer inserted into the center of the brisket registers 200°.

10. REST AND SLICE. Remove the brisket from butcher paper, and place on a cutting board, reserving some drippings in butcher paper. Slice the meat across the grain into ¼-inch-thick slices. Combine reserved drippings and El Sancho Barbecue Sauce (page 318), and serve immediately.

tip from the **PITS**

I trim the fat of the brisket before cooking, and cook fat side down. I don't wrap the brisket in aluminum foil while it smokes—the point of smoking is to let the flavor of the wood infuse the meat.

HARRISON SAPP, SOUTHERN SOUL BARBEQUE, ST. SIMONS ISLAND, GEORGIA

SMOKED BEEF BRISKET
(pictured on previous page)

The brisket is considered one of the hardest meats to master, but that's why it's also one of the most popular, especially in Texas. Look for a brisket with a lot of fat and plenty of marbling, and always cook it to medium-rare.

YIELD: 10 TO 15 SERVINGS   TOTAL: 10 TO 12 HOURS

1   (12- to 14-lb.) beef brisket, trimmed
½   cup Worcestershire sauce
1   cup Beef Rub (page 326)

3   to 4 pecan, hickory, or oak wood chunks
15   lb. charcoal briquettes
El Sancho Barbecue Sauce (page 318)

1. Brush or rub brisket generously with Worcestershire sauce. Coat entire brisket with Beef Rub and chill 1 to 4 hours.

2. Remove brisket from refrigerator, and let stand 1 hour.

3. Meanwhile prepare charcoal fire in smoker according to Minion Method (see page 39). Place water pan in smoker; add water to depth of fill line. Regulate temperature with a thermometer to 250° to 260° for 15 to 20 minutes.

4. Place brisket, fat side down, on top food grate and close smoker. Smoke 5 hours or until a meat thermometer inserted into the center of the brisket where the point and flat meet registers 165°.

5. Remove brisket from smoker, and wrap tightly in wax-free butcher paper; return brisket to smoker. Cook 3 to 5 more hours, checking temperature each hour until meat thermometer inserted into the center of the brisket registers 200°.

6. Remove brisket from smoker; open butcher paper, and allow steam to escape for 2 to 4 minutes. Re-wrap and let brisket stand in butcher paper 2 hours.

7. Remove brisket from butcher paper, and place on a cutting board, reserving ¼ cup drippings in butcher paper. Slice meat across the grain into ¼-inch-thick slices. Combine reserved drippings and El Sancho Barbecue Sauce, and serve immediately.

COWBOY SANDWICH
(pictured)

This brisket sandwich is a twist on the traditional French dip, minus the jus. It gets its kick from the pepper Jack cheese and pickled jalapeños.

YIELD: 4 SERVINGS.   TOTAL: 10 MINUTES

8   thick bread slices
4   (1-oz.) pepper Jack cheese slices

Smoked Beef Brisket
Pickled jalapeño slices

Preheat oven to 400°. Arrange bread slices on a baking sheet. Top 4 bread slices with pepper Jack cheese slices. Bake at 400° for 5 minutes or until bread is toasted and cheese is melted. Top cheese-covered bread slices with warm Smoked Beef Brisket and remaining 4 bread slices. Serve sandwiches topped with pickled jalapeño slices.

BEEF BRISKET TOSTADAS

These tasty tostadas get a Texas twist when topped with Smoked Beef Brisket. You can make this meal in minutes by picking up brisket from your favorite local barbecue joint.

YIELD: 6 SERVINGS   TOTAL: 18 MINUTES

- ½ cup fresh salsa
- 1 Tbsp. chopped fresh cilantro
- 1 (16-oz.) can refried beans
- 6 corn tostada shells
- ¼ cup chopped red onion
- 1 lb. chopped Smoked Beef Brisket without sauce, warmed (page 54)
- Garnishes: shredded lettuce, queso fresco, chopped tomatoes, lime wedges

1. Preheat oven to 400°. Stir together salsa and cilantro. Spread beans on tostada shells. Place shells on a jelly-roll pan; top with onion, brisket, and salsa.

2. Bake at 400° for 8 to 10 minutes or until thoroughly heated. Serve immediately.

CHEF'S SIDE
FOX BROS. BAR-B-Q, ATLANTA

FRITO PIE
YIELD: 10 SERVINGS   TOTAL: 50 MINUTES

- 1 Tbsp. olive oil
- 1 Tbsp. butter
- 2 cups finely chopped onion
- ¾ cup chopped jalapeño pepper
- 1 tsp. freshly ground black pepper
- 4 garlic cloves, minced
- 2 Tbsp. kosher salt
- 5 Tbsp. chili powder
- 2 Tbsp. adobo sauce from canned chipotle peppers in adobo sauce
- 1½ tsp. sugar
- 1½ tsp. granulated garlic
- 1½ tsp. freshly ground black pepper
- 1½ tsp. chipotle chile powder
- 1½ Tbsp. tomato paste
- ¼ tsp. ground cumin
- 1 (32-oz.) container beef stock
- 1 (28-oz.) can crushed tomatoes, undrained
- 3½ cups chopped Smoked Beef Brisket without sauce, warmed (page 54)
- 2 Tbsp. instant masa harina (corn flour)
- 1 cup warm water
- 10 (2-oz.) bags original corn chips
- Toppings: shredded Cheddar cheese, diced red onions, sour cream, sliced fresh jalapeño peppers, sliced green onions

1. Heat oil and butter in a Dutch oven until butter melts. Add onion and next 3 ingredients. Cover and cook over medium heat 5 minutes or until onion is tender, stirring occasionally.

2. Add salt and next 10 ingredients. Bring to a boil; reduce heat, and simmer, uncovered, 20 minutes. Stir in brisket.

3. Whisk together masa harina and warm water until blended; stir into brisket mixture. Simmer, uncovered, 10 minutes, stirring often.

4. Cut open corn chip bags at tops or sides. Place 1 bag corn chips into each of 10 bowls. Ladle 1 cup brisket mixture on top of corn chips in each bag. Top with desired toppings. Serve immediately.

BRISKET & RICE NOODLES WITH PINEAPPLE SALSA

Serving as a colorful garnish, the pickled Peppadew peppers are a briny, sweet addition to this Asian-inspired dish. Find them in the pickle and olive aisle at the grocery store.

YIELD: 4 SERVINGS   TOTAL: 30 MINUTES

1 Tbsp. kosher salt
½ (8.8-oz.) package thin rice noodles
½ fresh pineapple, peeled, cored, and finely chopped
1½ small Kirby cucumbers, seeded and sliced
⅓ cup thinly sliced red onion
2 Tbsp. chopped fresh cilantro
1½ Tbsp. seasoned rice wine vinegar
3 Tbsp. hoisin sauce
2 Tbsp. roasted peanut oil

2 Tbsp. fresh lime juice
1 Tbsp. fish sauce
1 tsp. Asian hot chili sauce (such as Sriracha)
4 cups shredded romaine lettuce
1 lb. shredded Smoked Beef Brisket, warmed (page 54)
½ cup sliced pickled Peppadew peppers
½ cup assorted torn mint, basil, and cilantro

1. Microwave 8 cups water and 1 Tbsp. kosher salt at HIGH in a large microwave-safe glass bowl 2 minutes. Submerge rice noodles in water; let stand 20 minutes or until tender. Drain.

2. Meanwhile, toss together pineapple and next 4 ingredients; add table salt and black pepper to taste.

3. Whisk together hoisin sauce, next 4 ingredients, and 2 Tbsp. water. Combine drained noodles and 2 Tbsp. hoisin sauce mixture in a medium bowl, tossing to coat.

4. Divide lettuce among 4 bowls. Top with noodles, pineapple mixture, brisket, and peppers. Drizzle with desired amount of remaining hoisin mixture. Sprinkle with herbs, and serve immediately.

The general rule of thumb is to cook a brisket for 1 hour per pound. But pay close attention to the smoker's temperature—don't let it go above 185°.

For a 12-lb. brisket, I like to cook it for a total of about 12 hours. About three-quarters of the way through, I remove it from the pit and wrap it in butcher paper, and then return it to the smoker. The natural grease soaks into the brisket instead of onto the fire and insulates the meat, creating a moist texture.

TIM BYRES, SMOKE, DALLAS

BEEF CHUCK ROLL

This massive cut of meat takes time to cook, but the end product is worth it. Christopher Prieto's low-and-slow method will yield mouthwatering meat every time.

The beef chuck roll is a unique beast of a meat, but it will provide you the best chopped beef sandwich you've ever tasted.

WHERE'S THE BEEF?

The chuck roll is considered a subprimal cut of the chuck—essentially the shoulder of the cow. This flavorful cut of beef is made up of mostly the larger, more tender muscles found in the chuck, and can be further butchered into smaller cuts, including chuck eye steaks, boneless country-style beef chuck ribs, chuck eye roast, and chuck pot roast, as well as ground beef and ground chuck. The beef chuck roll is excellent if you need to cook for a large group,

or want leftovers to freeze. Fat and collagen run throughout the meat, so it requires a long, slow cook to tenderize properly. Because the chuck roll is such a large cut of meat, cook times will be especially long (10 hours or more) so an overnight cook is ideal if you can pull it off.

FINDING AND BUYING

Don't confuse the beef chuck roll with a typical chuck roast from your local grocery store. They're not the same piece of meat by a long shot. The average chuck roll is large—about 15 to 25 pounds or more. But you can find them at some big-box grocery stores, or request one special from your butcher.

what to look for	Chris' top tips	best served with
❯ A chuck roll with very little water or blood in the packaging—too much could indicate that the meat was frozen at some point ❯ A large chuck roll that has an even shape; and a layer of soft, white fat (not yellow); consistent marbling	❯ Since the beef chuck roll consists of many different cuts of beef, rotate it on your pit if it has hot spots. ❯ Once the chuck comes off the smoker, make sure to rest it in foil so the natural juices can redistribute and be used after the meat is pulled.	❯ **SAUCE:** Smoky barbecue sauce cut with beef drippings ❯ **SIDES:** Barbecue pinto beans Slaw Potato salad Double-stuffed potato Plain white sliced bread

1. TRIM EXCESS FAT. Remove any large or hard patches of fat from the beef chuck roll so the rub will adhere to the meat and create a nice bark during cooking.

2. REMOVE SILVERSKIN. Using a sharp knife, cut off the silverskin in thin strips, angling your knife against the membrane. Continue to slide the knife along the silverskin, and pull on the membrane until it releases.

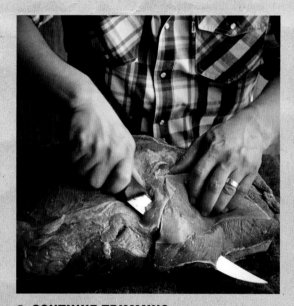

3. CONTINUE TRIMMING. The beef chuck roll has many layers of fat, silverskin, and connective tissue, so continue rotating and trimming as needed until you have an even, square piece of meat with a thin layer of fat.

4. INJECT WITH FLAVOR. Using an injector, inject the chuck roll with Beef Injection (page 334) at 1-inch intervals, making sure to fully flavor the entire chuck roll.

5. COVER WITH INJECTION. Use the remainder of your Beef Injection to liberally coat the outside of the chuck roll so the rub will stick.

6. SPRINKLE WITH RUB. Apply a heavy coating of Beef Rub (page 326) to the outside of the chuck roll. This will help create a dark, mahogany bark.

7. COAT WITH COFFEE. Apply a light coat of instant coffee granules after the rub to give the beef a unique flavor. Tip: Be sure to use instant coffee, as it will dissolve during the cooking process.

8. LET THE MEAT REST. Allow the chuck roll to chill for 1 to 4 hours before placing it on your smoker so the salt and other spices can penetrate the meat.

BEEF

9. SMOKE IT. Place beef, fat side down, on upper food grate and close the smoker. Smoke 5 to 6 hours or until a meat thermometer inserted into the thickest portion of the chuck roll registers 165°. At this point, the meat should have a rich, mahogany bark, and the meat will no longer take any smoke.

10. WRAP AND REST. Remove the chuck roll from the smoker, wrap tightly in a double layer of heavy-duty aluminum foil, and return it to the smoker. Cook another 4 to 8 hours, or until a meat thermometer inserted into the thickest portion of the chuck roll registers 205° to 210°. Remove beef from smoker; open foil, and allow steam to escape. Let chuck roll rest in foil 1 hour. Remove it from foil, and reserve drippings. Chop beef, and place in a large bowl; stir in reserved drippings. Serve immediately.

BBQ&A

ELIZABETH KARMEL, CAROLINACUETOGO.COM

What are the best spices for creating a delicious rub?

I'm a fan of not overdoing it. A lot of rubs overwhelm and cover up the meat so I like to use salt and pepper. The reason why I go only with salt and pepper is so you can taste the smoke flavor better, and the natural meat as well. I also love smoked paprika.

BEEF CHUCK ROLL

The beef chuck roll is a large cut of meat—it's like the beef version of the pork shoulder. You can find it at your local butcher shop, or at some big-box grocery stores. Choose a high-grade cut with even marbling, and cook it low and slow for delicious shredded beef.

YIELD: 15 TO 20 SERVINGS   **TOTAL: 14 TO 16 HOURS**

1   (15- to 20-lb.) beef chuck roll
2   cups Beef Injection (page 334)
½   cup Beef Rub (page 326)
½   cup instant coffee granules

4   to 6 hickory, pecan, or oak wood chunks
15   to 20 lb. charcoal briquettes
El Sancho Barbecue Sauce (page 318)

1. Remove silverskin from beef, and trim excess fat, leaving a thin layer of fat.

2. Using an injector, inject beef with Beef Injection at 1-inch intervals; sprinkle with Beef Rub and coffee granules. Chill 1 to 4 hours.

3. Remove beef from refrigerator, and let stand 1 hour.

4. Meanwhile, prepare charcoal fire in smoker according to Minion Method (see page 39). Place water pan in smoker; add water to depth of fill line. Regulate temperature with a thermometer to 250° to 260° for 15 to 20 minutes.

5. Place beef, fat side down, on upper food grate and close smoker. Smoke 5 to 6 hours or until a meat thermometer inserted into the thickest portion of the chuck roll registers 165°. Remove beef from smoker, and wrap tightly in a double layer of heavy-duty aluminum foil; return beef to smoker. Cook 4 to 8 more hours, checking temperature each hour until a meat thermometer inserted into the thickest portion registers 205° to 210°.

6. Remove beef from smoker; open foil, and allow steam to escape for 2 to 4 minutes. Let beef rest in foil 1 hour.

7. Remove beef from foil, and place on a cutting board, reserving drippings in foil. Using a meat cleaver, chop beef, and place in a large bowl; stir in reserved drippings. Serve immediately with El Sancho Barbecue Sauce.

tip from the **PITS**

I use only fruitwood to smoke with because it is the most gentle and doesn't overpower the meat. Depending on the time of year, I use different types. For instance, apple is more readily available at the first of the year.

SKIP STEELE, PAPPY'S SMOKEHOUSE, ST. LOUIS

BEEF SHORT RIBS

Christopher Prieto doesn't discriminate against any meat on his pit but says beef short ribs have a certain moisture and rich flavor that are unmatched.

Beef short ribs are some of the most fantastic ribs available. They are considered a subprimal cut of bone-in beef, and are butchered from a single rib or from several ribs of the steer. A single rib can weigh as much as 2 pounds.

BACK RIBS VS. SHORT RIBS

There are two sections of beef ribs: back ribs and short ribs. The meat is between the bones on back ribs and on top of the bone on short ribs. I prefer short ribs; they are similar to the St. Louis cut on pork ribs and are cut from the short plate. We call it the short plate because of its location on the steer—the sixth, seventh, and eighth bones just in front of the flank steak

and behind the brisket. The bones of a short plate are huge, nearly straight, and topped with 1 to 2 inches of beef.

BEEF OR PORK?

Beef and pork ribs have little in common. Beef short ribs are meatier, more flavorful, and have more connective tissues. But that also means they can be tougher if they're not cooked properly. They benefit most from low-and-slow cooking so the fat and tissues can melt, similar to beef brisket and pork ribs. Texans have perfected the art of smoking the beef short rib—a staple at nearly every barbecue restaurant in the Lone Star State.

what to look for	Chris' top tips	best served with
▶ Beef chuck ribs—also known as beef plate ribs—in a 3-bone rack ▶ Large racks with even fat and marbling throughout ▶ Avoid small back ribs. Beef plate ribs have huge bones, and the meat can weigh 1.5 to 2 pounds.	▶ Beef ribs love coarse black pepper, so don't be afraid to load them up before you put them on the smoker. ▶ When removing the membrane from the beef rib, use a paper towel to help grip the membrane and avoid damaging the rib.	▶ SAUCE: Beef ribs are actually best without sauce, but a smoky sauce on the side is OK. ▶ SIDES: Slaw Sliced white onion Mac and cheese Plain white sliced bread

1. TRIM THE FAT. Beef short ribs are already relatively lean, so they shouldn't require too much trimming.

2. REMOVE SILVERSKIN. Using a sharp knife, cut off the silverskin in thin strips, angling your knife against the membrane. Continue to slide the knife along the silverskin, and pull on the membrane until it releases.

3. REMOVE MEMBRANE. Remove the thick membrane from the back of ribs by pulling it off with a paper towel.

4. WET WITH WORCESTERSHIRE. Rub or brush the ribs generously with Worcestershire sauce to ensure the salt-and-pepper rub mixture will stick.

5. APPLY RUB. Cover ribs with a generous coating of salt-and-pepper mixture. Chill for 1 to 4 hours. Let stand at room temperature for 30 minutes before smoking.

6. SMOKE THEM. Place ribs, meat side up, on food grate, and smoke 4 to 6 hours or until a meat thermometer inserted into thickest portion registers 200°. Remove ribs from smoker, and let rest 30 minutes. Cut between the bones to separate ribs. Serve immediately.

BEEF SHORT RIBS

YIELD: 6 SERVINGS   TOTAL: 6 TO 8 HOURS

1   3-bone slab beef plate short ribs (8 to 10 lbs.)
2   Tbsp. kosher salt
2   Tbsp. coarsely ground black pepper
¼   cup Worcestershire sauce
3   to 4 pecan, hickory, or oak wood chunks
8   to 10 lb. charcoal briquettes

1. Rinse and pat ribs dry. Remove thick membrane from back of ribs by pulling it off with a paper towel. (This will make ribs more tender.) Trim excess fat.

2. Stir together salt and pepper in a medium bowl. Generously brush or rub ribs with Worcestershire sauce. Coat ribs with salt and pepper mixture. Chill for 1 to 4 hours.

3. Remove ribs from refrigerator, and let stand 30 minutes.

4. Meanwhile, prepare charcoal fire in smoker according to Minion Method (see page 39). Place water pan in smoker; add water to depth of fill line. Regulate temperature with a thermometer to 275° for 15 to 20 minutes.

5. Place ribs, meat side up, on upper food grate; close smoker. Smoke 4 to 6 hours or until a meat thermometer inserted into thickest portion registers 200°, checking temperature every hour.

6. Remove ribs from smoker, and let rest 30 minutes. Cut between bones to separate ribs. Serve immediately.

PORK SPARERIBS

Pork spareribs are more forgiving than baby backs. Christopher Prieto explains why, and how you can smoke juicy spareribs on your first try.

Pork spareribs are cut from the ends of baby back ribs, farther down the side of the hog. The bones are straighter and flatter than baby backs as well, and the meat has more marbling, which makes spareribs very flavorful. The most popular trim of the sparerib is known as the St. Louis cut. This cut is best made by removing the rib tips from the primary rack to create a nice rectangular slab to cook on the smoker.

WHY SPARERIBS?

One of the biggest advantages to cooking spareribs is they are very forgiving during the cooking process. So if you are new to trimming and smoking your own ribs, you have a good chance of ending up with a perfectly tender rack on your first or second try. Spareribs also have more bone than meat (unlike baby back ribs), and the meat is concentrated between the bones rather than on top. But the bones, connective tissues, and fat help give spareribs their exceptional flavor. Finally, spareribs are typically less expensive than baby back ribs, despite their ease to prepare and delicious flavor. For these reasons, most chefs and pitmasters actually prefer pork spareribs to baby backs—and with my simple smoking method you probably will, too.

what to look for	*Chris' top tips*	*best served with*
▶ Thick and meaty racks with fat that is evenly distributed ▶ Always look at the top side (meat side) of the rack for exposed rib bones (shiners). These can ruin the integrity of a rack during cooking. ▶ Whole sparerib racks you can trim to St. Louis cut	▶ Don't season your spareribs overnight because it can make them taste hammy. ▶ Don't over-sauce your spareribs. Barbecue sauce is just another layer of flavor that is best when applied as a light glaze that is allowed to set on the grill.	▶ **SIDES:** Barbecue pinto beans Slaw Potato salad Sliced white onion Mac and cheese Dill pickles Plain white sliced bread

1. REMOVE EXCESS FAT. Before you can trim your spareribs to St. Louis cut, remove the excess flap of meat and fat from the bone-side of the slab—it will likely run the entire length of the rack.

2. TRIM TO ST. LOUIS CUT. First remove the small flap of meat at the end of the rack by making a vertical cut parallel to, and about ½-inch away from, the last bone. Next, separate the breastbone and cartilage by cutting perpendicular to the ribs, cutting through soft spots where rib meets breastbone.

3. REMOVE MEMBRANE. Starting at the bone end, pull off the thin membrane from the back of the ribs using a paper towel. Trim any excess fat from ribs.

4. OIL THEM DOWN. Coat both sides of each rack of ribs with peanut oil to ensure the rub will stick.

5. APPLY RUB. Cover each rack of ribs with a liberal coating of Season All Rub (page 329) and black pepper, and let them stand 1 hour.

6. SMOKE THEM. Place ribs, bone side down, on upper food grate and smoke 1 to 1½ hours. Using a spray bottle, spritz with apple juice every 30 minutes, checking to prevent charring on the edges of the ribs.

7. WRAP AND REAPPLY. Remove ribs from smoker, and spray generously with apple juice. Wrap ribs tightly in a double layer of heavy-duty aluminum foil, and return to smoker. Cook, meat side down, 1½ more hours. Remove ribs from smoker and remove from aluminum foil. Brush ribs with El Sancho Barbecue Sauce (page 318).

8. SET THE SAUCE. Carefully return sauced ribs to smoker, bone side down. Cook 10 minutes or until barbecue sauce is set. Remove ribs from smoker, and cut between bones to separate ribs. Serve immediately with remaining El Sancho Barbecue Sauce.

PORK

PORK SPARERIBS *(pictured on page 46)*

Many pitmasters prefer pork spareribs to baby back ribs because they are easier to prepare, have more connective tissue and fat, and are just more flavorful.

YIELD: 8 TO 10 SERVINGS   TOTAL: 4 HOURS, 25 MINUTES

3   (4- to 5-lb.) racks pork spareribs
⅓   cup peanut oil
1½ cups Season All Rub, divided (page 329)
3   Tbsp. freshly ground black pepper
4   pecan, hickory, or cherry wood chunks

8   to 10 lb. charcoal briquettes
¾   cup apple juice
2   cups El Sancho Barbecue Sauce, divided (page 318)

1. Rinse and pat ribs dry. Remove thin membrane from back of ribs by pulling it off using a paper towel. (This will make ribs more tender.) Trim ribs to St. Louis cut (see technique on page 71).

2. Brush or rub ribs generously with peanut oil. Coat each rack with Season All Rub and black pepper, and let stand 1 hour.

3. Meanwhile, prepare charcoal fire in smoker according to Minion Method (see page 39). Place water pan in smoker; add water to depth of fill line. Regulate temperature with a thermometer to 275° for 15 to 20 minutes.

4. Place ribs, bone side down, on upper food grate; close smoker. Smoke 1 to 1½ hours, and using a spray bottle, spritz with apple juice every 30 minutes, checking to prevent charring on edges of ribs.

5. Remove ribs from smoker, and spray generously with apple juice. Wrap ribs tightly in a double layer of heavy-duty aluminum foil, and return to smoker. Cook, meat side down, 1½ more hours.

6. Remove ribs from smoker; open foil, and allow steam to escape for 2 to 4 minutes. Drain and discard liquid and aluminum foil.

7. Brush ribs with ½ cup El Sancho Barbecue Sauce each. Carefully return ribs to smoker, bone side down; close smoker. Cook 10 minutes or until barbecue sauce is set. Remove ribs from smoker, and cut between bones to separate ribs. Serve immediately with remaining ½ cup El Sancho Barbecue Sauce.

BABY BACK RIBS

The bones of the baby back curve, which makes the meat sensitive to overcooking. Christopher Prieto's method ensures a consistent temperature so you can cook perfect baby backs every time.

Baby back ribs, also known as loin back ribs, are the most popular ribs of a hog. They are the ribs closest to the hog's backbone, and sit just beneath the loin muscle (hence the name). A typical rack of baby back ribs has between 11 and 13 bones. The bones are curved and longer at one end of the slab than the other—about 6 inches at the longest end and 3 inches at the shortest end. Most of the meat sits on top of the bones, which makes it sensitive to being overcooked. Some baby back ribs can have as much as ½ inch of loin meat on top, but slabs generally weigh about 2 pounds (much of that is bone), making it easy for one adult to put down an entire rack in one sitting.

CONSISTENT HEAT IS KEY

Because of the different size bones, and the naturally lean meat, it's important to keep a very consistent temperature on your smoker when cooking baby backs. And contrary to what you might have heard, the meat should never "fall off the bone." The sign of a perfectly cooked baby back rib is when you can easily take a bite of the meat and the rest of the meat stays intact on the bone.

what to look for	Chris' top tips	best served with
▶ Thick racks with bright pink meat and evenly distributed fat throughout.	▶ The meat of a properly cooked baby back rib does not fall off the bone. You should be able to bite into it and the rest of the meat should stay on the bone.	▶ **SAUCE:** Any sweet red barbecue sauce. (Add 2 Tbsp. of honey to every 1 cup of barbecue sauce to enhance the shine on the ribs.)
▶ Racks with uniform-size bones and not too much curvature		
▶ Loin back ribs (another name for baby backs) because they're cut from the loin of the hog	▶ Baby back ribs cook faster than spareribs because the meat is leaner, so pay close attention during cooking.	▶ **SIDES:** Barbecue pinto beans Slaw Potato salad Mac and cheese

1. TRIM THE FAT. Baby backs are lean, so they shouldn't require too much trimming.

2. REMOVE MEMBRANE. Starting at the bone end, pull off the thin membrane from the back of the ribs using a paper towel.

3. OIL THEM DOWN. Coat both sides of each rack of ribs with peanut oil to ensure the rub will stick.

4. APPLY RUB. Cover each rack of ribs with a liberal coating of Season All Rub (page 329) and black pepper, and let them stand 1 hour.

5. SMOKE THEM. Place ribs, bone side down, on upper food grate; close the smoker. Smoke 1 to 1½ hours, checking periodically to prevent excess charring.

6. PREPARE FOIL. Cover the bottom of 3 double-layered, heavy-duty aluminum foil packets with brown sugar, squeeze margarine, and honey. Set one rack of ribs, meat side down, in each packet atop mixture. Sprinkle both sides of ribs with Season All Rub and granulated onion.

7. ADD MORE MARGARINE. Coat the rib side of each rack with honey and squeeze margarine.

8. TOP WITH BROWN SUGAR. Add a final topping of brown sugar to the mixture, and wrap the ribs tightly in foil. Return the packets to the smoker, meat side down, and cook for 1½ more hours.

PORK

9. BASTE WITH RIB APPLE GLAZE.
Remove ribs from the smoker and carefully open the foil packets to allow steam to escape. Drain and discard liquid and aluminum foil. Brush ribs with Rib Apple Glaze (page 318).

10. SET THE GLAZE.
Carefully return ribs to smoker, bone side down, and cook 10 more minutes or until glaze is set. Remove ribs from the smoker, and cut between bones to separate ribs. Serve immediately.

tip from the
PITS

The membrane on the back of a rack of ribs is meant to hold in the organs of the animal—meaning it keeps them from moving in or out of the chest cavity. It also prevents the rub, smoke, or flavor from penetrating the ribs. You'll produce a more flavorful rack of ribs by removing this membrane with a paper towel (see image 2 on page 75). Also, I think cooking ribs with the membrane on gives them an unpleasant texture.

CHRISTOPHER PRIETO, PRIME BARBECUE, WENDELL, NORTH CAROLINA

BABY BACK RIBS

Baby back ribs have curved bones that are longer at one end than the other, which makes them prone to overcooking. This method ensures the ribs stay moist on the smoker and guarantees you'll end up with delicious results.

YIELD: 8 TO 10 SERVINGS   TOTAL: 4 HOURS, 10 MINUTES

3 slabs pork baby back ribs, trimmed (about 9 lb.)	Heavy-duty aluminum foil
½ cup peanut oil	2 cups firmly packed light brown sugar
1½ cups plus 6 Tbsp. Season All Rub, divided (page 329)	1 (12-oz.) container squeeze margarine
10 lb. charcoal briquettes	2 cups honey
3 to 4 pecan, hickory, or cherry wood chunks	6 Tbsp. granulated onion
	2 cups Rib Apple Glaze, divided (page 318)

1. Rinse and pat ribs dry. Remove thick membrane from back of ribs by pulling it off using a paper towel. (This will make ribs more tender.)

2. Brush or rub ribs generously with peanut oil. Coat racks with ½ cup Season All Rub, each, and let stand 1 hour.

3. Meanwhile, prepare charcoal fire in smoker according the Minion Method (see page 39). Place water pan in smoker; add water to depth of fill line. Regulate temperature with a thermometer to 275° for 15 to 20 minutes.

4. Place ribs, bone side down, on upper food grate; close smoker. Smoke 1 to 1½ hours, checking periodically to prevent excess charring.

5. While ribs are smoking, prepare 3 sets of double-layered, heavy-duty aluminum foil packets (about 20-inches long but large enough to tightly wrap each rack individually). Cover the bottom of each packet with ⅓ cup of brown sugar, ¼ cup squeeze margarine, and ⅓ cup of honey.

6. Remove ribs from smoker, and set one rack, meat side down, in each foil packet atop the brown sugar and honey mixture. Sprinkle both sides of ribs with ½ Tbsp. Season All Rub and ½ Tbsp. granulated onion. Coat rib side of each rack with ⅓ cup brown sugar, ¼ cup squeeze margarine, and ⅓ cup of honey. Wrap ribs tightly in foil, and return to smoker, bone side down. Cook 1½ more hours.

7. Remove ribs from smoker; open foil, and allow steam to escape for 2 to 4 minutes. Drain and discard liquid and aluminum foil.

8. Brush ribs with ½ cup Rib Apple Glaze each. Carefully return ribs to smoker bone side down; close smoker. Cook 10 minutes or until glaze is set. Remove ribs from smoker, and cut between bones to separate ribs. Serve immediately with remaining ½ cup Rib Apple Glaze.

Note: We tested with Parkay Squeeze.

PORK BUTT

Christopher Prieto's smoking method and Season All Rub create a flavorful bark for the perfect pulled pork.

The pork butt is an inexpensive hunk of meat that is full of flavorful fat and connective tissue. Because it is so well marbled, it is very forgiving during the cooking process, making it one of the best meats for first-time barbecuers. The process, however, still requires a consistent heat and moist environment on the smoker, but when cooked low and slow so the fat can render, you can achieve a meat that is tender, moist, and hard to beat.

WHAT'S IN A NAME?
It's pretty ironic that we refer to this cut of meat as a pork butt. It's actually butchered from the top of the hog's shoulder, and is also known as a Boston butt, Boston shoulder roast, shoulder blade roast, or a variation of those names. Pork butts are sold bone-in and boneless, and typically weigh between 6 and 10 pounds. They are easy to find at local supermarkets and big-box grocers.

BONE-IN VS. BONELESS
I prefer to always buy bone-in pork butt. The bone helps keep the meat together during the cooking process and helps impart a bit of flavor, as well. The bone also is a good indicator of the meat's doneness. The bone of a properly cooked pork butt should pull out clean, with no meat attached at all.

what to look for	Chris' top tips	best served with
▶ 8- to 10-lb. bone-in butts with consistent marbling throughout, and a nice milky fat cap ▶ Fresh, never frozen or enhanced, pork butts ▶ A properly butchered pork butt that is nice and square in shape	▶ I always cook my pork butt fat side down. ▶ Always wrap the pork once it reaches 165° to help protect the meat from oversmoking. ▶ Don't put any meat on your smoker until the intense early smoke clears.	▶ **SAUCE:** Vinegar-based Eastern Carolina sauce; sticky sweet Kansas City sauce; or a South Carolina mustard sauce ▶ **SIDES:** Corn sticks Potato rolls Barbecue pinto beans Cheesy potatoes Hush puppies

1. INSPECT THE MEAT. Feel the surface of the pork butt for any shaved bones, or any especially hard patches of fat that need removing.

2. TRIM THE FAT. Remove any large or hard patches of fat from the pork butt so the rub will adhere to the meat and create a nice bark during cooking.

3. REMOVE SILVERSKIN. Using a sharp knife, cut off the silverskin or excess connective tissue in thin strips, angling your knife against the membrane. Continue to slide the knife along the silverskin or connective tissue, and pull until it releases.

4. OIL IT DOWN. Coat all sides of the pork butt with peanut oil to ensure the rub will stick.

5. APPLY RUB. Cover the pork butt with a liberal coating of Season All Rub (page 329).

6. APPLY MORE RUB. Don't be afraid to use too much. You want to generously coat the butt with the Season All Rub—it's this rub that helps create the dark mahogany bark and rich outer layer of flavor.

7. INJECT WITH FLAVOR. Using an injector, inject Pork Brine Injection (page 330) into the pork butt at 1-inch intervals. Let pork butt chill for 4 to 6 hours.

8. SMOKE IT. Place your pork on the upper food grate of your smoker and smoke 4 to 6 hours or until a meat thermometer inserted into thickest portion registers 165°. Spritz with apple juice every hour.

PORK

9. WRAP IN FOIL. Once the pork reaches 165°, it will no longer take on any smoke, so remove it from smoker, and wrap tightly in a double layer of heavy-duty aluminum foil. Return it to the smoker and continue cooking until a meat thermometer inserted into thickest portion registers 200°. Remove pork from smoker and open foil to allow steam to escape. Rewrap and let pork rest in foil 2 to 4 hours.

10. PULL THE PORK. While wearing insulated gloves, remove pork from foil, and place it on a cutting board, reserving drippings in foil. Pull pork into large chunks and discard all visible fat; coarsely chop the pork and drizzle it with reserved pork drippings. Serve immediately with El Sancho Barbecue Sauce or North Cackalacky Barbecue Sauce (both on page 318).

BBQ&A

WITH PITMASTER TROY BLACK

What are your 5 top tips to a perfect pork butt?

1. Start with a quality piece of meat.
2. Use a dry rub to season the pork, and allow the meat to stand for an hour before smoking.
3. Use only wood for smoking during the first 2 to 3 hours. Beyond that, use charcoal to maintain the heat. Using wood during the entire course of smoking a pork butt will most likely oversmoke the meat.
4. Use a good meat thermometer, and allow the pork butt to smoke until the internal temperature reaches 195°.
5. Don't baste during the cooking process. By not basting, you allow the outside of the meat to form what is known as the bark, which is the highly desirable part of the pork butt.

SMOKED PORK BUTT

Pork butts may very well be the most forgiving meat to barbecue, so if you're trying out a smoker for the first time, this cut of pork is a good one. Just coat it with a good dry rub, let it rest, and leave everything else up to your smoker.

YIELD: 8 TO 10 SERVINGS   TOTAL: 8 TO 16 HOURS

1	(8- to 10-lb.) bone-in pork shoulder roast (Boston butt)
½	cup peanut oil
2	cups Season All Rub (page 329)
1	cup Pork Brine Injection (page 330)

3	to 4 sugar maple or cherry wood chunks
10	lb. charcoal briquettes
¾	cup apple juice
	El Sancho Barbecue Sauce (page 318)
	North Cackalacky Barbecue Sauce (page 318)

1. Trim excess fat from pork butt. Coat pork butt with peanut oil, followed by a liberal coating of Season All Rub. Using an injector, inject 1 cup Pork Brine Injection into pork butt at 1-inch intervals. Chill for 4 to 6 hours.

2. Remove pork butt from refrigerator, and let stand 30 minutes.

3. Meanwhile, prepare charcoal fire in smoker according to Minion Method (see page 39). Place water pan in smoker; add water to depth of fill line. Regulate temperature with a thermometer to 275° for 15 to 20 minutes.

4. Place pork on upper food grate; close smoker. Smoke 4 to 6 hours or until a meat thermometer inserted into thickest portion registers 165°, spritzing with apple juice every hour.

5. Remove pork from smoker, and wrap tightly in a double layer of heavy-duty aluminum foil; return pork to smoker. Continue cooking until a meat thermometer inserted into thickest portion registers 200°.

6. Remove pork butt from smoker; open foil, and allow steam to escape for 2 to 4 minutes. Let pork rest in foil 2 to 4 hours.

7. Remove pork from foil, and place on a cutting board, reserving drippings in foil. Pull pork into large chunks, and discard all visible fat; coarsely chop and drizzle with reserved pork drippings. Serve with El Sancho Barbecue Sauce or North Cackalacky Barbecue Sauce.

BBQ&A

WITH TIM BYRES, SMOKE, DALLAS

What are some common barbecue mistakes made by novices?

I think the biggest mistake is thinking you need the most expensive tools and equipment to do a good job. An $80 Weber charcoal grill works great. You don't need to spend a ton to cook good barbecue. Another mistake is overthinking the process. Don't let it intimidate you. Sure, there is often pressure when you have eight to 10 people over, but do yourself a favor and make things ahead.

PORK

PULLED PORK SANDWICH *(pictured)*

This ultimate barbecue sandwich has it all: smoky flavor, sweet sauce, and a tangy slaw.

YIELD: 1 SERVING   TOTAL: 5 MINUTES

Smoked Pork Butt (page 84)
El Sancho Barbecue Sauce (page 318)

Memphis Slaw (page 268)
Grilled barbecue bread

Layer the smoked pork, barbecue sauce, and slaw on grilled barbecue bread. Serve immediately.

HUNGARIAN PULLED PORK SANDWICH

YIELD: 15 SERVINGS   TOTAL: 8 HOURS PLUS CHILL AND STAND TIMES

1 Tbsp. Hungarian sweet paprika	7½ cups hickory wood chips
1 Tbsp. Spanish smoked paprika	2 cups apple cider vinegar
1 Tbsp. firmly packed light brown sugar	¾ cup ketchup
1 tsp. table salt	2 Tbsp. granulated sugar
1 tsp. onion powder	1 Tbsp. hot pepper sauce
1 tsp. dry mustard	1 tsp. table salt
1 tsp. freshly ground black pepper	1 tsp. dried crushed red pepper
1 tsp. ground red pepper	½ tsp. freshly ground black pepper
1 (4½-lb.) bone-in pork shoulder (Boston butt)	1 (16-oz.) package shredded coleslaw mix
	15 hamburger buns

1. Combine first 8 ingredients in a large bowl. Rub spice mixture onto pork; place pork in bowl. Cover and chill at least 8 hours or overnight. Soak wood chips in water 1 to 24 hours.

2. Remove pork from refrigerator; let stand at room temperature 20 minutes. Prepare smoker according to manufacturer's directions, bringing internal temperature to 225° to 250°; maintain temperature for 15 to 20 minutes. Drain wood chips, and place on coals. Place pork on upper cooking grate; cover with smoker lid. Smoke pork, maintaining temperature inside smoker between 225° and 250°, for 8 to 10 hours or until a meat thermometer inserted into thickest portion registers 190°. Replace wood chips every 2 hours.

3. Meanwhile, combine ½ cup water, cider vinegar and next 6 ingredients in a microwave-safe bowl. Microwave at HIGH 2 to 3 minutes or until sugar dissolves. Cool and set aside.

4. Combine coleslaw and ½ cup sauce in a large bowl; toss well. Set aside to cool.

5. Remove meat from smoker; let stand 20 minutes. Shred meat with 2 forks; discard bone and fat. Combine shredded pork and 2 cups sauce in a large bowl; toss to coat. Spoon 3 oz. pork and ⅓ cup coleslaw on each hamburger bun. Cover and serve with sauce for dipping.

I like to coat pork butt with a dry rub and store it all day in the refrigerator. I cook it low, around 225°, and smoke the butt until it reaches 195°. Then, I wrap it in aluminum foil and let it rest about an hour until it continues to cook over 200°.

I use natural sugar instead of white sugar in my rubs because white sugar burns. Turbinado and dark brown sugar are my favorites—I use about 50% sugar and then the remaining 50% is salt, pepper, and spices.

**HARRISON SAPP,
SOUTHERN SOUL BARBEQUE,
ST. SIMONS ISLAND, GEORGIA**

BARBECUE CHILI

Enjoy chili in a new way starring smoky barbecue pork and a spicy seasoning blend. It comes together quickly with convenience items and canned tomatoes.

**YIELD: 8 SERVINGS
TOTAL: 35 MINUTES, INCLUDING SEASONING MIX**

1½ lb. shredded Smoked Pork Butt, without sauce (page 84)
2 (14.5-oz.) cans diced tomatoes with green pepper, celery, and onion
1 (8-oz.) can tomato sauce
1 cup barbecue sauce
⅓ cup Chili Seasoning Mix
Toppings: shredded cheese, sour cream, sliced jalapeños, tortilla chips, sliced green onions, chopped avocado

1. Stir together shredded pork and next 4 ingredients in a Dutch oven; bring to a boil over medium-high heat, stirring occasionally.

2. Cover, reduce heat to low, and simmer, stirring occasionally, 15 minutes. Serve with desired toppings.

CHILI SEASONING MIX

Keep this versatile spice blend on hand all year-round. It's loaded with flavor and pairs well with everything from seafood and beef to pork and chicken.

YIELD: ABOUT 1⅓ CUPS   TOTAL: 5 MINUTES

¾ cup chili powder
1 Tbsp. ground cumin
2 Tbsp. dried oregano
2 Tbsp. dried minced onion
2 Tbsp. seasoned salt
2 Tbsp. sugar
2 tsp. dried minced garlic

Stir together all ingredients. Store seasoning mix in an airtight container up to 4 months at room temperature. Shake or stir well before using.

GRILLED PORK TOSTADAS

Give a Mexican twist to leftover pulled pork. These crispy tostadas are super quick to make and are equally delicious with shredded rotisserie chicken.

YIELD: 4 SERVINGS   TOTAL: 15 MINUTES

4   (8-inch) tortillas
2   Tbsp. olive oil, divided
½   tsp. chili powder
½   tsp. ground cumin
2   avocados, halved, pitted, and peeled
1   (16-oz.) can refried beans

2   cups shredded lettuce
1   lb. Smoked Pork Butt, without sauce, warmed (page 84)
1   cup fresh salsa
1   cup crumbled queso fresco
Garnish: fresh cilantro

1. Preheat grill to 350° to 400° (medium-high) heat. Brush tortillas with 1 Tbsp. oil. Sprinkle with chili powder and cumin.

2. Brush avocado with remaining oil. Grill tortillas and avocado 1 to 2 minutes on each side or until tortillas are toasted and avocado is slightly charred.

3. Spread beans onto each tostada. Top evenly with lettuce, pork, salsa, cheese, and sliced avocado.

PULLED PORK NACHOS

If you prefer grated cheese to queso, spread out your chips on a baking sheet, sprinkle with cheese (try pepper Jack for a little extra kick), and bake at 350° just until the cheese melts. Then finish with remaining toppings.

YIELD: 4 SERVINGS   **TOTAL: 15 MINUTES**

Tortilla chips
1½ (15-oz.) cans black beans, drained and rinsed
2 cups Smoked Pork Butt, without sauce, warmed (page 84)
1 cup fresh salsa
⅔ cup chopped tomatoes

⅔ cup chopped fresh cilantro
½ cup sliced black olives
½ cup minced red onion
2 thinly sliced jalapeño peppers
1 (12-oz.) container refrigerated queso, warmed
4 lime wedges

Layer tortilla chips on a platter; top with beans, warmed pork, salsa, tomatoes, cilantro, olives, onion, and jalapeño peppers. Serve with warmed queso and lime wedges.

BBQ&A

WITH TIM BYRES, SMOKE, DALLAS

What's your favorite barbecue sauce?

Personally, I like them all, even though in West Texas they don't believe in sauce. We have a variety of sauces at Smoke: a Carolina-style sauce with cayenne, cider vinegar, and a little sorghum syrup or honey; a Creole mustard sauce; and a Mexican-inspired Tejano red sauce that's a blend of slow-cooked dried guajillo peppers, roasted garlic, and tomatillos. The red sauce is perfect paired with chicken or fish.

PORK

PULLED PORK GRIDDLE CAKES

Topped with tart and spicy cherry salsa, these cornmeal pancakes make fun appetizers and can even be served as a meal. Use pulled pork from your favorite barbecue restaurant or leftovers from the Smoked Pork Butt recipe on page 84.

YIELD: 16 GRIDDLE CAKES   TOTAL: 25 MINUTES

1½ cups self-rising white cornmeal mix
½   cup all-purpose flour
1   Tbsp. sugar
1⅔ cups buttermilk
3   Tbsp. butter, melted

2   large eggs, lightly beaten
2   cups chopped Smoked Pork Butt, without sauce, warmed (page 84)
Fresh Cherry Salsa

1. Whisk together cornmeal mix and next 5 ingredients just until moistened; stir in pulled pork.

2. Pour about ¼ cup batter for each griddle cake onto a hot, lightly greased griddle or large nonstick skillet. Cook 3 to 4 minutes or until tops are covered with bubbles and edges look dry and cooked; turn and cook other side 2 to 3 minutes or until done. Serve immediately with Fresh Cherry Salsa.

FRESH CHERRY SALSA

With a spicy kick from pepper jelly and crushed red pepper, this nod to summer is great served as a chip dipper or atop grilled chicken or pork.

YIELD: 2½ CUPS   TOTAL: 15 MINUTES

½   cup red pepper jelly
1   Tbsp. lime zest
¼   cup fresh lime juice
¼   tsp. dried crushed red pepper
2   cups pitted, coarsely chopped fresh cherries

¾   cup diced fresh nectarines
⅓   cup chopped fresh cilantro
⅓   cup chopped fresh chives

Whisk together red pepper jelly, lime zest, lime juice, and dried crushed red pepper in a small bowl. Stir in cherries, nectarines, cilantro, and chives. Refrigerate in an airtight container for up to 5 days.

PORK

PORK NOODLE BOWLS

This fresh and tasty Asian dish is a great way to utilize pulled pork. Make it a party and serve the toppings in small bowls for everyone to garnish as they like.

YIELD: 4 SERVINGS   TOTAL: 45 MINUTES

1   Tbsp. kosher salt
1   (8.8-oz.) package thin rice noodles
½   (8-oz.) package sliced fresh mushrooms
2   tsp. olive oil
2   cups Smoked Pork Butt, without sauce (page 84)
½   (16-oz.) package angel hair coleslaw mix

4   green onions (white and light green parts only), sliced
¼   cup loosely packed fresh cilantro leaves
6   cups chicken broth
1   Tbsp. grated fresh ginger (optional)
Lime wedges
Toppings: soy sauce, dried crushed red pepper, chopped dry-roasted peanuts

1. Microwave 8 cups water and kosher salt at HIGH in a large microwave-safe glass bowl 2 minutes. Submerge noodles; let stand 20 minutes or until tender. Drain. Divide noodles among 4 bowls.

2. Sauté mushrooms in hot oil in a medium skillet over medium-high heat 5 minutes or until tender. Spoon over noodles. Add pork to skillet, and cook, stirring occasionally, 5 minutes or until hot; spoon over mushrooms. Divide coleslaw mix and next 2 ingredients among bowls.

3. Bring broth and, if desired, ginger to a boil in a 3-qt. saucepan over medium heat. Remove from heat, and divide among bowls. Serve with lime wedges and desired toppings.

BBQ&A

WITH CHRISTOPHER PRIETO, PRIME BARBECUE, WENDELL, NORTH CAROLINA

What do you look for when selecting a pork butt?

Most pork butts come in packs of two, so I always look for uniformity in size so that the pork butts will cook evenly together. I prefer fresh (never frozen) pork butts that are between 8 and 10 pounds with good marbling throughout and a nice milky fat cap. And I always check to make sure the shoulder blade bone hasn't been broken.

KOREAN CABBAGE WRAPS WITH
SWEET-&-SOUR CUCUMBER SALAD

Gochujang is Korea's version of Sriracha; it adds a sweet and spicy kick to this dish. You can find it in the Asian foods aisle at the grocery store.

YIELD: 18 WRAPS   TOTAL: 30 MINUTES, INCLUDING SALAD

Sweet-&-Sour Cucumber Salad
- ½ cup soy sauce
- ¼ cup rice wine vinegar
- 2 Tbsp. firmly packed light brown sugar
- 2 Tbsp. dark sesame oil
- 2 Tbsp. gochujang (Korean chili paste)*

- 1 Tbsp. grated fresh ginger
- 1 garlic clove, pressed
- 1 lb. Smoked Pork Butt, without sauce (page 84)
- 18 savoy or napa cabbage leaves
- Chopped oil-roasted cocktail peanuts

1. Prepare Sweet-&-Sour Cucumber Salad.

2. While salad chills, process soy sauce and next 6 ingredients in a blender or food processor until smooth.

3. Spoon about ¼ cup pork into each cabbage leaf; drizzle with soy sauce mixture. Spoon Sweet-&-Sour Cucumber Salad over pork, using a slotted spoon. Top with desired amount of peanuts.

* 2 tsp. Asian hot chili sauce (such as Sriracha) can be substituted.

SWEET-&-SOUR CUCUMBER SALAD

This crunchy salad is also wonderful as a side dish or as a cooling relish to tame the heat of spicy dishes.

YIELD: 8 TO 10 SERVINGS   TOTAL: 20 MINUTES

- 3 Tbsp. rice wine vinegar
- 2 Tbsp. sugar
- 1 tsp. Dijon mustard
- ¼ tsp. table salt
- ¼ tsp. freshly ground black pepper

- 3 Tbsp. canola oil
- 1 English cucumber, seeded and thinly sliced into half-moons
- 2 shallots, minced
- 2 Tbsp. chopped fresh cilantro

Whisk together vinegar, sugar, Dijon mustard, salt, and pepper in a bowl. Add canola oil in a slow, steady stream, whisking constantly until well blended. Add cucumber, shallots, and cilantro. Toss to coat. Cover and chill 15 minutes.

PORK

BARBECUE PEACH SUMMER ROLLS

This Asian-Southern fusion appetizer may become one of your go-to dishes. You can find rice paper sheets in the Asian foods aisle, and they stay fresh for a while, making these summer rolls perfect for prepping ahead. Just be sure to keep them covered with a damp paper towel while you're preparing them so they don't dry out.

YIELD: 12 TO 16 ROLLS   TOTAL: 45 MINUTES, INCLUDING DIPPING SAUCE

Hot water
12 to 16 (8- to 9-inch) round rice paper sheets
2 small peaches, peeled and thinly sliced
12 to 16 Bibb lettuce leaves
1 English cucumber, cut into thin strips
1 large ripe avocado, thinly sliced
1 lb. Smoked Pork Butt, without sauce, warmed (page 84)

1 Granny Smith apple, peeled and cut into thin strips
½ cup torn fresh mint
½ cup torn fresh cilantro
½ cup torn fresh basil
Sweet Pepper-Peanut Sauce

1. Pour hot water to depth of 1 inch into a large shallow dish. Dip 1 rice paper sheet in hot water briefly to soften (about 15 to 20 seconds). Pat dry with paper towels.

2. Place softened rice paper on a flat surface. Place 1 or 2 peach slices in center of rice paper; top with 1 lettuce leaf, 2 cucumber strips, 1 avocado slice, about 3 Tbsp. pork, 3 or 4 apple strips, and 1½ to 2 Tbsp. herbs. Fold sides over filling, and roll up, burrito style. Place roll, seam side down, on a serving platter. Cover with damp paper towels to keep them from drying out.

3. Repeat procedure with remaining rice paper and filling ingredients. Serve with Sweet Pepper-Peanut Sauce.

SWEET PEPPER-PEANUT SAUCE

One of the key ingredients in this sauce is spicy fresh ginger. To peel ginger easily, use the side of a spoon to scrape off the papery skin.

YIELD: ABOUT 1½ CUPS   TOTAL: 10 MINUTES

1 cup sweet pepper relish (such as Howard's)
½ cup finely chopped cocktail peanuts
3 Tbsp. fresh lime juice
2 Tbsp. soy sauce
4 tsp. toasted sesame oil

1 Tbsp. grated fresh ginger
2 finely chopped green onions
2 garlic cloves, minced
2 tsp. Asian hot chili sauce (such as Sriracha)

Stir together sweet pepper relish, and next 8 ingredients. Cover and chill until ready to serve. Refrigerate in an airtight container for up to 3 days.

SMOKED CHICKEN

Christopher Prieto's pan chicken technique is a foolproof way to achieve perfectly juicy smoked chicken every time.

Smoked chicken isn't one of the most popular meats on barbecue restaurant menus, but that is one of the reasons it makes such a great meat to master at home. First, chicken is relatively inexpensive compared to most red meats, and second, you can change the flavor of the meat dramatically with different seasonings, rubs, brines, and marinades.

TO BRINE OR NOT TO BRINE?

For this particular smoked chicken method, I'm a firm believer in brining the chicken first. It instills extra moisture and flavor to the meat before it goes on the smoker, and it helps ensure the bird won't dry out during the cooking process. The key is to prepare and apply the brine properly and to wash it off before you season the chicken. The biggest difference in this cooking method and others is I smoke my chickens in a disposable aluminum pan. This allows the birds to constantly baste in their own juices, but the skin also ends up nice and brown because of the Chicken Slather (page 333). So what you end up with is incredibly juicy and flavorful chickens with dark, crispy skin.

what to look for	*Chris' top tips*	*best served with*
◗ Chicken that has white skin—it should not have any yellow color. ◗ Buy chicken that is as fresh as possible (not frozen). I prefer locally butchered chicken, but air-chilled chicken from out of state works well, too.	◗ Chicken always benefits from a brine or marinade. ◗ Chicken cooks best at higher barbecue temperatures, 250° or higher. ◗ Basting the chicken with butter or apple juice while it cooks will help keep it moist and create a crispy skin.	◗ **SAUCE:** Vinegar-based sauce; sticky sweet Kansas City sauce; or Alabama white-style barbecue sauce ◗ **SIDES:** Slaw Barbecue pinto beans Potato salad Hush puppies or potato rolls

1. BRINE IT. Place each chicken in a 2-gal., heavy-duty zip-top plastic bag and cover chickens in brine. Chill at least 3 hours or up to 5 hours. Remove chickens from brine, discarding brine; drain well, rinse, and pat dry.

2. SEASON IT. Rub a generous amount of Chicken Slather (page 333) over the skin and inside the cavity of the chickens.

3. BUTTER INSIDE CAVITY. Spread unsalted butter cubes inside the cavity of the chickens.

4. TOP WITH MORE BUTTER. Place both chickens, breasts down, in a disposable pan. Scatter unsalted butter cubes on top and around chickens.

5. SMOKE THEM. Place chickens in pan on upper food grate and smoke 2 hours. Check temperature using a meat thermometer inserted into the thickest portion of the thighs, and baste chickens with pan juices and 12-oz. bottle of squeeze margarine. Continue smoking for 30 minutes to 1 hour or until a meat thermometer inserted into the thickest portion of thighs registers 170°.

6. REST AND PULL. Remove chickens from pan, reserving drippings. Cover chickens loosely with aluminum foil, and let stand 30 minutes. Remove and discard bones (or reserve for another use). Shred chickens with 2 forks or chop with a meat cleaver, and place meat in a bowl. Stir together ¼ cup drippings and North Cackalacky Barbecue Sauce (page 318). Stir sauce mixture into chicken, and serve immediately.

BBQ&A

WITH CAREY BRINGLE, PEG LEG PORKER, NASHVILLE

Do you brine your poultry before you smoke it?

We don't. We smoke ours hot and fast—at 275° to 300° for about 2½ hours until the internal temperature reaches between 165° and 170°. We rub it with garlic salt and because we cook it hot and fast, the garlic crisps up the skin. A good tip: Don't ever poke the breast when you're taking the temperature. Instead take the temp on the back of the thigh.

CHICKEN

SMOKED CHICKEN *(pictured on page 34)*

YIELD: 8 TO 10 SERVINGS   TOTAL: 8 HOURS

2   (5-lb.) whole chickens
2   qt. Chicken Brine (page 333)
3   to 4 pecan, sugar maple, cherry,
     or applewood chunks
10   lb. charcoal briquettes
1½   cups Chicken Slather (page 333)

1   (16⅛- x 11¾-inch) disposable aluminum
     roasting pan
2   cups unsalted butter, cubed
1   (12-oz.) container squeeze margarine
¾   cup North Cackalacky Barbecue Sauce
     (page 318)

1. Remove and discard giblets and necks from chickens. Prepare Chicken Brine, and chill thoroughly. Place each chicken in a 2-gal., heavy-duty zip-top plastic bag, and cover chickens in brine. Chill at least 3 hours or up to 5 hours.

2. Meanwhile, prepare charcoal fire in smoker according the Minion Method (see page 39). Place water pan in smoker; add water to depth of fill line. Regulate temperature with a thermometer to 250° to 260° for 15 to 20 minutes.

3. Remove chickens from brine, discarding brine; drain well, rinse, and pat dry. Rub Chicken Slather over skin and inside cavities of chickens. Place chickens, breast side down, in disposable pan. Scatter butter cubes on tops and around sides of chickens.

4. Place chickens in pan on upper food grate; close smoker. Smoke 2 hours. Check temperature using a meat thermometer inserted into the thickest portion of the thighs, and baste chickens with pan juices and bottle of squeeze margarine. Continue smoking for 30 minutes to 1 hour or until meat thermometer inserted into thickest portion of the thighs registers 170°.

5. Remove chickens from pan, and place on a cutting board, reserving drippings in pan. Cover chickens loosely with aluminum foil, and let stand 30 minutes.

6. Remove and discard bones from chickens (or reserve for another use). Shred chicken with 2 forks or chop with a meat cleaver, and place meat in a bowl. Pour reserved pan drippings through a fine wire-mesh sieve into a medium bowl. Stir together ¼ cup strained drippings and North Cackalacky Barbecue Sauce, discarding remaining drippings. Stir sauce mixture into chicken. Serve immediately.

Note: We tested with Parkay Squeeze.

CHICKEN

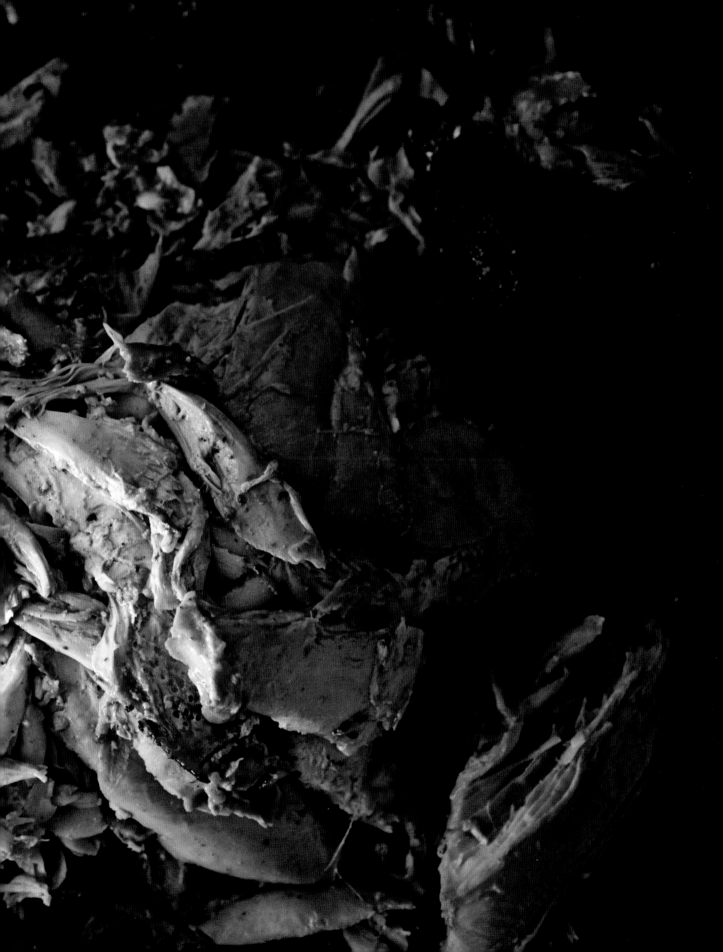

BEER-CAN CHICKEN

This simple technique lets you "roast" a whole chicken on the grill using beer to keep the bird moist.

YIELD: 4 SERVINGS   TOTAL: 2 HOURS, 35 MINUTES, INCLUDING RUB

1   (4-lb.) whole chicken
1   Tbsp. vegetable oil
1½ Tbsp. BBQ Chicken Rub

1½ tsp. kosher salt
1   (12-oz.) can beer

1. If applicable, remove neck and giblets from chicken, and reserve for another use. Pat chicken dry with paper towels. Brush cavity and outside of chicken with oil. Stir together BBQ Chicken Rub and kosher salt; sprinkle mixture inside cavity and on outside of chicken. Chill chicken 30 minutes to 12 hours.

2. Let chicken stand at room temperature 30 minutes. Light 1 side of grill, heating to 350° to 400° (medium-high) heat; leave other side unlit. Open beer. Place chicken upright onto beer can, fitting can into cavity. Pull legs forward to form a tripod, so chicken stands upright.

3. Place chicken upright on unlit side of grill. Grill, covered with grill lid, 1 to 1½ hours or until golden and a meat thermometer inserted into thickest portion of thighs registers 165°. Carefully remove chicken from can. Cover chicken loosely with aluminum foil; let stand 10 minutes before serving.

BBQ CHICKEN RUB

Smoked paprika, red pepper, cumin, and thyme are just a few of the spices that give this chicken rub its depth and flavor. It's also ideal for beef and pork.

YIELD: 6 TBSP.   TOTAL: 5 MINUTES

2   Tbsp. kosher salt
1   Tbsp. smoked paprika
1   Tbsp. onion powder
1½ tsp. ground red pepper
1½ tsp. ground cumin

1   tsp. garlic powder
1   tsp. dried thyme
1   tsp. dried oregano
1   tsp. freshly ground black pepper

Stir together salt, and next 8 ingredients. Store in an airtight container up to 6 months.

CHICKEN WINGS

These chicken wings get a boost of flavor from Christopher Prieto's two-process cooking method. They're first smoked before being finished on the grill.

YIELD: 8 TO 10 SERVINGS   TOTAL: 3 HOURS, 10 MINUTES

1 to 3 lb. chicken wings (about 25 wings)	2 to 3 pecan, sugar maple, or apple wood chunks
½ cup peanut oil	5 lb. charcoal briquettes
1 cup Season All Rub (page 329)	1 cup Rib Apple Glaze (page 318)

1. Toss wings in peanut oil. Apply a liberal coating of Season All Rub to wings, and let stand in a zip-top bag for 2 hours.

2. Meanwhile, prepare charcoal fire in smoker according the Minion Method (see page 39). Place water pan in smoker; add water to depth of fill line. Regulate temperature with a thermometer to 250° to 260° for 15 to 20 minutes.

3. Place chicken wings on upper food grate; close smoker. Smoke 1 hour. Remove wings from smoker, and let stand in a large bowl.

4. Meanwhile, preheat grill to 300° to 350° (medium) heat.

5. Toss wings in Rib Apple Glaze and grill chicken wings, covered with grill lid, 10 minutes, turning occasionally to set glaze.

6. Remove wings from grill, and serve immediately.

tip from the **PITS**

At Bogart's, we smoke our chicken wings at 250° for 2 hours and we blowtorch them to get the skin crisp. We toss them in a spicy-sweet sauce, such as peach-habanero or cranberry-chipotle sauce.

SKIP STEELE, BOGART'S SMOKEHOUSE, ST. LOUIS

SMOKY CHICKEN CHILI

Smoked pulled pork and turkey are equally delicious in this white chili and work well as substitutes for chicken.

YIELD: 6 TO 8 SERVINGS   TOTAL: 1 HOUR, 30 MINUTES

2   poblano chile peppers, chopped
1   large red bell pepper, chopped
1   medium-size sweet onion, chopped
3   garlic cloves, minced
2   Tbsp. olive oil
2   (14½-oz.) cans zesty chili-style diced tomatoes
3   cups shredded or chopped Smoked Chicken, about 1 lb. (page 105)
1   (16-oz.) can navy beans

1   (15-oz.) can black beans, drained and rinsed
1   (12-oz.) can beer*
1   (1.25-oz.) envelope white chicken chili seasoning mix
Toppings: shredded Cheddar cheese, chopped fresh cilantro, sour cream, lime wedges, baby corn, sliced black olives, chopped red onion, tortilla chips

Sauté first 4 ingredients in hot oil in a large Dutch oven over medium-high heat 8 minutes or until vegetables are tender. Stir in diced tomatoes and next 5 ingredients. Bring to a boil over medium-high heat. Reduce heat to low, and simmer, stirring occasionally, 1 hour. Serve with desired toppings.

* 1½ cups chicken broth may be substituted.

tip from the PITS

My favorite woods to use for smoking meats are pecan, cherry, and sugar maple. Each of these woods provides a delicate smoke and unique flavor. Hickory, oak, apple, and peach are also great choices, but I think you should go with what is most prevalent where you live. I also always try to recommend people stay away from mesquite wood. It has an acidic smoke, which is bad for your meat and can also eat away at the metal inside your grill or smoker.

CHRISTOPHER PRIETO, PRIME BARBECUE, WENDELL, NORTH CAROLINA

CHICKEN

CORNMEAL CAKES WITH SMOKED CHICKEN & COLESLAW

Reinvent a favorite Southern staple using smoked chicken in this dish. The fresh corn in the pillowy cornmeal cakes adds a sweet crunch for an extra layer of flavor.

YIELD: 8 TO 10 SERVINGS   TOTAL: 1 HOUR, 30 MINUTES

1 (6-oz.) package buttermilk cornbread mix	1 pt. prepared coleslaw
²/₃ cup milk	1 lb. chopped Smoked Chicken (page 105)
2 Tbsp. butter, melted	½ cup barbecue sauce
1 cup fresh corn kernels (2 ears)	2 avocados, sliced

1. Stir together first 3 ingredients in a small bowl until smooth. Stir in corn kernels. Drop mixture by ¼ cupfuls for each cornmeal cake onto a hot, lightly greased griddle or large nonstick skillet. Cook over medium heat 3 to 4 minutes on each side or until golden.

2. Divide coleslaw among cornmeal cakes; layer with Smoked Chicken, barbecue sauce, and avocado slices.

CHEF'S SIDE

TIM BYRES, SMOKE, DALLAS

HOMINY CASSEROLE

YIELD: 12 SERVINGS   TOTAL: 40 MINUTES

1 cup uncooked stone-ground yellow grits	¼ cup chopped pickled jalapeño
½ cup yellow cornmeal	1 (15.5-oz.) can white hominy, drained
½ cup masa harina (corn flour)	2 Tbsp. pickled jalapeño juice
1 lb. hickory-smoked bacon slices, cut into ½ inch pieces	½ cup sour cream
1 tsp. black peppercorns, crushed	2¾ cups shredded sharp Cheddar cheese, divided
1 qt. chicken or ham stock	1 Tbsp. Louisiana hot sauce
½ cup heavy cream	2 Tbsp. minced fresh chives

1. Combine first 3 ingredients in a bowl. Set aside.

2. Cook bacon and crushed peppercorns over medium-high heat in a Dutch oven 8 minutes or until crisp. Gradually add chicken stock, heavy cream, and 1 cup water. Bring to a boil; slowly whisk in grits mixture, in 3 additions. Reduce heat to low, and cook 15 minutes or until thick and smooth. Stir in chopped jalapeño, hominy and jalapeño juice. Remove from heat; stir in sour cream, 2 cups cheese, and hot sauce.

3. Preheat broiler. Divide grits mixture evenly into 12 (8-oz.) broiler-proof casserole dishes. Sprinkle evenly with remaining ¾ cup cheese. Place dishes on a baking sheet. Broil 3 minutes or until golden brown. Sprinkle with chives, and serve immediately.

CHICKEN

CHICKEN ENCHILADA CASSEROLE

Layered with corn tortillas and creamy filling, this casserole is just one way to make use of leftover Smoked Chicken (page 105).

YIELD: 8 TO 10 SERVINGS   **TOTAL: 1 HOUR, 30 MINUTES**

1½ cups diced sweet onion
2   large poblano peppers, seeded and diced
2   Tbsp. canola oil
3   garlic cloves, minced
2   (10¾-oz.) cans cream of chicken soup
1   (8-oz.) container sour cream
2   (4.5-oz.) cans chopped or diced green chiles

1   cup chicken broth
1   (1-oz.) envelope taco seasoning mix
18   (6-inch) corn tortillas, quartered
6   cups shredded Smoked Chicken, about 2 lb. (page 105)
2   cups (8 oz.) shredded extra-sharp Cheddar cheese
2   cups (8 oz.) shredded pepper Jack cheese

1. Preheat oven to 350°. Sauté first 2 ingredients in hot oil in a large skillet over medium-high heat 5 minutes or until tender. Add garlic, and sauté 1 minute. Stir in soup and next 4 ingredients; remove from heat.

2. Spread 1 cup soup mixture in a lightly greased 13- x 9-inch baking dish. Arrange 24 tortilla quarters, slightly overlapping, over soup mixture; top with 3 cups chicken, ¾ cup each Cheddar and pepper Jack cheeses, and 1½ cups soup mixture. Repeat layers once. Top with remaining 24 tortilla quarters, soup mixture, and cheeses.

3. Bake at 350° for 45 to 50 minutes or until bubbly and golden. Remove from oven to a wire rack, and let stand 15 minutes before serving.

BBQ&A

WITH ELIZABETH KARMEL, CAROLINACUETOGO.COM

Why is it so important to keep your smoker/grill clean?

The cleaner your grill, the better your results. To keep it clean, you need to burn off any drippings with high heat, and never use soap or water. Just use a brush to scrape it clean. A grill is like a cast-iron skillet. The more you use it, the better your food will taste.

SMOKED CHICKEN SUMMER SALAD

Transform the classic shredded chicken sandwich into a crunchy salad drizzled with sweet vinaigrette and topped with crispy croutons.

YIELD: 6 SERVINGS   TOTAL: 1 HOUR, 20 MINUTES, INCLUDING VINAIGRETTE AND CROUTONS

Sweet Onion Vinaigrette
Toasted Bun Croutons
1   (4-oz.) package watercress
1   cup thinly sliced radishes (about 8 large radishes)
1   cup loosely packed fresh cilantro leaves
½   cup fresh corn kernels (about 1 ear)

½   English cucumber, thinly sliced into half moons
½   lb. shredded Smoked Chicken, without sauce (page 105)
⅓   cup crumbled queso fresco
1   jalapeño pepper, halved, seeded, and thinly sliced

1. Prepare Sweet Onion Vinaigrette and Toasted Bun Croutons.

2. Toss together watercress, next 5 ingredients, and ¼ cup vinaigrette in a large bowl. Arrange mixture on a serving platter. Sprinkle with queso fresco, and top with jalapeño pepper slices and croutons. Serve salad with remaining vinaigrette.

SWEET ONION VINAIGRETTE

YIELD: 1¼ CUPS   TOTAL: 40 MINUTES

½   cup finely chopped sweet onion
⅓   cup apple cider vinegar
3   Tbsp. sugar
2   Tbsp. coarse-grained mustard

1   tsp. kosher salt
¼   tsp. ground cumin
⅛   tsp. ground red pepper
½   cup canola oil

Whisk together first 7 ingredients. Gradually add oil in a slow, steady stream, whisking constantly until smooth. Cover and chill 30 minutes or until ready to serve.

TOASTED BUN CROUTONS

YIELD: ABOUT 2½ CUPS   TOTAL: 50 MINUTES

1   Tbsp. sugar
4   Tbsp. canola oil
1   tsp. chili powder
1   tsp. kosher salt

½   tsp. freshly ground black pepper
4   hot dog or hamburger buns, cut into ½-inch cubes (about 4 cups)

1. Preheat oven to 375°. Whisk together first 5 ingredients. Add bun cubes, and toss.

2. Spread in a single layer on a lightly greased 15- x 10-inch jelly-roll pan. Bake 10 to 12 minutes or until golden brown, stirring halfway through. Cool 30 minutes.

BARBECUE CHICKEN SANDWICHES WITH CREAMY SLAW

Leftover Smoked Chicken reappears in this comforting all-in-one dish. You can also pick up chicken from your favorite barbecue joint, or use shredded rotisserie chicken. To speed up the process further, replace the homemade barbecue sauce with bottled.

YIELD: 4 SERVINGS   TOTAL: 25 MINUTES

½   cup mayonnaise
1   Tbsp. fresh lemon juice
½   tsp. granulated sugar
1   (12-oz.) package angel hair coleslaw mix
     or broccoli slaw mix
⅓   cup chopped fresh flat-leaf parsley
1½ cups ketchup
¼   cup spicy brown mustard
1   Tbsp. apple cider vinegar

1   Tbsp. Worcestershire sauce
1   tsp. firmly packed light brown sugar
½   tsp. garlic powder
½   tsp. onion powder
¼   tsp. kosher salt
2   cups shredded Smoked Chicken
     (page 105)
8   Texas toast slices, toasted
Memphis Slaw (page 268)

1. Stir together mayonnaise, lemon juice, and granulated sugar until smooth. Stir in coleslaw mix and parsley. Add table salt and black pepper to taste.

2. Combine ketchup and next 7 ingredients in a medium saucepan. Cook over medium-low heat, stirring occasionally, 15 minutes or until bubbly. Toss shredded Smoked Chicken and ½ cup barbecue sauce in a bowl. Spoon Memphis Slaw and barbecue mixture over 4 Texas toast slices and top with remaining 4 slices. Serve with remaining barbecue sauce.

CHICKEN

SPATCHCOCK SMOKED TURKEY

"Spatchcocking" a turkey simply means to split the bird down the back and flatten it out so it can smoke evenly and quickly. Pitmaster Christopher Prieto explains the advantages of the process.

I am a strong believer in cooking turkey on a hot smoker—fast (in two to three hours or less, depending on the size) because it produces a dark, crispy skin, and prevents the meat from oversmoking. This method works particularly well when you spatchcock a large bird, because you're opening the turkey to sit flat on the grill grates so it smokes evenly and more quickly. There are also several other advantages to spatchcocking a turkey before you smoke it. Because the bird's cavity is exposed, it's much easier to season, which impacts the flavor of the entire turkey. And since the turkey will lie flat on the smoker, both the outside skin and the inside cavity will brown during the cooking process (this is simply impossible with an upright, intact bird). The breast meat won't dry out as much, either, since hot smoke is circulating from all sides. Don't be intimidated by the butchering process—it is relatively simple and will result in a moist, delicious turkey every time.

---

what to look for

* Fresh (not frozen) turkey weighing between 15 and 18 pounds.

* Never buy a brand you don't recognize, especially during the holidays when these pop up. Either buy from your local butcher or buy a brand you know.

Chris' top tips

* Always dry the outside skin as much as possible before applying any oil.

* Turkey is best when smoked with lighter woods, such as apple, cherry, pecan, or sugar maple. Heavier woods like hickory or mesquite should be avoided.

best served with

* **SAUCE:**
South Carolina mustard sauce; a 50/50 mix of Eastern Carolina and sweet Kansas City sauces

* **SIDES:**
Slaw
Barbecue pinto beans
Potato salad

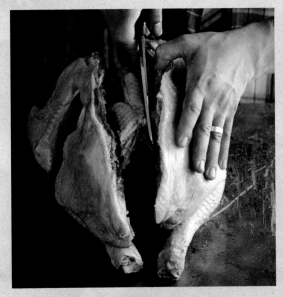

1. REMOVE BACKBONE. Place turkey, breast side down, on a cutting board. Using poultry shears, cut along both sides of the backbone and open turkey like a book.

2. BREAK THE BREASTBONE. Using the heel of your hands, press firmly against the inside of the breast cavity until the breastbone cracks and the turkey will lie flat. Tip: It may be easier to flip the turkey over and press directly on the breasts.

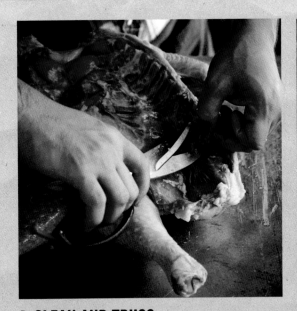

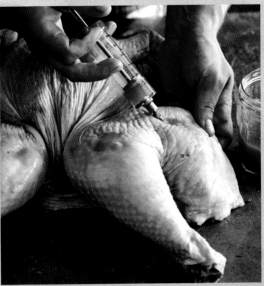

3. CLEAN AND TRUSS. Next, flatten out the thighs, and tuck the wings under so they're secure for cooking. Once the turkey will lie fully flat, use your poultry shears to remove any large pieces of fat or remains of organs.

4. INJECT WITH FLAVOR. Using an injector, inject Creole-style butter marinade into the turkey at 1-inch intervals. Cover and chill for at least 5 hours or up to 8 hours.

5. OIL IT DOWN. After you've injected your turkey and it has chilled for at least 5 hours, remove from the refrigerator and pat dry. Next coat the skin with an even layer of olive oil.

6. APPLY RUB. Finally, coat the oil-covered skin with a liberal layer of Season All Rub (page 329). This will not only flavor the turkey, but also give it a crisp, mahogany skin.

7. SMOKE IT. Place the turkey, breast side up, on the smoker's top food grate; close the smoker. Smoke 2 hours. Check temperature using a meat thermometer inserted into the thickest portion of the thigh.

8. BASTE THE SKIN. At the 2-hour mark, baste the entire turkey with a 12-oz. bottle of squeeze margarine. Continue smoking for 1 hour, or until a meat thermometer inserted into the thickest portion of the thigh registers 165°. Tip: At this stage, you can shield the breasts with heavy-duty aluminum foil, if needed, to prevent excess browning.

TURKEY

9. PULL AND CHOP. Remove the turkey from smoker; let it stand in a clean pan for 30 minutes. Place turkey on a cutting board, reserving drippings in pan. Remove and discard bones (or reserve for another use).

10. PULL AND CHOP. Shred turkey with 2 forks or chop with a meat cleaver, and place the meat in a large bowl. Add reserved drippings, tossing to coat. Serve immediately.

tip from the
PITS

Duck is great smoked. The trick is to poach it first in a pot of vinegar, salt, and water for about 5 minutes. It also allows some of the fat to release into the water and cut down on greasiness. After removing it from the poaching liquid, I season the duck and smoke it. You can also spatchcock the duck and finish smoking it in a cast-iron skillet, breast side down. The skillet renders the fat and creates a crispy crust.

TIM BYRES, SMOKE, DALLAS

SPATCHCOCK SMOKED TURKEY

Smoking turkey is a foolproof way to cook a large bird and end up with delicious meat that is flavorful and juicy. This technique allows the bird to lie flatter on the grill grates and cook more evenly.

YIELD: 8 TO 10 SERVINGS   TOTAL: 8 TO 11 HOURS

- 1 (10- to 15-lb.) whole turkey
- 1 (17-oz.) bottle injectable Creole-style butter marinade
- 3 to 4 pecan or sugar maple wood chunks
- 8 to 10 lb. charcoal briquettes
- 3 Tbsp. olive oil
- ¾ cup Season All Rub (page 329)
- 1 (12-oz.) container squeeze margarine

1. Cut turkey lengthwise along either side of backbone using kitchen shears; remove backbone. Open turkey, and place, breast side up, on a cutting board. Using the palms of your hands, break breastbone so turkey will lie flat. Place turkey, breast side up, in a large roasting pan. Using an injector, inject all of marinade into turkey at 1-inch intervals. Cover and chill for at least 5 hours or up to 8 hours.

2. Meanwhile prepare charcoal fire in smoker according the Minion Method (see page 39). Place water pan in smoker; add water to depth of fill line. Regulate temperature with a thermometer to 275° for 15 to 20 minutes.

3. Remove turkey from refrigerator and pat dry; coat skin with olive oil. Sprinkle turkey with Season All Rub.

4. Place turkey, breast side up, on top food grate; close smoker. Smoke 2 hours. Check temperature using a meat thermometer inserted into the thickest portion of the thighs, and baste with bottle of squeeze margarine. Shield breast with heavy-duty aluminum foil, if needed, to prevent excess browning. Continue smoking for 30 minutes to 1 hour or until meat thermometer inserted into thickest portion of the thighs registers 165°.

5. Remove turkey from smoker; let stand in clean pan 30 minutes. Place turkey on a cutting board, reserving drippings in pan. Remove bones from turkey and discard (or reserve for another use). Shred turkey with 2 forks or chop with a meat cleaver, and place meat in a large bowl. Add reserved drippings, tossing to coat. Serve immediately.

Note: We tested with Parkay Squeeze and Tony Chachere's Creole Style Butter Marinade.

HOPPIN' JOHN SOUP

Smoked turkey and country ham are substituted for sliced bacon in this traditional New Year's Day soup of black-eyed peas and collard greens.

YIELD: 11 CUPS   TOTAL: 2 HOURS, 30 MINUTES, INCLUDING CROUTONS

½ (16-oz.) package dried black-eyed peas, rinsed and sorted

1½ lb. Smoked Turkey, preferably dark meat (page 126)

⅓ cup finely chopped country ham

¼ tsp. dried crushed red pepper

2 garlic cloves, minced

1 jalapeño pepper, seeded and minced

2 carrots, cut into 1-inch pieces

1 celery rib, diced

1 large sweet onion, diced

1 bay leaf

2 Tbsp. canola oil

½ (16-oz.) package fresh collard greens, trimmed and finely chopped

1 Tbsp. hot sauce

1 Tbsp. apple cider vinegar

Hot cooked brown rice

Cornbread Croutons

Flat-leaf parsley leaves

1. Bring peas, turkey, and 6 cups water to a boil in a large Dutch oven. Cover, reduce heat to medium, and simmer 45 minutes or until peas are tender, skimming any foam from surface. Drain peas, reserving 1¼ cups liquid.

2. Sauté ham and next 7 ingredients in hot oil in Dutch oven over medium-high heat 10 minutes or until vegetables are tender. Add peas, reserved 1¼ cups liquid, turkey meat, collards, hot sauce, and 6 cups water. Bring to a boil; reduce heat to medium, and simmer, stirring occasionally, 30 minutes. Stir in vinegar. Season with table salt and freshly ground black pepper. Discard bay leaf. Serve over rice with Cornbread Croutons and parsley.

CORNBREAD CROUTONS

YIELD: MAKES 6 DOZEN USING A 9-INCH PAN   TOTAL: 20 MINUTES

½ cup chopped fresh cilantro

2 jalapeño peppers, seeded and chopped

Cornbread batter

1. Preheat oven to 375°.

2. Stir cilantro and jalapeño peppers into your favorite cornbread batter. Bake as directed; cool 10 minutes. Cut into 1-inch cubes. Bake at 375° in a lightly greased jelly-roll pan until edges are golden, stirring halfway through.

TURKEY TORTILLA SOUP

This soup is a simple way to utilize the leftover cooked meat from the Smoked Turkey on page 126, and you'll reap the rewards of a delicious meal with minimal effort.

YIELD: 8 CUPS   TOTAL: 40 MINUTES

10 (6-inch) fajita-size corn tortillas, cut into ½-inch-wide strips
Vegetable cooking spray
1 small onion, chopped
2 garlic cloves, chopped
1 small jalapeño pepper, seeded and minced
1 Tbsp. olive oil
1 (32-oz.) container chicken broth
1 (10-oz.) can medium enchilada sauce
2 cups chopped Smoked Turkey, without sauce (page 126)
1 tsp. ground cumin
Toppings: chopped avocado, shredded sharp Cheddar cheese, chopped fresh cilantro, chopped tomatoes

1. Preheat oven to 450°. Place half of tortilla strips in a single layer on a baking sheet. Coat strips with cooking spray; bake 10 minutes or until browned and crisp, stirring once. Set aside.

2. Sauté onion and next 2 ingredients in hot olive oil in a Dutch oven over medium-high heat 5 to 6 minutes or until browned.

3. Add chicken broth and remaining unbaked tortilla strips to onion mixture. Cook broth mixture over medium heat 3 to 5 minutes or until tortilla strips soften and broth mixture thickens slightly.

4. Stir in enchilada sauce and next 2 ingredients, and cook 6 to 8 minutes or until mixture is thoroughly heated. (Do not boil.) Garnish with baked tortilla strips and desired toppings.

OVEN-GRILLED LOADED TURKEY MELTS

Thinly sliced Smoked Turkey and avocado spread come together with bacon and mozzarella cheese for one knockout sandwich.

YIELD: 4 SERVINGS   TOTAL: 30 MINUTES

2	ripe avocados, peeled and mashed	4	tomato slices
2	Tbsp. mayonnaise	4	sliced red onion rings
1	tsp. garlic powder	8	center-cut bacon slices, cooked
8	bread slices	¼	lb. smoked mozzarella cheese slices
1	lb. thinly sliced Smoked Turkey, without sauce (page 126)	3	Tbsp. butter, softened

1. Preheat oven to 400°.

2. Stir together avocado, mayonnaise, and garlic powder. Spread avocado mixture on 1 side of 4 bread slices. Top evenly with Smoked Turkey, tomato, onion, bacon, cheese, and remaining bread slices.

3. Spread butter evenly on both sides of sandwiches. Place buttered sandwiches on a baking sheet. Place a second baking sheet on top of sandwiches. Bake for 20 minutes or until golden.

BBQ&A

WITH PITMASTER TROY BLACK

How do you flavor your poultry before you smoke it?

I cover the outside with butter and use a dry rub. Sometimes I brine it for flavor in a simple brine of salt, sugar, and water. I've also added things such as orange slices, apple juice, herbs, and even different types of sugars and salts.

STRAWBERRY-TURKEY-BRIE PANINI *(pictured)*

Break out your panini press. The flavorful combination of strawberry, basil, Smoked Turkey, and Brie make this sandwich worthy of that little bit of extra effort.

YIELD: 4 SERVINGS   TOTAL: 10 MINUTES

1   (8-oz.) Brie round
8   Italian bread slices
8   oz. thinly sliced Smoked Turkey, without sauce (page 126)
8   fresh basil leaves
½   cup sliced fresh strawberries
2   Tbsp. red pepper jelly
2   Tbsp. butter, melted

1. Trim and discard rind from Brie. Cut Brie into ½-inch-thick slices. Layer 4 bread slices evenly with Smoked Turkey, basil leaves, strawberries, and Brie.

2. Spread pepper jelly on 1 side of each of remaining 4 bread slices; place bread slices, jelly sides down, on top of Brie. Brush sandwiches with melted butter.

3. Cook sandwiches, in batches, in a preheated panini press 2 to 3 minutes or until golden brown.

SMOKED TURKEY-BLUE CHEESE OPEN-FACED SANDWICHES

Forget about turkey and Swiss. This open-faced sandwich takes your leftover Smoked Turkey to another level.

YIELD: 6 SERVINGS   TOTAL: 15 MINUTES

Fig paste
12 (¼-inch-thick) toasted French bread slices
Sliced Smoked Turkey, without sauce (page 126)
Soft-ripened blue-veined Brie
Parchment paper
Arugula

Preheat oven to 425°. Spread desired amount of fig paste on toasted bread slices; top with Smoked Turkey slices and Brie. Place on a parchment paper-lined baking sheet. Bake for 8 minutes. Remove from oven. Top with arugula, and sprinkle with freshly ground pepper to taste just before serving.

TURKEY

HOT & FAST

Quick grilling is ideal for tender cuts of meat. Burgers, steaks, chicken breasts, pork chops, and fish fillets need high heat to sear on the outside without overcooking on the inside.

COFFEE-RUBBED SKIRT STEAK

Serve this tender, flavor-packed skirt steak with grilled corn and sliced tomatoes. If you can't find chicory coffee, you can substitute espresso or regular coffee.

YIELD: 6 TO 8 SERVINGS   TOTAL: 50 MINUTES

- 2 Tbsp. chili powder
- 1 Tbsp. sugar
- 1 Tbsp. kosher salt
- 1 Tbsp. finely ground chicory coffee
- 1 tsp. coarsely ground black pepper

- 2 (1½-lb.) boneless skirt, flank, or tri-tip steaks
- Fresh fruit salsa
- Lime wedges

1. Preheat grill to 400° to 450° (high) heat. Stir together first 5 ingredients; rub over steaks. Let stand 30 minutes.

2. Grill, covered with grill lid, 3 to 5 minutes on each side or to desired degree of doneness. Let stand 5 minutes. Cut across the grain into thin strips; serve with salsa and lime wedges.

tip from the **PITS**

When I use coffee as a rub on different cuts of beef, I use instant coffee instead of regular ground coffee. Instant crystals melt into the meat better and don't leave a mealy texture. They also add the same smoky notes and color as regular coffee grounds.

CHRISTOPHER PRIETO, PRIME BARBECUE, WENDELL, NORTH CAROLINA

GRILLED TRI-TIP

Tri-tip is a relatively inexpensive cut of beef ideal for quick grilling. It's the lean triangular muscle cut from the bottom sirloin. After grilling, let the steak stand at least 10 minutes before slicing to prevent the juices from escaping.

YIELD: 8 TO 10 SERVINGS   TOTAL: 40 MINUTES, INCLUDING BUTTER

2   (2-lb.) tri-tip steaks
2   tsp. table salt, divided
1¼ tsp. freshly ground black pepper, divided
Citrus-Chile Butter

3   bunches baby Vidalia or green onions, trimmed
3   Tbsp. olive oil

1. Preheat grill to 350° to 400° (medium-high) heat. Sprinkle steaks with 1½ tsp. salt and 1 tsp. pepper. Grill steaks, covered with grill lid, 9 to 12 minutes on each side or to desired degree of doneness.

2. Remove from grill, and rub 3 Tbsp. Citrus-Chile Butter onto steaks. Cover steaks with aluminum foil; let stand 5 minutes.

3. Meanwhile, toss onions with olive oil; season with remaining ½ tsp. salt and ¼ tsp. pepper. Grill onions, without grill lid, 2 minutes; turn and grill 1 more minute.

4. Uncover steaks, and cut diagonally across the grain into thin slices. Serve with grilled onions and remaining Citrus-Chile Butter.

CITRUS-CHILE BUTTER

This compound butter is a mixture of lime and lemon zests and jalapeño pepper. If you love spicy food, don't seed the jalapeño before mincing.

YIELD: 1 CUP   TOTAL: 10 MINUTES

1   cup butter, softened
2   Tbsp. lime zest
2   Tbsp. lemon zest
3   garlic cloves, minced

1   Tbsp. seeded and minced jalapeño pepper
1   tsp. chopped fresh thyme

1. Stir together butter, and next 5 ingredients.

2. Season with table salt and freshly ground black pepper to taste.

3. Cover and chill until ready to serve, or shape into a log with plastic wrap, and freeze up to 1 month.

SMOKED BEEF TENDERLOIN

Beef tenderloin is ideal for a special occasion and is deliciously tender and flavorful in this application. Substitute more budget-friendly steaks if you wish. Try a 1½-lb. tri-tip steak and smoke for 20 minutes or a 1-lb. flank steak and smoke for 15 minutes. For each, reduce the seasoning to 1¼ teaspoons.

YIELD: 8 TO 10 SERVINGS
TOTAL: 15 HOURS, 20 MINUTES, INCLUDING CHILL TIME, RUB, AND SAUCE

1   (5-lb.) beef tenderloin, trimmed
Wood chips
2   Tbsp. olive oil
2   Tbsp. Hill Country Rub (page 325)
Vegetable cooking spray
Chimichurri Sauce

1. Cover tenderloin, and let stand at room temperature 1 hour.

2. Meanwhile, soak wood chips in water 30 minutes. Prepare smoker according to manufacturer's directions, bringing internal temperature to 300°; maintain temperature for 15 to 20 minutes.

3. Pat tenderloin dry; brush with olive oil, and sprinkle with Hill Country Rub.

4. Drain wood chips, and place on coals. Place tenderloin on cooking grate; cover with smoker lid.

5. Smoke tenderloin, maintaining temperature inside smoker at 300°, for 45 minutes or until a meat thermometer inserted into thickest portion registers 130°. Let stand at room temperature 30 minutes; cover and chill 12 to 24 hours.

6. Coat cold cooking grate of grill with cooking spray, and place on grill. Preheat grill to 400° to 450° (high) heat. Place chilled tenderloin on cooking grate, and grill 2 minutes on each side. Let stand 5 minutes before slicing. Serve with Chimichurri Sauce.

CHIMICHURRI SAUCE

Argentina's equivalent to ketchup, chimichurri is an herbal dipping sauce perfect for serving with smoky grilled meats.

YIELD: 1¾ CUPS   TOTAL: 10 MINUTES

4   cups firmly packed fresh flat-leaf parsley leaves
¾   cup olive oil
4   garlic cloves
3   Tbsp. fresh lemon juice
3   Tbsp. sherry vinegar or red wine vinegar
2   Tbsp. minced shallot
1   tsp. kosher salt
½   tsp. freshly ground black pepper
½   tsp. dried crushed red pepper

Process ingredients in a food processor until finely chopped. Refrigerate in an airtight container for up to 5 days.

GRILLED MOLASSES FLANK STEAK

Molasses is the syrupy mixture left over when sugar crystals are extracted from boiled-down sugar cane and sugar beet juice. The potent flavor is ideal for the marinade, and the longer you marinate, the more time it has to infuse the flank steak.

YIELD: 6 TO 8 SERVINGS
TOTAL: 5 HOURS, 25 MINUTES, INCLUDING MARINADE TIME AND SALSA

¾   cup molasses
⅓   cup soy sauce
¼   cup canola oil
¼   cup fresh lemon juice
2   Tbsp. Worcestershire sauce

2   Tbsp. grated fresh ginger
3   garlic cloves, minced
1   tsp. dried crushed red pepper
1   (2-lb.) flank steak
Watermelon Salsa

1. Place first 8 ingredients in a 2-gal. zip-top plastic freezer bag; squeeze bag to combine. Add steak; seal bag, and chill 4 to 12 hours. Remove steak from marinade, discarding marinade.

2. Preheat grill to 400° to 450° (high) heat. Grill steak, covered with grill lid, 9 minutes on each side or to desired degree of doneness. Remove from grill, and let stand 10 minutes. Cut diagonally across the grain into thin slices. Season with table salt and freshly ground black pepper to taste. Top with Watermelon Salsa.

WATERMELON SALSA

The perfect topping for Grilled Molasses Flank Steak, this salsa is also great as a stand-alone dip for tortilla chips or served with grilled chicken or pork.

YIELD: ABOUT 4 CUPS   TOTAL: 35 MINUTES

1   cup diced unpeeled nectarine
2   jalapeño peppers, seeded and minced
1   Tbsp. sugar
3   Tbsp. fresh lime juice
2   tsp. orange zest

2   tsp. grated fresh ginger
2   cups seeded and diced watermelon
½   cup chopped fresh cilantro
⅓   cup diced red onion

1. Stir together first 6 ingredients in a large bowl; let stand 15 minutes.

2. Add watermelon and next 2 ingredients, and toss gently to coat.

3. Serve immediately, or cover and chill up to 24 hours.

FLANK STEAK SANDWICHES WITH BLUE CHEESE *(pictured)*

These sandwiches feature creamy, soft-ripened blue cheese, which has a gooey consistency that pairs well with the grilled steak.

YIELD: 6 SERVINGS   TOTAL: 30 MINUTES

- 2 large sweet onions, cut into ¼-inch-thick slices
- 4 Tbsp. olive oil, divided
- ½ tsp. table salt
- ½ tsp. freshly ground black pepper
- 3 red bell peppers, cut into 1-inch-wide strips
- 6 (2- to 3-oz.) ciabatta or deli rolls, split
- 5 oz. soft-ripened blue cheese
- 1½ cups loosely packed arugula
- Herb-Marinated Flank Steak
- 6 Tbsp. mayonnaise

1. Preheat grill to 400° to 450° (high) heat. Brush onions with 1 Tbsp. olive oil, and sprinkle with ¼ tsp. salt and ¼ tsp. pepper. Place pepper strips in a large bowl, and drizzle with 1 Tbsp. olive oil. Sprinkle with remaining ¼ tsp. salt and ¼ tsp. pepper; toss to coat.

2. Grill onions and bell pepper strips, covered with grill lid, 7 to 10 minutes on each side or until lightly charred and tender.

3. Brush cut sides of rolls with remaining 2 Tbsp. olive oil, and grill, cut sides down, without grill lid, over 400° to 450° (high) heat 1 to 2 minutes or until lightly browned and toasted.

4. Spread blue cheese on cut sides of roll bottoms; top with steak, bell pepper strips, onion, and arugula. Spread mayonnaise on cut sides of roll tops. Place roll tops, mayonnaise sides down, on top of arugula, pressing lightly.

HERB-MARINATED FLANK STEAK

The herb marinade is also great on chicken. Substitute boneless, skinless breasts, and grill 7 minutes on each side or until done.

YIELD: 6 SERVINGS   TOTAL: 1 HOUR, INCLUDING MARINADE TIME

- ½ small sweet onion, minced
- 3 garlic cloves, minced
- ¼ cup olive oil
- 2 Tbsp. chopped fresh basil
- 1 Tbsp. chopped fresh thyme
- 1 Tbsp. chopped fresh rosemary
- 1 tsp. table salt
- ½ tsp. dried crushed red pepper
- 1¾ lb. flank steak
- 1 lemon, halved

1. Place first 8 ingredients in a 2-gal. zip-top plastic freezer bag, and squeeze bag to combine. Add steak; seal bag, and chill 30 minutes to 1 hour and 30 minutes. Remove steak from marinade, discarding marinade.

2. Preheat grill to 400° to 450° (high) heat. Grill steak, covered with grill lid, 9 minutes on each side or to desired degree of doneness. Remove from grill; squeeze juice from lemon over steak. Let stand 10 minutes. Cut across the grain into thin slices.

BULGOGI FLANK STEAK (pictured)

This Korean barbecue steak gets its tenderness and flavor from a long marinating time. Serve it with a crisp salad to round out the meal.

YIELD: 6 SERVINGS   TOTAL: 12 HOURS, 45 MINUTES, INCLUDING MARINADE TIME

½   cup soy sauce
¼   cup firmly packed light brown sugar
¼   cup chopped green onions
¼   cup dark sesame oil
2   Tbsp. dry sherry

2   Tbsp. minced fresh garlic
1   Tbsp. grated fresh ginger
1   tsp. dried crushed red pepper
1   (2-lb.) flank steak

1. Combine first 8 ingredients in a 2-gal. zip-top plastic freezer bag; add steak. Seal bag, and chill 12 hours. Remove steak from marinade, discarding marinade.

2. Preheat grill to 400° to 450° (high) heat. Grill steak, covered with grill lid, 9 minutes on each side or to desired degree of doneness. Let stand 10 minutes. Cut diagonally across the grain into thin slices. Sprinkle with table salt and freshly ground black pepper to taste.

SPICY FLANK STEAK

If you prefer your flank steak even spicier, increase the crushed red pepper in the rub to 1 teaspoon.

YIELD: 4 TO 6 SERVINGS   TOTAL: 40 MINUTES

1   (1½- to 2-lb.) flank steak
2   tsp. vegetable oil
2   tsp. ground cumin
2   tsp. chili powder

1   tsp. kosher salt
¾   tsp. freshly ground black pepper
½   tsp. dried crushed red pepper
¼   tsp. ground cinnamon

1. Preheat grill to 350° to 400° (medium-high) heat. Rub both sides of steak evenly with vegetable oil.

2. Stir together ground cumin and next 5 ingredients. Rub cumin mixture evenly over both sides of steak. Let stand 10 minutes.

3. Grill, covered with grill lid, 5 to 7 minutes on each side or to desired degree of doneness. Remove from grill. Cover steak loosely with aluminum foil, and let stand 10 minutes. Cut across the grain into thin slices.

GRILLED BALSAMIC-MOLASSES BACON

It doesn't get better than this: sticky-sweet bacon infused with herbaceous rosemary. Serve this bacon for breakfast, on top of your favorite burger, or just by itself.

YIELD: 6 TO 8 SERVINGS   TOTAL: 1 HOUR

14 (8-inch) wooden skewers
6   Tbsp. molasses
3   Tbsp. balsamic vinegar
¼   tsp. ground red pepper

14 thick applewood-smoked bacon slices
3   fresh rosemary sprigs

1. Soak wooden skewers in water 30 minutes. Preheat grill to 250° to 300° (low) heat.

2. Stir together molasses and next 2 ingredients. Thread 1 bacon slice onto each skewer.

3. Grill bacon, covered with grill lid, 15 to 18 minutes or until bacon begins to brown, turning every 6 minutes. Baste with half of molasses mixture, using rosemary sprigs as a brush; grill, covered with grill lid, 5 minutes. Turn bacon, and baste with remaining molasses mixture, using rosemary sprigs. Grill, covered with grill lid, 5 minutes or until browned and crisp. Remove from grill. Sprinkle with freshly ground black pepper to taste. Serve bacon immediately.

tip from the
PITS

I'm a big fan of cooking on either charcoal or gas grills because they're both so approachable. But when it comes to wood, use what is indigenous to your area. In North Carolina, you'll find hickory. In Texas, it's post oak, and in St. Louis it's applewood because of the orchards.

ELIZABETH KARMEL, CAROLINACUETOGO.COM

BROWN SUGAR PORK CHOPS WITH PEACH BARBECUE SAUCE

These pork chops are quickly brined in a salty-sweet brown sugar mixture, preparing them to caramelize beautifully when they hit the hot grill. The fresh peach barbecue sauce is infused with spicy ginger for a fragrant and fresh result.

YIELD: 4 SERVINGS   TOTAL: 1 HOUR, 10 MINUTES

¾ cup firmly packed dark brown sugar
¼ cup kosher salt
2 cups boiling water
3 cups ice cubes
4 bone-in pork loin chops (about 2 lb.)
1 medium-size sweet onion, finely chopped
1 Tbsp. canola oil
1 garlic clove, minced

1 (1-inch) piece fresh ginger, peeled and grated
1½ cups ketchup
½ cup peach preserves or jam
2 large peaches (about 1 lb.), peeled and cut into ¾-inch chunks
2 Tbsp. apple cider vinegar
Garnish: fresh thyme

1. Combine sugar and salt in a large bowl; add boiling water, stirring until sugar and salt dissolve. Stir in ice cubes to cool mixture. Add pork chops; cover and chill 30 minutes.

2. Meanwhile, sauté onion in hot oil in a medium saucepan over medium heat 2 minutes or until tender. Add garlic and ginger; cook, stirring constantly, 45 to 60 seconds or until fragrant. Add ketchup, peach preserves, and peaches. Reduce heat to low, and simmer, stirring occasionally, 30 minutes or until sauce thickens. Add vinegar; season with table salt and freshly ground black pepper to taste. Remove from heat.

3. Remove pork from brine, discarding brine. Rinse pork well, and pat dry with paper towels.

4. Preheat grill to 350° to 400° (medium-high) heat. Pour half of peach mixture into a bowl; reserve remaining mixture. Season both sides of pork with desired amount of table salt and freshly ground pepper.

5. Grill pork, covered with grill lid, 5 to 6 minutes on each side or until a meat thermometer inserted into thickest portion of each chop registers 145°, basting pork occasionally with peach mixture in bowl. Remove pork from grill; let stand 5 minutes before serving. Serve with reserved peach mixture.

PORK TENDERLOINS WITH BALSAMIC STRAWBERRIES

This recipe screams summer with sweet strawberries, pork wrapped in bacon, and tender French green beans. Be sure to wrap the pork tightly in bacon to give it a smoky flavor and a crispy crust.

YIELD: 6 TO 8 SERVINGS   **TOTAL: 1 HOUR**

1 (3-lb.) package pork tenderloins	2 Tbsp. olive oil, divided
½ tsp. freshly ground black pepper	4 garlic cloves, divided
2 tsp. kosher salt, divided	½ cup balsamic vinegar
10 center-cut bacon slices	⅓ cup strawberry preserves
2 (8-oz.) packages haricots verts (thin green beans)	½ cup quartered fresh strawberries

1. Light 1 side of grill, heating to 400° to 500° (high) heat; leave other side unlit. Remove silverskin from tenderloins, leaving a thin layer of fat. Sprinkle with pepper and 1 tsp. salt; wrap 5 bacon slices around each tenderloin, and secure with wooden picks.

2. Place green beans, 1 Tbsp. olive oil, 2 garlic cloves, and remaining 1 tsp. salt in center of a 24- x 18-inch piece of heavy-duty aluminum foil; toss to coat. Bring up sides of foil over beans; double-fold top and side edges to seal, making a packet.

3. Arrange pork and foil packet over unlit side, and grill, covered with grill lid, 25 to 30 minutes or until a meat thermometer inserted into thickest portion registers 145°.

4. Meanwhile, mince remaining 2 garlic cloves; sauté in remaining 1 Tbsp. hot olive oil in a medium skillet over medium-high heat 2 to 3 minutes or until golden. Add vinegar; bring to a boil over medium-high heat. Boil 5 minutes. Remove from heat, and stir in preserves. Reserve half of mixture for basting. Stir fresh strawberries into remaining mixture.

5. Remove foil packet from grill; transfer pork to lit side. Baste pork with reserved strawberry mixture. Grill 5 more minutes over lit side, turning once. Remove pork from grill; let stand 10 minutes. Slice and serve with strawberry mixture and green beans.

BOURBON-BROWN SUGAR PORK TENDERLOIN

Pork tenderloins are often sold two to a package, so when buying the pork for this recipe, look for a 2-lb. package.

YIELD: 6 TO 8 SERVINGS
TOTAL: 18 HOURS, 30 MINUTES, INCLUDING MARINADE TIME

2	(1-lb.) pork tenderloins	¼	cup soy sauce
¼	cup firmly packed dark brown sugar	¼	cup Dijon mustard
¼	cup minced green onions	½	tsp. freshly ground black pepper
¼	cup bourbon	½	tsp. cornstarch

1. Remove silverskin from tenderloins, leaving a thin layer of fat. Combine brown sugar and next 5 ingredients in a large zip-top plastic freezer bag; add pork. Seal bag, and chill 8 to 18 hours, turning bag occasionally. Remove pork from marinade, reserving marinade.

2. Preheat grill to 350° to 400° (medium-high) heat. Grill pork, covered with grill lid, 8 minutes on each side or until a meat thermometer inserted into thickest portion registers 145°. Remove from grill, and let stand 10 minutes.

3. Meanwhile, combine reserved marinade and cornstarch in a saucepan. Bring to a boil over medium heat; cook, stirring constantly, 1 minute. Cut pork diagonally into thin slices, and arrange on a serving platter; drizzle with warm sauce.

—— TRY THIS ——

BOURBON-BROWN SUGAR FLANK STEAK: Substitute 1½ lb. flank steak for pork tenderloin. Reduce grill time to 6 to 8 minutes on each side or to desired degree of doneness.

GRILLED PORK TENDERLOIN SANDWICHES

The flavor of these simple pork sandwiches is enhanced by the sweet Vidalia Onion Barbecue Sauce. Be sure to get real Vidalia onions when you're preparing the barbecue sauce.

YIELD: 6 SERVINGS   TOTAL: 45 MINUTES

1	tsp. garlic powder	2	(¾-lb.) pork tenderloins
1	tsp. table salt		Vegetable cooking spray
1	tsp. dry mustard	6	whole wheat hamburger buns
½	tsp. coarsely ground black pepper	6	Tbsp. Vidalia Onion Barbecue Sauce

1. Preheat grill to 350° to 400° (medium-high) heat. Stir together first 4 ingredients; rub pork tenderloins evenly with seasoning mixture. Lightly coat pork with cooking spray.

2. Grill, covered with grill lid, 10 to 12 minutes on each side or until a meat thermometer inserted into thickest portions registers 145°. Remove from grill, and let stand 10 minutes. Chop or slice, and serve on hamburger buns. Drizzle each sandwich with 1 Tbsp. Vidalia Onion Barbecue Sauce.

VIDALIA ONION BARBECUE SAUCE

Sweet, succulent Vidalia onions hail from the namesake Vidalia, Georgia. The soil and climate where they're grown give them their characteristic flavor. And this barbecue sauce is the perfect accompaniment with the pork tenderloin sandwich.

YIELD: ABOUT 2½ CUPS   TOTAL: 30 MINUTES

1	medium Vidalia onion, finely chopped	2	Tbsp. Worcestershire sauce
1	cup ketchup	1	Tbsp. olive oil
2	Tbsp. firmly packed brown sugar	1	garlic clove, minced
2	Tbsp. fresh lemon juice	½	tsp. table salt
2	Tbsp. apple cider vinegar	½	tsp. freshly ground black pepper

Stir together all ingredients and ½ cup water in a large saucepan; bring to a boil over medium heat. Reduce heat to low, and simmer, stirring occasionally, 20 minutes. Refrigerate in an airtight container for up to a week.

SMOKED PAPRIKA PORK ROAST

The pork in this recipe is "dry brined," allowing the salt in the seasoning mixture to pull the flavor into the meat and improve the juiciness. Don't be alarmed with the long, uncovered chilling time; it helps keep the rub dry.

YIELD: 8 SERVINGS   TOTAL: 1 HOUR, 30 MINUTES, PLUS 24 HOURS CHILL TIME

2   Tbsp. smoked paprika
2   Tbsp. firmly packed brown sugar
1   Tbsp. kosher salt
1   garlic clove, pressed
1   tsp. coarsely ground black pepper

4   tsp. chopped fresh thyme, divided
1   (3½- to 4-lb.) boneless pork loin roast
Kitchen string
Sticky Stout Barbecue Sauce

1. Stir together first 5 ingredients and 2 tsp. thyme. Trim pork roast. Rub paprika mixture over pork. Tie roast with kitchen string at 1½-inch intervals, and place in a 13- x 9-inch baking dish. Chill, uncovered, 24 hours.

2. Light 1 side of grill, heating to 350° to 400° (medium-high) heat; leave other side unlit. Place pork over lit side, and grill, covered with grill lid, 8 minutes on each side or until browned. Transfer pork to unlit side, and grill, covered with grill lid, 35 to 45 minutes or until a meat thermometer inserted into thickest portion registers 145°. Let stand 10 minutes. Brush with Sticky Stout Barbecue Sauce. Sprinkle with remaining 2 tsp. thyme. Serve with remaining sauce.

STICKY STOUT BARBECUE SAUCE

This Kansas City-inspired thick and sweet sauce gets its rich flavor from robust stout beer. It can be made up to three days in advance. Cover and chill, and reheat when ready to use.

YIELD: ABOUT 2 CUPS   TOTAL: 30 MINUTES

1   small onion, finely chopped
1   Tbsp. vegetable oil
2   garlic cloves, minced
1   (11.2-oz.) bottle stout beer

1   cup spicy barbecue sauce
¼   cup fig preserves
2   Tbsp. apple cider vinegar

1. Sauté onion in hot oil in a large saucepan over medium-high heat 4 to 5 minutes or until tender. Add garlic; sauté 1 minute. Gradually stir in beer. Cook 8 to 10 minutes or until mixture is reduced by half. Reduce heat to medium.

2. Stir in barbecue sauce and next 2 ingredients, and cook 4 to 5 minutes or until thoroughly heated.

SERRANO PEPPER BURGERS *(pictured on page 164)*

Serrano chiles are small and yellow and are available at your local supermarket. Substitute milder Anaheim or poblano peppers if you'd like something with a little less kick.

YIELD: 12 SERVINGS   TOTAL: 1 HOUR

1   lb. serrano peppers
2   Tbsp. olive oil
3   lb. ground chuck
1   lb. pepper Jack cheese, thinly sliced

Butter, softened
12 hamburger buns
Toppings: mayonnaise, ketchup,
      mustard, lettuce, tomato slices

1. Light 1 side of grill, heating to 350° to 400° (medium-high) heat; leave other side unlit. Toss together peppers and olive oil. Arrange peppers in a grill basket or on an aluminum-foil tray over unlit side, and grill, covered with grill lid, 10 to 15 minutes or until peppers begin to shrivel. Transfer peppers to lit side of grill, and grill, covered with grill lid, 8 to 10 minutes or until lightly charred, turning halfway through. Remove from grill to a wire rack, and cool completely (about 15 minutes).

2. Remove and discard stems; slice peppers in half lengthwise. Remove seeds, and sprinkle peppers with desired amount of salt.

3. Preheat both sides of grill to 350° to 400° (medium-high) heat. Shape ground chuck into 12 patties; sprinkle with desired amount of table salt and freshly ground black pepper. Grill patties, without grill lid, 4 to 5 minutes on each side or to desired degree of doneness. Place 2 to 3 pepper halves on each patty; top with cheese. Grill, covered with grill lid, until cheese melts.

4. Butter buns, and toast on grill. Serve patties on toasted buns with desired toppings.

BACON-WRAPPED BARBECUE BURGERS *(pictured on page 165)*

The best part about this burger is convenience items make it easy to prep. Don't skip the step to precook the bacon in the microwave. It helps crisp it up to perfection on the grill.

YIELD: 4 SERVINGS   TOTAL: 1 HOUR

8   center-cut bacon slices
1   (4.5-oz.) jar sliced mushrooms, drained
    and chopped
½   cup chopped Vidalia or sweet onion
2   tsp. olive oil
½   cup bottled honey barbecue sauce,
    divided

1½ lb. ground beef
Wooden picks
¼   tsp. table salt
4   sesame seed hamburger buns, toasted

1. Arrange bacon on a paper towel-lined microwave-safe plate; cover with a paper towel. Microwave bacon at HIGH 2 minutes or until edges begin to crinkle and bacon is partially cooked.

2. Sauté mushrooms and onion in hot oil in a small nonstick skillet over medium heat 4 to 5 minutes or until tender and liquid is absorbed. Remove from heat, and stir in 2 Tbsp. barbecue sauce.

3. Preheat grill to 350° to 400° (medium-high) heat. Shape ground beef into 8 (5-inch) thin patties. Place 2 Tbsp. mushroom mixture in center of each of 4 patties. Top with remaining patties, pressing edges to seal. Shape into 4-inch patties. Wrap sides of each patty with 2 bacon slices, overlapping ends of each slice. Secure bacon using wooden picks. Sprinkle patties with salt. Cover and chill 10 minutes.

4. Grill patties, covered with grill lid, 5 to 6 minutes on 1 side. Turn and baste with half of remaining barbecue sauce. Grill 5 to 6 minutes or until beef is no longer pink in center. Turn and baste with remaining barbecue sauce. Remove from grill, and let stand 5 minutes. Remove wooden picks. Serve burgers on buns, and topped with remaining mushroom mixture.

LAMB SLIDERS WITH LEMONY PICKLES & HERB-CAPER MAYO

(pictured on page 164)

These mini lamb burgers will disappear in a flash. The homemade lemony pickles and creamy flavor-packed mayonnaise pair perfectly with the lamb. Grill the buns for even smokier flavor.

YIELD: 12 SLIDERS   TOTAL: 45 MINUTES

¼ cup mayonnaise
¼ cup plain Greek yogurt
2 Tbsp. drained capers
1 Tbsp. chopped fresh mint
1 Tbsp. chopped fresh rosemary
1 tsp. lemon zest

1 cup thinly sliced English cucumber
3 Tbsp. fresh lemon juice
1 lb. ground lamb
2 oz. crumbled feta cheese
12 slider buns or dinner rolls, split
2 cups baby arugula

1. Preheat grill to medium-high (350° to 400°) heat. Combine mayonnaise, and next 5 ingredients. Set aside.

2. Combine cucumber slices and lemon juice in a small bowl. Let stand at least 30 minutes, tossing occasionally.

3. Gently combine lamb and feta cheese. Shape mixture into 12 patties. Grill burgers 2 minutes on each side or until done.

4. Spread mayonnaise mixture on insides of buns. Top each bun bottom with 1 slider, lemony pickles, arugula, and bun top.

Lamb Sliders
(page 163)

Grilled Chicken Tequila
Burger (page 166)

Serrano Pepper
Burger (page 162)

Bacon-Wrapped
Barbecue Burger
(page 162)

Shrimp Burger
(page 167)

GRILLED CHICKEN TEQUILA BURGERS *(pictured on page 164)*

Add some *olé!* to your plate with these tequila-bathed burgers. The creamy and cool cilantro-lime mayo tames the flames of spicy jalapeño.

YIELD: 5 SERVINGS   TOTAL: 25 MINUTES, INCLUDING MAYONNAISE

1   lb. ground chicken breast
3   Tbsp. chopped fresh cilantro
2   garlic cloves, chopped
1   jalapeño pepper, seeded and chopped
½   cup panko (Japanese breadcrumbs) or
    ¼ cup uncooked regular or
    quick-cooking oats
2   Tbsp. tequila

1   tsp. lime zest
¾   tsp. table salt
½   tsp. freshly ground black pepper
¼   tsp. soy sauce
Sliced bell peppers
Sliced onions
5 hamburger buns
Cilantro-Lime Mayonnaise

1. Preheat grill to 350° to 400° (medium-high) heat. Pulse ground chicken, cilantro, garlic, and jalapeño pepper in a food processor 3 or 4 times or until combined. Add panko or oats, tequila, lime zest, salt, pepper, and soy sauce; pulse until combined.

2. Shape into 5 patties. Grill, covered with grill lid, 4 to 5 minutes on each side or until a meat thermometer inserted into thickest portion registers 165°; remove from grill. Keep warm.

3. Reduce grill temperature to 300° to 350° (medium) heat. Grill sliced bell peppers and onions 4 minutes on each side or until tender. Serve burgers, bell peppers, and onions on buns with Cilantro-Lime Mayonnaise.

CILANTRO-LIME MAYONNAISE

This simple herb-and-lime mayonnaise comes together quickly and is an easy way to add a boost of flavor to your favorite sandwich.

YIELD: ABOUT ½ CUP   TOTAL: 5 MINUTES

¼   cup mayonnaise
1   tsp. chopped fresh cilantro
1   tsp. chopped fresh chives

1   tsp. lime zest
1   tsp. fresh lime juice

Stir together mayonnaise, cilantro, chives, lime zest, and fresh lime juice. Refrigerate in an airtight container for up to a week.

SHRIMP BURGERS *(pictured on page 165)*

The preparation for these shrimp burgers is similar to that of crab cakes. The shrimp are held together with a spicy mixture of egg and cracker crumbs, and then the patties are grilled until lightly crisp.

YIELD: 4 SERVINGS   TOTAL: 1 HOUR, 30 MINUTES

1¼ lb. unpeeled, medium-size raw shrimp
Vegetable cooking spray
1   large egg, lightly beaten
1   Tbsp. mayonnaise
2   tsp. fresh lemon juice
½   tsp. table salt
⅛   tsp. ground red pepper
3   Tbsp. finely chopped celery

2   Tbsp. chopped green onion
1   Tbsp. chopped fresh parsley
1¼ cups crushed cornbread crackers
    (about 1 sleeve or 24 crackers)
4   kaiser rolls with poppy seeds, split
Sweet 'n' Spicy Tartar Sauce
4   Bibb lettuce leaves

1. Peel shrimp; devein, if desired. Cut each shrimp into thirds.

2. Line a 15- x 10-inch jelly-roll pan with aluminum foil. Coat with cooking spray.

3. Stir together egg and next 4 ingredients until blended; stir in celery, green onion, and parsley. Fold in shrimp and cracker crumbs (mixture will be very thick). Shape into 4 (4-inch-wide, 1-inch-thick) patties. Place patties on prepared pan. Cover and chill 1 to 24 hours. Transfer to freezer, and freeze 30 minutes.

4. Coat cold cooking grate with cooking spray, and place on grill. Preheat grill to 350° to 400° (medium-high) heat. Grill burgers, covered with grill lid, 4 to 5 minutes or until burgers lift easily from cooking grate using a large spatula. Turn burgers, and grill 4 to 5 minutes or until shrimp turn pink and burgers are cooked through and lightly crisp.

5. Grill rolls, cut sides down, 1 to 2 minutes or until lightly toasted. Serve burgers on buns with Sweet 'n' Spicy Tartar Sauce and lettuce.

SWEET 'N' SPICY TARTAR SAUCE

Our shrimp burgers need a healthy dollop of this spicy tartar sauce. You can whip it up in minutes, and also serve it with your favorite grilled white fish.

YIELD: 1 CUP   TOTAL: 35 MINUTES

1   cup mayonnaise
2   Tbsp. chopped fresh parsley
2   Tbsp. prepared horseradish

1½ tsp. Cajun seasoning
1½ tsp. fresh lemon juice
¼   tsp. paprika

Stir together all ingredients in a bowl. Cover and chill 30 minutes to 24 hours. Refrigerate in an airtight container for up to 3 days.

GREEK TURKEY BURGERS

Traditional Greek flavors like feta, red onion, yogurt, and mint make this burger a real winner. For a fun presentation, use a mandoline to thinly slice the cucumber lengthwise into long strips.

YIELD: 4 SERVINGS   TOTAL: 25 MINUTES

1⅓ lb. ground turkey breast
1   (4-oz.) package crumbled feta cheese
¼   cup finely chopped red onion
1   tsp. dried oregano
1   tsp. lemon zest
½   tsp. table salt
Vegetable cooking spray
½   cup grated English cucumber

1   (6-oz.) container fat-free Greek yogurt
1   Tbsp. chopped fresh mint
½   tsp. table salt
4   French hamburger buns, split and toasted
Toppings: lettuce leaves, tomato slices, thinly sliced cucumber, sliced red onion rings

1. Stir together first 6 ingredients. Shape mixture into 4 (½-inch-thick) patties.

2. Heat a grill pan over medium-high heat. Coat grill pan with cooking spray. Add patties; cook 5 minutes on each side or until done.

3. Stir together cucumber, yogurt, mint, and ½ tsp. salt in a small bowl. Serve burgers on buns with cucumber sauce and desired toppings.

GRILLED APPLE-SMOKED STRIPED BASS

The "apple" in this recipe refers to the apple-wood chips that lend a great smoky flavor to tender and flaky fish. Applewood is a hard-wood and burns very long.

YIELD: 8 SERVINGS   TOTAL: 2 HOURS

¼   cup applewood chips
2   dried habanero chiles
1   Tbsp. peanut or vegetable oil
1   tsp. table salt
½   tsp. freshly ground black pepper
1   (3-lb.) striped bass fillet (about 1-inch thick)
Vegetable cooking spray
1   lemon, thinly sliced

1. Cover applewood chips with water, and soak for 1 hour. Drain well.

2. Place chiles in a spice or coffee grinder; process until finely ground. Place ⅛ tsp. ground chile in a small bowl (reserve remaining ground chile for another use). Add oil, salt, and black pepper, stirring to combine. Rub spice mixture over fish; refrigerate 30 minutes.

3. Preheat grill to 300° to 350° (medium) heat. Place wood chips on hot coals. Coat a large piece of heavy-duty aluminum foil with cooking spray; pierce foil several times with a fork.

4. Place foil on grill rack coated with cooking spray. Place fish on foil; arrange lemon slices over fish. Grill 20 minutes or until fish flakes with a fork. Serve immediately.

BBQ&A

WITH TIM BYRES, SMOKE, DALLAS

What are your favorite types of wood?

It really depends on what I'm cooking. I really like mesquite because it's dense and very smoky. Hickory is probably the most well known and lends a milder smoky flavor. Pecan wood is one of the mildest and is great for poultry and fish. Oak gives a heavier, smoky, and floral flavor. Fruitwoods like peach, apple, and cherry are great for fish, poultry, and pork.

GRILLED SEA BASS WITH MANGO SALSA

The fresh fruit salsa is delicious with grilled sea bass, but it's also tasty with chicken, pork, or shrimp. Keep some in the fridge for a simple topping, or to snack on with tortilla chips.

YIELD: 4 SERVINGS   TOTAL: 2 HOURS, 25 MINUTES, INCLUDING CHILL TIME

1   cup diced fresh mango (about 1 mango)
½   cup diced red bell pepper
2   green onions, chopped (about 2 Tbsp.)
1   jalapeño pepper, seeded and minced
¼   cup chopped fresh cilantro
1   garlic clove, minced

⅛   tsp. table salt
2   Tbsp. fresh lime juice
4   (6-oz.) sea bass or halibut fillets
    (about 1¼-inches thick)
Vegetable cooking spray

1. Combine first 8 ingredients in a bowl. Cover and chill at least 2 hours.

2. Preheat grill to 300° to 350° (medium) heat.

3. Coat fish lightly with cooking spray; season with table salt and freshly ground black pepper.

4. Place fish on grill rack coated with cooking spray. Grill, covered with grill lid, 5 minutes on each side or just until fish flakes with a fork. Serve with mango salsa.

— TRY THIS —

GRILLED SEA BASS WITH PEACH SALSA: Replace first 8 ingredients with 3 cups coarsely chopped peeled peaches (about 6 small peaches); 1 cup diced red onion; ¼ cup fresh lemon juice; 3 Tbsp. minced fresh cilantro; 2 Tbsp. minced shallots; 1 tsp. chopped seeded serrano chile; 1 tsp. honey; ¼ tsp. kosher salt. Combine ingredients in a bowl; toss gently. Prepare remaining recipe as directed in Step 2.

GRILLED GROUPER WITH WATERMELON SALSA

This delicious fish dish is perfectly poised to become a fish taco with a twist. Serve it alongside the salsa with some shredded cabbage, and enclose in grilled corn tortillas.

YIELD: 4 SERVINGS   TOTAL: 25 MINUTES

4   (4-oz.) grouper fillets
1   tsp. freshly ground black pepper
1   tsp. table salt, divided
3   Tbsp. olive oil, divided
2   cups chopped seedless watermelon
¼   cup chopped pitted kalamata olives
½   English cucumber, chopped
1   small jalapeño pepper, seeded and minced
2   Tbsp. minced red onion
2   Tbsp. white balsamic vinegar
Garnish: sliced jalapeño pepper

1. Preheat grill to 350° to 400° (medium-high) heat. Sprinkle grouper with pepper and ½ tsp. salt. Drizzle with 2 Tbsp. olive oil.

2. Grill fish, covered with grill lid, 3 to 4 minutes on each side or just until fish flakes with a fork.

3. Combine chopped watermelon, next 5 ingredients, and remaining ½ tsp. salt and 1 Tbsp. olive oil. Serve with grilled fish. Garnish with jalapeño slices.

GRILLED SALT-CRUSTED RED SNAPPER

Salt-crusting the snapper ensures a moist and flaky texture while seasoning the fish perfectly. After cooking, the salt creates a crust that can be easily removed before serving. Don't let the fish stand with the salt crust too long before or after it cooks, or it will become too salty.

YIELD: 4 SERVINGS   TOTAL: 40 MINUTES

4   lb. kosher salt
1   lemon
1   Tbsp. chopped fresh dill
2   (1½-lb.) whole red snappers, cleaned
    and scaled

1   cup thinly sliced fennel
4   dill sprigs

1. Preheat grill to 350° to 400° (medium-high) heat. Combine salt and 1½ cups water (mixture should resemble slushy wet sand). Grate zest from lemon to equal 1 tsp. Cut lemon into 6 slices. Stir lemon zest and chopped dill into salt mixture.

2. Place 2 large sheets of heavy-duty aluminum foil on a large baking sheet. Spread 2 cups salt mixture into a 13- x 7-inch rectangle on each piece of foil.

3. Top each salt portion with 1 fish. Place 3 lemon slices, ½ cup fennel, and 2 dill sprigs inside the cavity of each fish. Pat remaining 4 cups salt mixture evenly over both fish to cover completely.

4. Carefully slide foil with fish onto grill. Grill, covered with grill lid, 25 to 30 minutes, or until a meat thermometer inserted into thickest part of fish reaches 145°. Remove fish from grill.

5. Crack salt crust away from fish, and serve immediately.

GRILLED TUNA WITH FRESH SALSA

This dish is ideal for entertaining. Make the salsa ahead of time and throw the tuna steaks on the grill while your guests enjoy appetizers and cocktails.

YIELD: 4 SERVINGS   TOTAL: 40 MINUTES

- 2 cups diced plum tomatoes (about 6 tomatoes)
- ¼ cup thinly sliced green onions
- ¼ cup fresh lime juice
- 2 Tbsp. chopped fresh cilantro
- 2 Tbsp. minced seeded jalapeño pepper
- 1 Tbsp. olive oil
- 2 tsp. balsamic vinegar
- ½ tsp. table salt, divided
- ½ tsp. freshly ground black pepper, divided
- 4 (6-oz.) tuna steaks (about 1-inch thick)
- Vegetable cooking spray
- Lime wedges (optional)

1. Combine first 7 ingredients in a bowl; stir in ¼ tsp. salt and ¼ tsp. black pepper. Let stand 30 minutes.

2. Preheat grill to 350° to 400° (medium-high) heat.

3. Lightly coat both sides of tuna steaks with cooking spray; sprinkle with remaining ¼ tsp. salt and ¼ tsp. freshly ground black pepper. Place steaks on grill rack; grill 3 minutes on each side or until fish is medium-rare or to desired degree of doneness. Serve with salsa and, if desired, lime wedges.

— TRY THIS —

GRILLED TUNA WITH PUTTANESCA SALSA: Omit first 9 ingredients (and lime wedges) and combine ¼ cup basil, lemon zest, lemon juice, and 2 minced garlic cloves in a shallow dish. Add tuna, and turn to coat. Cover and chill 30 minutes. For salsa: Combine 2 cups chopped tomato; ¼ cup coarsely chopped kalamata olives; 1 Tbsp. drained capers; 1 garlic clove, minced; ¼ cup basil; and ⅛ tsp. black pepper in a medium bowl. Prepare remaining recipe as directed in Step 2.

GRILLED OYSTERS WITH HORSERADISH-GARLIC PANKO TOPPING

When buying oysters, look for those that are similar in size so they'll all cook in the same amount of time.

YIELD: 2 DOZEN   TOTAL: 35 MINUTES

¼ cup butter
2 garlic cloves, minced
1 cup panko (Japanese breadcrumbs)
1 tsp. lemon zest

2 Tbsp. prepared horseradish
2 Tbsp. chopped fresh parsley
2 dozen oysters in the shell

1. Preheat grill to 300° to 350° (medium) heat. Melt butter in a large skillet over medium heat. Add garlic and panko. Cook 3 to 4 minutes, stirring constantly, until breadcrumbs are toasted.

2. Remove pan from heat, and stir in lemon zest, horseradish, and parsley.

3. Place oysters in single layer on grill rack. Grill oysters, covered with grill lid, 15 minutes or until oysters open. Top with crumb mixture before serving.

CEDAR-PLANKED BARBECUE SALMON *(pictured)*

The barbecue rub on this salmon enhances the flavor and color, while grilling on the cedar plank provides a hint of smokiness.

YIELD: 4 SERVINGS   TOTAL: 24 HOURS, 30 MINUTES, INCLUDING SOAK TIME

1 cedar plank
1 (2-lb.) salmon fillet

2 Tbsp. Prize-Winning Barbecue Rub
   (page 326)

1. Soak cedar plank in water overnight; drain. Place salmon fillet, skin side down, on soaked plank. Sprinkle 2 Tbsp. Prize-Winning Barbecue Rub evenly over flesh side of salmon.

2. Preheat grill to 350° to 400° (medium-high) heat. Grill, covered with grill lid, 25 minutes or until salmon flakes with a fork.

FIRECRACKER GRILLED SALMON

For ease, try grilling the salmon flesh side down first and then turning to finish skin side down. The skin will be easier to remove.

YIELD: 6 SERVINGS   TOTAL: 40 MINUTES, INCLUDING MARINADE TIME

6 (6-oz.) salmon fillets
½ cup vegetable oil
¼ cup soy sauce
¼ cup balsamic vinegar
1 Tbsp. honey
2 tsp. finely chopped garlic

2 tsp. dried crushed red pepper
1½ tsp. ground ginger
1 tsp. sesame oil
½ tsp. table salt
¼ tsp. onion powder
Vegetable cooking spray

1. Place salmon fillets in a large zip-top plastic freezer bag. Whisk together vegetable oil and next 9 ingredients. Pour over salmon, reserving ¼ cup mixture. Seal and chill 30 minutes.

2. Coat cold cooking grate of grill with cooking spray, and place on grill. Preheat grill to 350° to 400° (medium-high) heat. Remove salmon from marinade; discard marinade.

3. Grill salmon, without grill lid, 4 to 5 minutes or until fish flakes with a fork, turning occasionally and basting with reserved marinade. Remove and discard skin. Serve immediately.

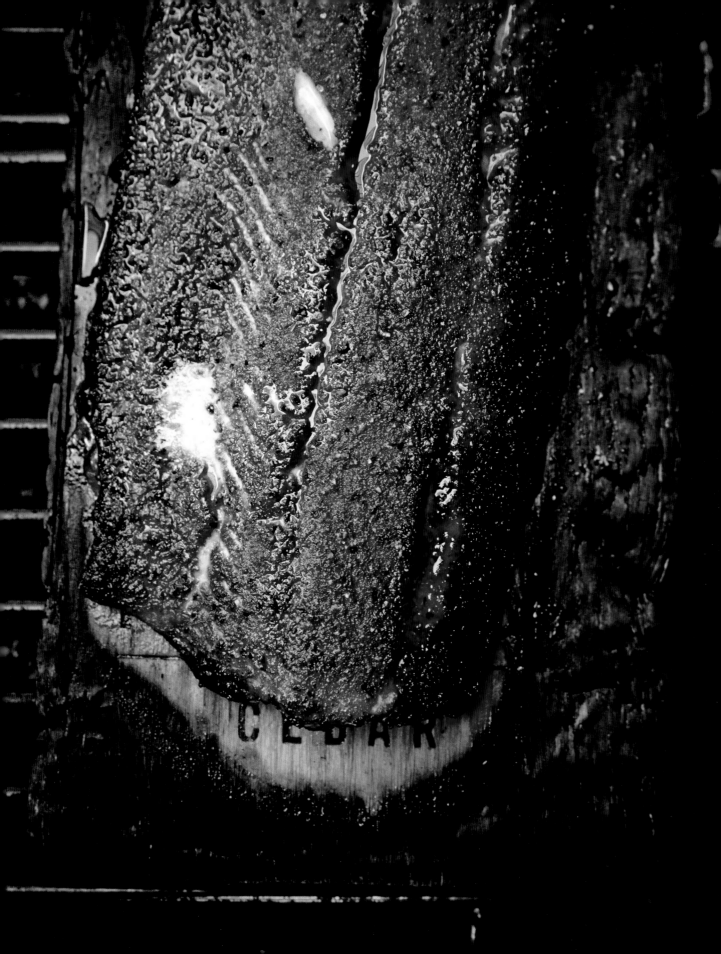

LOWCOUNTRY BOIL KABOBS WITH SPICY OLD BAY BUTTER

Enjoy this coastal Georgia favorite in a new way with all the elements skewered on kabobs. Grilling the lemons heightens their flavor, and the Old Bay butter mixture infuses the kabobs as they grill. Keep a spray bottle nearby to help tame flare-ups.

YIELD: 6 SERVINGS   **TOTAL: 35 MINUTES**

1   lb. small new potatoes
3   ears fresh corn
1½ lb. peeled large raw shrimp
1   lb. smoked sausage, cut into
     1-inch pieces

2   lemons, cut into wedges
12 (12-inch) wooden or metal skewers
½   cup butter, melted
2   Tbsp. Old Bay seasoning
½   tsp. ground red pepper

1. Preheat grill to 350° to 400° (medium-high) heat. Bring potatoes and water to a boil in a large Dutch oven. Boil 8 minutes. Add corn. Cook 5 more minutes or until potatoes are tender and corn is almost done. Drain.

2. Cut each ear of corn into 1-inch pieces. Thread potatoes, corn, shrimp, sausage, and lemon wedges onto skewers.

3. Combine melted butter, Old Bay, and ground red pepper.

4. Grill skewers 5 to 6 minutes, turning occasionally and basting with butter mixture.

SHRIMP, WATERMELON & HALLOUMI KABOBS

With a high melting point, halloumi cheese is a great choice for the grill. It is popular in Greek and Turkish cuisines and is made from a mixture of goat and sheep milk.

YIELD: 6 SERVINGS   TOTAL: 1 HOUR, 15 MINUTES, INCLUDING MARINADE TIME

36 unpeeled, jumbo raw shrimp
    (about 2 lb.)
12 (12-inch) wooden or metal skewers
Cilantro-Lime Marinade
12 oz. halloumi cheese, cut into 1½-inch
    cubes*

24 (2-inch) watermelon cubes
3   Tbsp. fresh cilantro leaves, torn
3   Tbsp. fresh mint leaves, torn

1. Peel shrimp, leaving tails on; devein, if desired.

2. Soak wooden skewers in water 30 minutes. (Omit if using metal skewers.)

3. Meanwhile, combine shrimp and ½ cup Cilantro-Lime Marinade in a large zip-top plastic freezer bag. Combine cheese and ⅓ cup Cilantro-Lime Marinade in another large zip-top plastic freezer bag. Seal bags, turning to coat; chill 30 minutes, turning occasionally.

4. Preheat grill to 350° to 400° (medium-high) heat. Remove shrimp and cheese from marinades, discarding marinades. Thread shrimp, watermelon, and cheese alternately onto skewers, leaving a ⅛-inch space between pieces.

5. Grill kabobs, covered with grill lid, 4 to 5 minutes on each side or just until shrimp turn pink. Sprinkle with cilantro and mint. Serve with remaining Cilantro-Lime Marinade.

*Firm feta cheese may be substituted.

CILANTRO-LIME MARINADE

This marinade also doubles as a vinaigrette and dipping sauce, and the sweetness can be adjusted by adding more sugar if you'd like.

YIELD: 2 CUPS   TOTAL: 5 MINUTES

1   cup red wine vinegar
⅓   cup chopped fresh cilantro
2   Tbsp. seeded and minced jalapeño pepper
1   Tbsp. sugar
2   Tbsp. lime zest

¼   cup fresh lime juice
2   Tbsp. Dijon mustard
2   garlic cloves, pressed
1   tsp. kosher salt
1   cup canola oil

Whisk together vinegar, and next 8 ingredients until blended. Add canola oil in a slow, steady stream, whisking constantly until smooth. Refrigerate in an airtight container for up to a week.

KOREAN BUTTERMILK CHICKEN KABOBS

Gochujang and buttermilk make these chicken skewers tender and flavorful. The Korean chili paste is sweet enough for kids and is great slathered onto other grilled meats.

YIELD: 6 TO 8 SERVINGS   **TOTAL: 4 HOURS, INCLUDING MARINADE TIME**

1½ cups buttermilk
1   (10-oz.) bottle gochujang (Korean chili paste)
2   tsp. kosher salt
1   tsp. freshly ground black pepper
3   lb. skinned and boned chicken thighs, cut into 2-inch pieces

10 (10-inch) wooden or metal skewers
3   lemons
Vegetable cooking spray
½   cup torn fresh cilantro leaves

1. Stir together first 4 ingredients in a large shallow dish or zip-top plastic freezer bag. Add chicken, turning to coat. Cover or seal, and chill 1 to 3 hours.

2. Meanwhile, soak wooden skewers in water 30 minutes. (Omit if using metal skewers.) Cut each lemon into 8 wedges.

3. Coat cold cooking grate of grill with cooking spray, and place on grill. Preheat grill to 350° to 400° (medium-high) heat. Remove chicken from marinade, discarding marinade. Thread chicken and lemon wedges alternately onto skewers, leaving a ⅛-inch space between pieces.

4. Grill kabobs, covered with grill lid, 6 to 8 minutes on each side or until chicken is done. Transfer to a serving platter. Sprinkle with cilantro leaves.

GRILLED CHICKEN THIGHS WITH WHITE BARBECUE SAUCE

This simple rub is only enhanced when put on the grill. The kicker that takes this dish to the next level, though, is the white barbecue sauce, an Alabama original.

YIELD: 5 SERVINGS
TOTAL: 4 HOURS, 30 MINUTES, INCLUDING CHILL TIME AND BARBECUE SAUCE

1	Tbsp. dried thyme	½	tsp. table salt
1	Tbsp. dried oregano	½	tsp. freshly ground black pepper
1	Tbsp. ground cumin	10	skin-on, bone-in chicken thighs
1	Tbsp. paprika		(about 3 lb.)
1	tsp. onion powder		White Barbecue Sauce (page 323)

1. Combine first 7 ingredients until blended. Rinse chicken, and pat dry; rub seasoning mixture over chicken. Place chicken in a zip-top plastic freezer bag. Seal and chill 4 hours.

2. Preheat grill to 350° to 400° (medium-high) heat. Remove chicken from bag, discarding bag.

3. Grill chicken, covered with grill lid, 8 to 10 minutes on each side or until a meat thermometer inserted into thickest portion registers 165°. Serve with White Barbecue Sauce.

GRILLED CHICKEN WINGS

YIELD: 6 TO 8 SERVINGS   TOTAL: 35 MINUTES

2   lb. chicken wings
2   Tbsp. olive oil
1½ tsp. kosher salt

½   tsp. freshly ground black pepper
Honey Drizzle of choice

1. Preheat grill to 350° to 400° (medium-high) heat. Toss together wings and oil in a large bowl. Sprinkle with salt and pepper; toss to coat.

2. Grill wings, covered with grill lid, 25 to 30 minutes or until skin is crisp and wings are done, turning occasionally. Toss with desired Honey Drizzle.

CIDER VINEGAR-BROWN BUTTER HONEY DRIZZLE

¼   cup butter
½   cup honey

1   Tbsp. apple cider vinegar

1. Cook butter in a saucepan over medium-high heat 5 minutes or until brown and fragrant. Transfer to a small bowl, and cool 5 minutes.

2. Cook honey and vinegar in a saucepan over medium heat, stirring often, 2 minutes or until thoroughly heated. Whisk in browned butter. Yield: about ¾ cup.

HORSERADISH-HONEY MUSTARD DRIZZLE

½   cup honey
3   Tbsp. prepared horseradish

2   Tbsp. coarse-grained mustard

Cook honey, horseradish, and mustard in a small saucepan over medium heat, stirring often, 2 minutes or until thoroughly heated. Yield: about ¾ cup.

CRACKED PEPPER-ROSEMARY HONEY DRIZZLE

½   cup honey
1   tsp. cracked black pepper

1   (3-inch) fresh rosemary sprig

Cook honey, 2 Tbsp. water, pepper, and rosemary sprig in a saucepan over medium heat, stirring often, 2 minutes or until thoroughly heated. Discard rosemary. Yield: about ½ cup.

CHILI-LEMON HONEY DRIZZLE

½   cup honey
¼   cup bottled chili sauce

2   Tbsp. fresh lemon juice

Cook honey, chili sauce, and lemon juice over medium heat, stirring often, 2 minutes or until thoroughly heated. Yield: about 1 cup.

GRILLED CHIPOTLE CHICKEN

Plain grilled chicken? Never again with this spicy upgrade. The smoky chipotle chile pepper delivers the right amount of heat to this five-ingredient dish.

YIELD: 4 SERVINGS   TOTAL: 20 MINUTES

2   lb. skinned and boned chicken thighs

2   Tbsp. firmly packed light brown sugar

½   tsp. dried oregano

½   tsp. ground chipotle chile pepper

½   tsp. kosher salt

1. Preheat grill to 350° to 400° (medium-high) heat. Place each chicken thigh between 2 sheets of heavy-duty plastic wrap, and flatten to ¼-inch thickness, using a rolling pin or flat side of a meat mallet. Combine sugar and next 3 ingredients; rub over chicken.

2. Grill chicken, covered with grill lid, 2 to 3 minutes on each side or until done. Remove from grill, and cover with aluminum foil until ready to serve.

When I make barbecue chicken, I like to apply a rub that has chili powder and paprika as part of the ingredients. I also always brine chicken, turkey, and quail overnight in a mixture of water, sugar, and salt before I smoke them.

JIMMY HAGOOD, FOOD FOR THE SOUTHERN SOUL, CHARLESTON, SOUTH CAROLINA

GRILLED TURKEY BREAST

The brine makes this turkey extra juicy, and the spice rub pairs perfectly with the homemade herb sauce. Use any leftovers to make the ultimate turkey sandwich.

YIELD: 8 SERVINGS   TOTAL: 9 HOURS, 35 MINUTES, INCLUDING BRINE TIME

⅓ cup kosher salt
⅓ cup sugar
3 bay leaves
2 jalapeño peppers, halved
2 Tbsp. cumin seeds
1 (5- to 6-lb.) boned, skin-on fresh turkey breast*
Vegetable cooking spray

1 Tbsp. table salt
1 Tbsp. cumin seeds
1 Tbsp. paprika
2 tsp. freshly ground black pepper
1 tsp. ground coriander
1 tsp. dried oregano
Parsley-Mint Salsa Verde

1. Stir together first 5 ingredients and 2 qt. water in a deep food-safe container or stockpot until sugar is dissolved. Add turkey. Chill 8 hours or overnight, turning once.

2. Coat cold cooking grate of grill with cooking spray, and place on grill. Light 1 side of grill, heating to 350° to 400° (medium-high) heat; leave other side unlit. Remove turkey from brine, discarding brine. Rinse turkey, drain well, and pat dry with paper towels.

3. Stir together table salt and next 5 ingredients. Rub skin of turkey with mixture.

4. Place turkey, skin side down, over lit side of grill, and grill, without grill lid, 4 to 5 minutes or until slightly charred. Transfer to unlit side, skin side up. Grill, covered with grill lid, 30 to 40 minutes or until a meat thermometer inserted into thickest portion registers 165°. Return turkey, skin side down, to lit side, and grill, covered with grill lid, 4 to 5 minutes or until skin is crisp.

5. Remove turkey from heat; cover loosely with aluminum foil. Let stand 10 minutes. Serve with Parsley-Mint Salsa Verde.

*Frozen turkey breast, thawed, may be substituted.

PARSLEY-MINT SALSA VERDE

An easy herb sauce adds a fresh punch of flavor to grilled turkey. But it's also great on chicken, beef, and pork.

YIELD: 1¾ CUPS   TOTAL: 35 MINUTES

⅔ cup extra virgin olive oil
⅓ cup sherry vinegar
¼ cup finely chopped shallots
2 garlic cloves, finely chopped

1 tsp. table salt
½ tsp. freshly ground black pepper
1 cup chopped fresh flat-leaf parsley
¾ cup chopped fresh mint

Whisk together first 6 ingredients and 2 Tbsp. water until salt dissolves. Whisk in parsley and mint. Let stand 20 minutes. Refrigerate in airtight container for up to 3 days.

GRILLED LAMB CHOPS

If you want a recipe to impress dinner guests, this is it. These simple grilled lamb chops are topped with a delicious flavored mayonnaise and citrus parsley relish to make them extra special. Just be careful not to overcook the lamb chops, as they could become tough and dry.

YIELD: 4 SERVINGS   TOTAL: 40 MINUTES

8 (1½- to 2-inch-thick) lamb loin chops (about 2½ lb.)	½ tsp. freshly ground black pepper
2 Tbsp. olive oil	1 navel orange
1 tsp. table salt	Lemon-Tarragon Aïoli
	Orange Gremolata

1. Trim fat from edges of lamb chops to ⅛-inch thickness. Brush both sides of lamb evenly with olive oil. Sprinkle evenly with salt and pepper. Let stand 15 minutes.

2. Preheat grill to 350° to 400° (medium-high) heat. Grill lamb chops, covered with grill lid, 4 to 5 minutes on each side (medium-rare) or to desired degree of doneness. Transfer lamb chops to a serving platter; cover loosely with aluminum foil, and let stand 5 minutes.

3. Cut orange into 8 wedges. Grill orange wedges, covered with grill lid, 1 to 2 minutes on each side or until grill marks appear. Serve lamb chops with grilled orange wedges, Lemon-Tarragon Aïoli, and Orange Gremolata.

LEMON-TARRAGON AÏOLI

YIELD: ABOUT 1 CUP   TOTAL: 15 MINUTES

1 shallot, chopped	2 Tbsp. fresh lemon juice
¾ cup mayonnaise	1 tsp. fresh minced garlic
2 Tbsp. chopped fresh tarragon	1½ tsp. Dijon mustard

Process all ingredients in a blender until smooth; transfer to a small bowl. Cover and chill at least 30 minutes or up to 3 days.

ORANGE GREMOLATA

YIELD: ABOUT ½ CUP   TOTAL: 15 MINUTES

½ cup minced fresh flat-leaf parsley	⅛ tsp. table salt
2 tsp. orange zest	Pinch of freshly ground black pepper
2 tsp. minced garlic	

Combine all ingredients. Serve immediately, or cover and chill up to 3 days.

GRILLED STUFFED SWEET PEPPERS

(pictured)

Covering the grill rack with aluminum foil helps keep the filling from dripping onto the grill while still infusing the sweet peppers with smoky flavor. If the weather outside is less than ideal, you can also cook these on a baking pan in the oven.

YIELD: 8 SERVINGS   TOTAL: 45 MINUTES

2   (8-oz.) packages mini bell peppers
1   (8-oz.) package cream cheese, softened
1   cup crumbled feta cheese
¼   cup sun-dried tomatoes in oil
2   garlic cloves, minced
2   Tbsp. chopped fresh basil
½   tsp. freshly ground black pepper
2   Tbsp. olive oil

1. Preheat grill to 350° to 400° (medium-high) heat. Carefully cut the stems from the top of the peppers, reserving tops, and remove membranes and seeds.

2. Pulse cream cheese, feta, sun-dried tomatoes, garlic, basil, and pepper in a food processor until smooth.

3. Place cream cheese mixture in a zip-top plastic bag. Snip the corner with scissors and pipe mixture into peppers. Replace pepper tops. Brush with oil.

4. Place a sheet of aluminum foil on grill. Grill peppers 7 minutes or until peppers are blistered and filling is warm.

GRILLED ASPARAGUS

Grilling asparagus is super easy and adds such a wonderful charred, smoky flavor that you simply can't get on the stovetop.

YIELD: 4 SERVINGS   TOTAL: 15 MINUTES

1   lb. fresh asparagus
1   Tbsp. olive oil
1   tsp. balsamic vinegar
¼   tsp. table salt
¼   tsp. freshly ground black pepper
1   tsp. lemon zest

1. Preheat grill to 350° to 400° (medium-high) heat. Snap off and discard tough ends of asparagus.

2. Combine olive oil, balsamic vinegar, salt, and pepper in a shallow dish or large zip-top plastic bag; add asparagus, turning to coat.

3. Remove asparagus from oil mixture.

4. Grill asparagus, covered with grill lid, 2 to 4 minutes or until tender, turning once. Remove asparagus, and sprinkle evenly with lemon zest; serve immediately.

GRILLED MEXICAN-STYLE STREET CORN

This is one of the best ways to enjoy summer-fresh corn. Shellacked in a seasoned cream sauce, this corn is rolled in savory grated cheese and sprinkled with tart lime juice. Similar to Parmesan cheese, Cotija can be found with other cheeses at the grocery store.

YIELD: 8 SERVINGS   TOTAL: 20 MINUTES

8 ears fresh corn
½ cup mayonnaise
½ cup crema
⅓ cup chopped fresh cilantro

2 garlic cloves, minced
1 Tbsp. smoked paprika
1 cup crumbled Cotija cheese
Lime wedges

1. Preheat grill to medium-high (350° to 400°) heat. Pull husks back from corn; remove silks and replace husks.

2. Grill corn 12 to 15 minutes, turning occasionally. Shuck corn.

3. Combine mayonnaise, crema, cilantro, garlic, and smoked paprika. Brush mixture over corn. Roll corn in cheese. Serve with lime wedges.

— TRY THIS —

CHARRED CORN WITH GARLIC-HERB BUTTER: Preheat grill to 350° to 400° (medium-high) heat. Brush corn with olive oil. Grill corn, covered with grill lid, 20 minutes or until charred, turning every 4 to 5 minutes. Remove from grill; brush corn with garlic-herb butter (mix together 1 [5.2-oz.] container buttery garlic-and-herb spreadable cheese, ½ cup butter, 2 tsp. minced curly leaf parsley, and sea salt to taste). Sprinkle with salt and pepper to taste. Serve immediately with remaining butter.

GRILLED SQUASH & SALSA VERDE

Choose an assortment of summer squash and zucchini at your local farmers' market or grocery store to make this simple side dish sing. Topped with tangy goat cheese, toasted pumpkin seeds, and fresh Salsa Verde, this grilled summer vegetable dish is anything but boring.

YIELD: 4 TO 6 SERVINGS   TOTAL: 20 MINUTES, INCLUDING SALSA

4 or 5 assorted medium squash (about 3½ lb.)	1 cup raw, unsalted, shelled pepitas (pumpkin seeds), toasted
3 Tbsp. olive oil	Salsa Verde
¼ tsp. kosher salt	¼ cup crumbled goat cheese

1. Preheat grill to 300° to 350° (medium) heat.

2. Cut squash lengthwise into ¼-inch-thick slices. Toss with olive oil and salt.

3. Grill 10 minutes or until lightly caramelized.

4. Place squash on a serving platter. Top with pepitas, Salsa Verde, and goat cheese.

SALSA VERDE

This slightly chunky green salsa adds a zing to grilled vegetables, meats, and even plain-Jane tortilla chips. Process the tomatillos to your desired thickness.

YIELD: ABOUT 1 CUP   TOTAL: 10 MINUTES

7 fresh tomatillos, husks removed	2 Tbsp. fresh lime juice
½ small onion	1 tsp. kosher salt
1 tsp. kosher salt	Garnish: fresh cilantro sprigs
2 Tbsp. chopped fresh cilantro	

1. Combine tomatillos, onion, 1 tsp. kosher salt, and water to cover in a deep saucepan. Bring to a boil; boil 3 to 5 minutes or until tender. Drain and cool.

2. Process tomatillo mixture, cilantro, lime juice, and 1 tsp. kosher salt in a blender 10 to 20 seconds or until slightly chunky.

GRILLED BEET KABOBS WITH LEMONY GOAT CHEESE DIP

Select beets of the same size so they'll cook evenly on the grill.

YIELD: 12 SERVINGS   **TOTAL: 1 HOUR, 10 MINUTES**

24 (6-inch) wooden skewers
6 large beets (about 4 lb.), scrubbed
3 Tbsp. olive oil, divided
¾ tsp. table salt, divided
¾ tsp. freshly ground black pepper, divided
1 Tbsp. chopped fresh dill

1½ tsp. lemon zest
1 Tbsp. fresh lemon juice
4 oz. goat cheese, softened
2 garlic cloves, minced
1 (5.3-oz.) container plain Greek yogurt

1. Soak skewers in warm water to cover for 30 minutes. Preheat oven to 350°. Trim tops of beets to ½ inch. Wrap each beet in aluminum foil; place on a baking sheet.

2. Bake for 1½ hours or until tender. Unwrap beets; cool 10 minutes.

3. Preheat grill to 350° to 400° (medium-high) heat. Peel beets and remove stems; cut each beet into 8 wedges. Place wedges in a large bowl. Drizzle with 1 Tbsp. oil and ½ tsp., each salt and pepper; toss until coated. Thread 4 wedges onto 1 pair of skewers. Repeat procedure with remaining wedges and skewers.

4. Grill beets 3 minutes; turn skewers over and grill 3 more minutes or until lightly browned.

5. Stir together dill, next 5 ingredients, remaining 2 Tbsp. oil, remaining ¼ tsp. salt, and remaining ¼ tsp. pepper in a small bowl until smooth. Serve with beet skewers.

WITH JUSTIN & JONATHAN FOX, FOX BROS. BAR-B-Q, ATLANTA

How do you prevent vegetables from burning on the grill?

Stay on top of them; you put in the effort so you want to have a great end product. Stay close and watch out for flare-ups. Always keep a hot side and a cool side on your grill and move the veggies to the cool side of the grill and cover them with the lid.

GRILLED BALSAMIC BRUSSELS SPROUTS WITH BACON

If your Brussels sprouts are on the small side, thread them onto skewers before grilling so they don't slip through the grill grates.

YIELD: 4 TO 6 SERVINGS   TOTAL: 40 MINUTES

2½ lb. Brussels sprouts, trimmed
　　and halved
¼　cup olive oil, divided
½　tsp. table salt
½　tsp. freshly ground black pepper

4　center-cut bacon slices
1　Tbsp. balsamic vinegar
2　tsp. whole grain mustard
2　tsp. honey

1. Preheat grill to 350° to 400° (medium-high) heat. Toss Brussels sprouts with 1 Tbsp. olive oil, salt, and pepper.

2. Grill Brussels sprouts 8 minutes on each side or until browned and tender. Transfer to a serving bowl.

3. Cook bacon in a large skillet over medium heat until crisp. Remove to paper towels to drain. Let cool, and crumble.

4. Meanwhile, whisk together vinegar, mustard, and honey. Slowly add remaining 3 Tbsp. olive oil in a slow, steady stream, whisking until combined. Pour dressing over Brussels sprouts. Add crumbled bacon. Toss well to combine.

GRILLED SUMMER VEGETABLE PLATTER

Great for using up leftover vegetables or adding a rainbow of color to the picnic spread, this cornucopia of veggies is sure to impress. Use what you have on hand, or add your favorites to throw on the grill.

YIELD: 8 TO 10 SERVINGS   TOTAL: 1 HOUR, 15 MINUTES, INCLUDING VINAIGRETTE

3   (12-inch) wooden or metal skewers
1   pt. cherry tomatoes
1   lb. fresh asparagus
4   small zucchini or yellow squash (about 1 lb.), cut lengthwise into ½-inch slices
2   small sweet potatoes (about ½ lb.), peeled and cut into ½-inch wedges
5   mini bell peppers, halved
1   (8-oz.) container fresh mushrooms
1   medium eggplant (about 1 lb.), cut into ½-inch slices
2   small bunches green onions
Olive oil
Veggie Vinaigrette

1. Soak wooden skewers in water 30 minutes. (Omit if using metal skewers.)

2. Preheat grill to 350° to 400° (medium-high) heat. Thread tomatoes 1 inch apart onto skewers. Snap off and discard tough ends of asparagus.

3. Brush tomatoes, and next 7 ingredients with olive oil; sprinkle with desired amount of salt and black pepper.

4. Grill sweet potatoes, covered with grill lid, 6 minutes on each side or until tender. At the same time, grill zucchini, peppers, mushrooms, and eggplant 4 to 6 minutes on each side or until crisp-tender. Grill green onions, asparagus, and tomatoes 2 to 3 minutes on each side or until tender and grill marks appear.

5. Remove from grill, and brush with vinaigrette. Arrange on a serving platter. Serve with remaining vinaigrette.

VEGGIE VINAIGRETTE

Grilled vegetables are never boring with this tangy dressing. Use it as a basting sauce and serve alongside your favorite produce for dipping.

YIELD: ABOUT 1 CUP   TOTAL: 5 MINUTES

¾   cup extra virgin olive oil
9   jarred anchovy fillets, drained
6   garlic cloves, chopped
3   Tbsp. red wine vinegar
2   Tbsp. drained capers
Pinch of freshly ground black pepper

Process ingredients in a food processor until smooth. Refrigerate in an airtight container for up to 3 days.

GRILLED EGGPLANT DIP

An easy take on traditional baba ghanoush, this smoky dip gets its flavor from grilled eggplant and bell pepper, as well as smoked paprika. Try it as a sandwich spread if you have any leftovers.

YIELD: 2½ CUPS   TOTAL: 20 MINUTES

- 1 large eggplant, cut lengthwise into ¼-inch-thick strips
- ¼ cup extra virgin olive oil, divided
- 1 red bell pepper, halved and seeded
- 2 garlic cloves
- 1 Tbsp. fresh lemon juice
- ¾ tsp. table salt
- ½ tsp. freshly ground black pepper
- ½ tsp. smoked paprika
- 1 Tbsp. chopped freshly parsley
- 1 tsp. chopped fresh oregano
- Pita chips

1. Preheat grill to 350° to 400° (medium-high) heat. Brush eggplant with 1 Tbsp. oil. Grill eggplant and red bell pepper 8 to 10 minutes or until tender, turning occasionally.

2. With food processor running, drop garlic through food chute. Process until minced.

3. Add eggplant, bell pepper, lemon juice, salt, pepper, paprika, and remaining 3 Tbsp. olive oil. Pulse to desired smoothness.

4. Stir in parsley and oregano. Serve with pita chips.

BBQ&A

WITH CAREY BRINGLE, PEG LEG PORKER, NASHVILLE

How do you keep foods from sticking to the grill?

It all depends on what type of grill or grate. But the best way is to season it beforehand with regular cooking oil.

GREEK PIZZA WITH CHICKEN & ARTICHOKES

Bypass the pizza parlor and grill up your own. This calls for homemade dough, but you can also pick up some from the grocery's bakery.

YIELD: 1 (14-INCH) PIZZA   TOTAL: 1 HOUR, 15 MINUTES, INCLUDING DOUGH

Vegetable cooking spray

1 (6-oz.) jar marinated artichoke hearts, drained and coarsely chopped

1 (4-oz.) jar roasted red peppers, drained and cut into strips

10 kalamata olives, drained, pitted, and thinly sliced

1 Tbsp. olive oil

1½ Tbsp. chopped fresh oregano

½ tsp. freshly ground black pepper

½ recipe Brick Oven Pizza Dough (page 219)

1 cup (4 oz.) shredded mozzarella cheese, divided

2 cups chopped cooked chicken

1 cup (4 oz.) crumbled feta cheese

1. Coat cold cooking grate of grill with cooking spray. Preheat grill to 300° to 350° (medium) heat.

2. Combine artichoke hearts and next 5 ingredients in a bowl; toss gently.

3. Place dough on a large baking sheet coated with cooking spray; lightly coat dough with cooking spray. Roll dough to ¼-inch thickness (about 14 inches in diameter). Slide pizza dough from baking sheet onto cooking grate.

4. Grill, covered with grill lid, 2 to 3 minutes or until lightly browned. Turn dough over, and reduce temperature to 250° to 300° (low) heat; top with ¾ cup mozzarella cheese and chicken.

5. Spoon artichoke mixture evenly over chicken. Sprinkle with remaining ¼ cup mozzarella cheese; top with feta cheese. Grill, covered with grill lid, 5 minutes or until cheese melts. Serve immediately.

GRILLED TOMATO-PEACH PIZZA

An ode to summer, this fresh-tasting pizza uses convenient store-bought dough to get dinner on the table in a flash. You can also use a half-recipe of the Brick Oven Pizza Dough (page 219) if you prefer.

YIELD: 1 (14-INCH) PIZZA   TOTAL: 30 MINUTES

Vegetable cooking spray
2   tomatoes, sliced
½   tsp. table salt
1   large peach, peeled and sliced

1   lb. bakery pizza dough
½   (16-oz.) package fresh
     mozzarella, sliced
6   to 7 fresh basil leaves

1. Coat cold cooking grate of grill with cooking spray, and place on grill. Preheat grill to 300° to 350° (medium) heat.

2. Sprinkle tomatoes with salt; let stand 15 minutes. Pat tomatoes dry with paper towels.

3. Grill peach slices, covered with grill lid, 2 to 3 minutes on each side or until grill marks appear.

4. Place dough on a large baking sheet coated with cooking spray; lightly coat dough with cooking spray. Roll dough to ¼-inch thickness (about 14 inches in diameter). Slide pizza dough from baking sheet onto cooking grate.

5. Grill, covered with grill lid, 2 to 3 minutes or until lightly browned. Turn dough over, and reduce temperature to 250° to 300° (low) heat; top with tomatoes, grilled peaches, and mozzarella. Grill, covered with grill lid, 5 minutes or until cheese melts. Arrange basil leaves over pizza. Serve immediately.

GRILLED SAUSAGE SALAD PIZZA

Dinner is complete with this equal parts salad and pizza combo. Spice up your pie with hot smoked sausage if you like it with a bit of kick.

YIELD: 1 (12-INCH) PIZZA   TOTAL: 45 MINUTES

1   medium-size sweet onion, cut into ¼-inch-thick slices
3   Tbsp. olive oil, divided
½   lb. smoked link sausage
1   (12-inch) prebaked Italian pizza crust

1½   cups (6 oz.) freshly shredded mozzarella cheese
1¼   tsp. kosher salt, divided
1   cup firmly packed arugula
½   cup fresh flat-leaf parsley
½   tsp. freshly ground black pepper
1   lemon, halved

1. Preheat grill to 350° to 400° (medium-high) heat. Brush onion with 1 Tbsp. oil. Grill onion, covered with grill lid, 6 minutes on each side. Grill sausage 4 minutes on each side; slice.

2. Brush pizza crust with 1 Tbsp. oil. Grill crust, oil side down, 2 minutes. Turn crust over, and brush with remaining 1 Tbsp. oil; sprinkle with cheese and ¼ tsp. salt. Grill 2 minutes or until cheese melts.

3. Toss together arugula, parsley, pepper, sausage, onion, and remaining 1 tsp. salt. Top pizza with salad; squeeze lemon juice over salad. Serve immediately.

BRICK OVEN PIZZA DOUGH

YIELD: 2 (14-INCH) PIZZA CRUSTS   TOTAL: 1 HOUR

2   (¼-oz.) envelopes active dry yeast
2   cups warm water (100° to 110°)
5   cups all-purpose unbleached flour, divided
1   cup coarse-ground whole wheat flour
2   tsp. table salt
2   tsp. sugar

1½   tsp. dried thyme
⅓   cup grated Parmesan cheese (optional)
½   cup plus 3 Tbsp. extra virgin olive oil, divided

1. Combine yeast and 2 cups warm water in a liquid measuring cup, and let stand 5 minutes.

2. Combine yeast mixture, 3 cups all-purpose flour, whole wheat flour, next 3 ingredients and, if desired, cheese in a large mixing bowl; add ½ cup olive oil. Beat at low speed with an electric mixer until blended, stopping to scrape down sides as necessary. Stir in enough remaining all-purpose flour to make a stiff dough. (Dough will be smooth.)

3. Place dough and 1 Tbsp. oil in a large lightly greased bowl, turning to coat top. Cover and let rise in a warm place for 45 minutes or until dough is doubled in bulk. Punch dough down.

4. Turn dough out onto a lightly floured surface, and knead 4 or 5 times. Divide dough in half, and shape into balls. Roll each ball into a 14-inch circle on a lightly floured surface. Place one 14-inch circle onto a lightly floured pizza peel; brush with 1 tablespoon oil, and prick with a fork. Add desired toppings and bake or grill until browned and bubbly.

RAINY DAY BBQ

Barbecue isn't just for the outdoor smoker. With recipes for your slow cooker, stovetop, and oven, you can produce delicious dishes all year-round.

5-INGREDIENT SLOW-COOKER PULLED PORK *(pictured)*

This sauceless pulled pork is wonderful for just about any recipe. Use it for pulled pork tacos topped with fresh salsa, to top a salad, or to stuff baked potatoes. It's also great served the traditional way—piled high on sandwich buns and drenched with your favorite sauce.

YIELD: 8 TO 10 SERVINGS   TOTAL: 8 HOURS, 10 MINUTES

2   large sweet onions, cut into
      ½-inch slices
1   (5- to 6-lb.) boneless pork shoulder roast
      (Boston butt)
2   Tbsp. garlic-oregano-red pepper
      seasoning blend

1   tsp. kosher salt
1   (10½-oz.) can condensed chicken
      broth

1. Place onions in a lightly greased 6-qt. slow cooker. Rub roast with seasoning blend and salt; place roast on onions. Pour broth over roast. Cover and cook on LOW 8 to 10 hours or until meat shreds easily with a fork.

2. Transfer roast to a cutting board or serving platter; shred with 2 forks, removing any large pieces of fat. Remove onions with a slotted spoon, and serve with pork.

BBQ PORK BUTT

A little magic happens in the slow cooker when you combine these three ingredients. The carbonation from the soft drink acts as a tenderizer and creates a delicious sauce that you'll want to spoon over the pulled pork.

YIELD: MAKES 6 SERVINGS   TOTAL: 8 HOURS, 5 MINUTES

1   (3- to 4-lb.) bone-in pork shoulder roast
      (Boston butt)

1   (18-oz.) bottle barbecue sauce
1   (12-oz.) can cola soft drink

1. Place pork roast in a 6-qt. slow cooker; pour barbecue sauce and cola over roast.

2. Cover and cook on HIGH 8 hours or until meat is tender and shreds easily.

CHICKEN & BRISKET BRUNSWICK STEW *(pictured)*

Here's a new twist on the standard, pulled-pork-loaded Brunswick stew. Pick up brisket from your local barbecue joint or use leftovers from the recipe on page 54.

YIELD: 10 TO 12 SERVINGS   TOTAL: 2 HOURS, 40 MINUTES

2 large onions, chopped	1 (9-oz.) package frozen baby lima beans
2 garlic cloves, minced	1 (12-oz.) bottle chili sauce
1 Tbsp. vegetable oil	1 Tbsp. firmly packed brown sugar
1½ Tbsp. jarred beef soup base	1 Tbsp. yellow mustard
2 lb. skinned and boned chicken breasts	1 Tbsp. Worcestershire sauce
1 (28-oz.) can fire-roasted crushed tomatoes	½ tsp. coarsely ground black pepper
1 (12-oz.) package frozen white shoepeg or whole kernel corn	1 lb. chopped Smoked Beef Brisket (page 54)
1 (10-oz.) package frozen cream-style corn, thawed	1 Tbsp. fresh lemon juice
	Hot sauce (optional)

1. Sauté onions and garlic in hot oil in a 7.5-qt. Dutch oven over medium-high heat 3 to 5 minutes or until tender.

2. Stir together beef soup base and 2 cups water, and add to Dutch oven. Stir in chicken and next 9 ingredients. Bring to a boil. Cover, reduce heat to low, and cook, stirring occasionally, 2 hours.

3. Uncover and shred chicken into large pieces using 2 forks. Stir in brisket and lemon juice. Cover and cook 10 minutes. Serve with hot sauce, if desired.

EASY BRUNSWICK STEW

Take advantage of the convenience of a slow cooker with this classic barbecue side.

YIELD: 8 SERVINGS   TOTAL: 10 HOURS, 30 MINUTES

3 lb. boneless pork shoulder roast (Boston butt)	1 (14-oz.) can chicken broth
2 medium new potatoes, peeled and chopped	1 (9-oz.) package frozen baby lima beans, thawed
1 large onion, chopped	1 (9-oz.) package frozen corn, thawed
1 (28-oz.) can crushed tomatoes	6 Tbsp. firmly packed brown sugar
1 (18-oz.) bottle barbecue sauce	1 tsp. table salt

1. Trim roast, and cut into 2-inch pieces. Stir together all ingredients in a 6-qt. slow cooker.

2. Cover and cook on LOW 10 hours or until potatoes are fork-tender. Remove pork and shred with 2 forks. Return shredded pork to slow cooker, and stir well. Serve immediately.

PORK CARNITAS NACHOS

This is the ultimate snack to munch on while watching the big game. Tender shredded pork seasoned with smoky adobo sauce, beer, and lime juice is the perfect topper for nachos and is sure to have everyone coming back for more.

YIELD: 10 SERVINGS   TOTAL: 6 HOURS, 20 MINUTES

1   (3- to 3½-lb.) boneless pork loin
5   garlic cloves, quartered
2   tsp. ground cumin
1   tsp. dried oregano
¾   tsp. table salt
1   (12-oz.) bottle beer
2   canned chipotle chiles in adobo sauce, chopped
2   Tbsp. fresh lime juice

2   Tbsp. adobo sauce from can
Tortilla chips
5   cups cooked brown rice
5   cups canned seasoned black beans, drained and rinsed
Toppings: chopped onion, pico de gallo, chopped fresh cilantro, sliced jalapeños, queso fresco, lime wedges

1. Make ½-inch-deep slits on outside of pork; stuff with garlic. Combine cumin, oregano, and salt in a small bowl. Place pork in a 3½-qt. slow cooker. Sprinkle pork on all sides with spice mixture.

2. Combine beer, chipotle chiles, lime juice, and adobo sauce. Pour mixture over pork. Cover and cook on HIGH for 6 to 8 hours or until meat is fork-tender.

3. Remove pork from slow cooker; shred with 2 forks. Combine shredded pork and ½ cup cooking liquid; toss well.

4. Layer tortilla chips on bottom of platter; spoon rice and beans over chips. Add shredded pork and toppings. Serve with lime wedges.

SLOW-COOKER PORK TACOS AL PASTOR *(pictured)*

These homemade pork tacos are simple and filling. If you prefer a little less heat, omit the crushed red pepper in the salsa, as the chipotle peppers already give the meat a nice kick.

YIELD: 8 TO 10 SERVINGS   TOTAL: 8 HOURS, 20 MINUTES

1   (4½- to 5-lb.) boneless pork shoulder roast (Boston butt), trimmed
2   tsp. kosher salt
1   (12-oz.) bottle white ale
2   (8-oz.) cans pineapple tidbits in juice
1   (7-oz.) can chipotle peppers in adobo sauce
1½ cups chopped fresh pineapple
⅓   cup chopped fresh cilantro

¼   cup minced red onion
2   Tbsp. fresh lime juice
1   tsp. kosher salt
½   tsp. dried crushed red pepper
16 (6-inch) fajita-size corn tortillas, warmed
Toppings: crumbled goat cheese, sliced radishes, fresh cilantro leaves, chopped avocado, shredded cabbage

1. Rub roast with salt, and place in a lightly greased 6-qt. slow cooker. Pour beer and 1 can of pineapple tidbits over roast. Process chipotle peppers and remaining can pineapple in a blender or food processor until smooth. Pour over roast. Cover and cook on LOW 8 to 10 hours or until meat shreds easily with a fork.

2. Transfer pork to a cutting board; shred with 2 forks, removing any large pieces of fat. Skim fat from sauce, and stir in shredded pork.

3. Stir together fresh pineapple and next 5 ingredients. Serve pork in warm tortillas with pineapple mixture and desired toppings.

PORK & SLAW SANDWICHES

YIELD: 15 SERVINGS   TOTAL: 8 HOURS, 15 MINUTES

1   (3-lb.) boneless pork loin roast, trimmed
1¾ cups barbecue sauce
2   Tbsp. firmly packed brown sugar
1½ Tbsp. hot sauce
½   tsp. freshly ground black pepper
2½ cups packaged cabbage-and-carrot coleslaw

¼   cup mayonnaise
1   Tbsp. white vinegar
¼   tsp. sugar
⅛   tsp. table salt
15 (2-oz.) hamburger buns

1. Place pork and 1 cup water in a 3- to 4-qt. slow cooker. Cover and cook on LOW for 7 hours or until meat shreds easily with a fork.

2. Drain pork, discarding cooking liquid. Return pork to slow cooker; shred with 2 forks. Stir in barbecue sauce and next 3 ingredients. Cover and cook on LOW for 1 hour.

3. Combine coleslaw and next 4 ingredients in a bowl; toss well. Place about ⅓ cup pork mixture and about 2 Tbsp. slaw on bottom half of each bun; cover with bun tops. Serve immediately.

MUSTARD BARBECUED PORK

If you're a fan of South Carolina-style mustard-sauced barbecue, this simple pulled pork is the recipe for you. Start it first thing in the morning and let the slow cooker do the work for you.

YIELD: 10 TO 12 SERVINGS   **TOTAL: 8 HOURS, 35 MINUTES**

⅓ cup firmly packed light brown sugar
2½ tsp. table salt
1½ tsp. garlic powder
1½ tsp. paprika
1   tsp. onion powder
½   tsp. ground red pepper

1   (4- to 5-lb.) bone-in pork shoulder roast (Boston butt), trimmed
1   cup yellow mustard
⅓ cup honey
¼   cup apple cider vinegar
1½ tsp. Worcestershire sauce

1. Stir together brown sugar, and next 5 ingredients. Rub mixture over pork roast; place roast in a lightly greased 6-qt. slow cooker.

2. Whisk together yellow mustard, and remaining 3 ingredients. Pour mixture over roast. Cover and cook on LOW 8 to 10 hours (or on HIGH 4 to 6 hours) or until meat shreds easily with a fork. Let stand 15 minutes. Shred pork with 2 forks, removing any large pieces of fat; stir until sauce is incorporated.

— TRY THIS —

SOUTH CAROLINA SLIDERS: Prepare recipe as directed. Bake 1 (15-oz.) package slider miniature sandwich buns according to package directions. Split buns. Spoon ¼ cup barbecued pork and ¼ cup South Carolina Slaw (page 268) onto each bun bottom. Cover with bun tops, and serve immediately.

EASY BARBECUED PORK CHOPS

Bone-in pork chops stay moister while cooking than boneless. Add a bottle of your favorite barbecue sauce and slow-simmer the chops for an easy and delicious meal.

YIELD: 6 SERVINGS   TOTAL: 6 HOURS, 25 MINUTES

6   (1-inch-thick) bone-in pork loin chops   1   (18-oz.) bottle barbecue sauce

Place pork chops and barbecue sauce in a 6-qt. slow cooker; cover and cook on LOW 6 to 8 hours or to desired degree of tenderness. Serve immediately.

CHEF'S SIDE

JIMMY HAGOOD, FOOD FOR THE SOUTHERN SOUL, CHARLESTON

MACARONI AND CHEESE

YIELD: 12 SERVINGS   TOTAL: 3 HOURS, INCLUDING CHILL TIMES

4   cups whole milk
1   cup heavy cream
2   large eggs
Vegetable cooking spray

2   cups cooked and chilled elbow macaroni
6   cups shredded Cheddar cheese, divided

1. Preheat oven to 325°. Whisk together milk, cream and eggs.

2. Coat a 13- x 9-inch baking dish with cooking spray.

3. Combine cooked macaroni with 4 cups Cheddar cheese, and season with salt and pepper. Pour noodle and cheese mixture into prepared baking dish. Press down with hands to form a dense layer.

4. Pour milk, cream, and egg mixture over macaroni until well saturated. Top macaroni mixture with remaining 2 cups Cheddar cheese.

5. Bake for 45 minutes, rotating so it browns evenly.

6. Cool until set (about 45 minutes).

HONEY-&-SOY-LACQUERED SPARERIBS

Wrapping the ribs tightly with aluminum foil seals in the moisture as the ribs cook to tender perfection. You'll know they are ready to be lacquered when the meat pulls away from the bone without much effort.

YIELD: 6 TO 8 SERVINGS   **TOTAL: 2 HOURS, 35 MINUTES**

2 (2- to 2½-lb.) slabs St. Louis-style pork spareribs	2 Tbsp. Asian hot chili sauce (such as Sriracha)
1 Tbsp. kosher salt	1 Tbsp. fresh lime juice
2 tsp. freshly ground black pepper	1 Tbsp. butter
½ cup honey	1 tsp. dry mustard
2 Tbsp. soy sauce	1 tsp. ground ginger

1. Preheat oven to 325°. Rinse ribs, and pat dry. Remove thin membrane from back of slabs by slicing into it and pulling it off. (This will make the ribs more tender.) Sprinkle salt and pepper over slabs; wrap each slab tightly in aluminum foil. Place slabs on a jelly-roll pan, and bake at 325° for 2 to 2½ hours or until tender and meat pulls away from bone.

2. Bring honey and next 6 ingredients to a boil in a saucepan over high heat, stirring occasionally. Reduce heat to medium-low; simmer 5 minutes or until reduced by half. Transfer to a bowl.

3. Remove slabs from oven. Increase oven temperature to broil. Carefully remove slabs from foil; place on a foil-lined baking sheet. Brush each slab with 3 Tbsp. honey mixture.

4. Broil 5 to 7 minutes or until browned and sticky. Brush with remaining honey mixture before serving.

BBQ&A

WITH JIMMY HAGOOD, FOOD FOR THE SOUTHERN SOUL, CHARLESTON

What's your favorite barbecue sauce?

I like to say that most people approach their barbecue sauce styles like religion, politics, and college basketball: They're very opinionated, so I always have three sauces available. Personally, I like a tomato-based barbecue sauce that is thinned with vinegar.

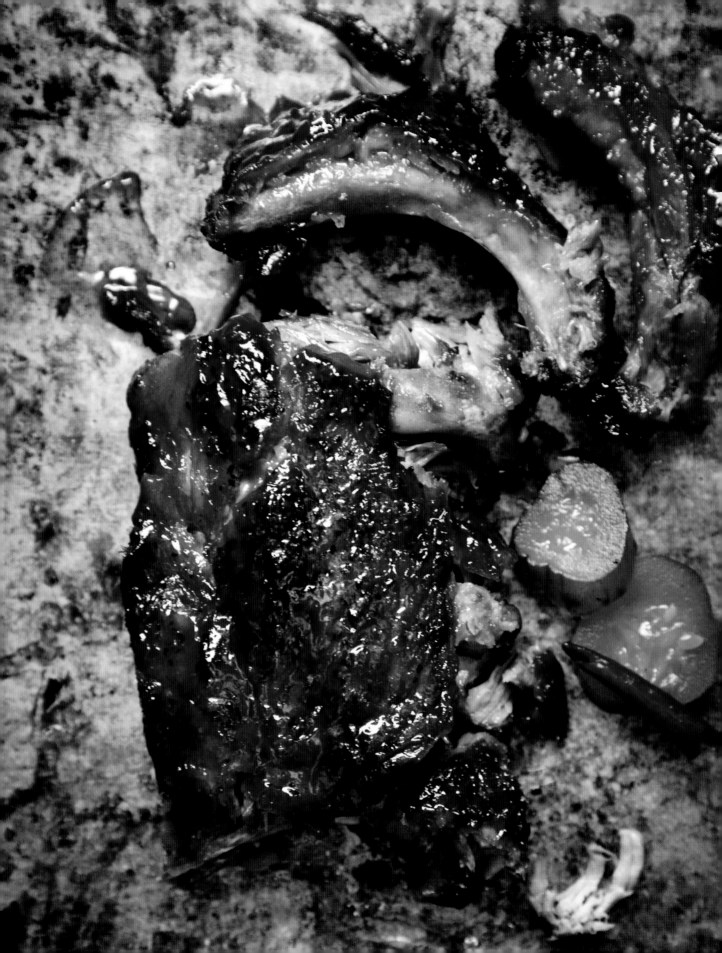

BOURBON BBQ BABY BACK RIBS

Depending on the shape of your slow cooker, you may need to cut the rib racks into thirds instead of in half. Be sure to brush the homemade barbecue sauce in between each layer so all of the ribs are covered.

YIELD: 5 SERVINGS   **TOTAL: 9 HOURS, 50 MINUTES**

5   lb. pork baby back ribs, racks cut in half
1½ tsp. table salt
1   tsp. freshly ground black pepper
1   cup ketchup
1   cup firmly packed light brown sugar
½   cup bourbon
¼   cup prepared horseradish
½   tsp. hot sauce

1. Preheat oven to 475°. Place ribs, meat side up, in a large roasting pan. Sprinkle ribs with salt and pepper.

2. Bake at 475° for 30 minutes. Meanwhile, combine ketchup and next 4 ingredients in a small bowl.

3. Arrange ribs in a 6-qt. slow cooker, adding sauce on each layer of ribs. Cover and cook ribs on LOW 9 hours. Remove ribs from slow cooker; cover to keep warm.

4. Pour drippings and sauce from slow cooker into a saucepan. (Skim a few ice cubes across the surface of sauce to remove fat, if desired, and discard.) Bring sauce to a boil; reduce heat, and simmer over medium heat 20 minutes or until sauce thickens. (Sauce will reduce by about half.) Brush sauce over ribs before serving.

BBQ&A

WITH JUSTIN & JONATHAN FOX, FOX BROS. BAR-B-Q, ATLANTA

What do you look for when selecting a rack of ribs?

I want to see good uniform ribs with nice thickness. I don't want a rack that is thick at one end and thin at the other. I also don't want to see "shiners," which is when the bone is sticking out of the meat.

BEEF RIBS WITH SORGHUM GLAZE

Most if not all pitmasters suggest removing the thin membrane from the back of the ribs to make them extra tender.

YIELD: 8 SERVINGS   TOTAL: 18 HOURS, 25 MINUTES, INCLUDING CHILL TIME

4 (2½-lb.) racks beef back ribs (center-cut)	1 tsp. onion powder
¼ cup sugar	1 tsp. smoked paprika
¼ cup kosher salt	½ tsp. ground red pepper
2 Tbsp. freshly ground black pepper	1 cup sorghum syrup
1 tsp. garlic powder	1 cup apple cider vinegar
	1 Tbsp. coarsely ground black pepper

1. Rinse and pat ribs dry. Remove thin membrane from back of ribs by slicing into it and pulling it off.

2. Stir together sugar and next 6 ingredients. Massage sugar mixture into rib meat, covering all sides. Wrap ribs tightly with plastic wrap, and place in zip-top plastic freezer bags; seal and chill 12 hours.

3. Bring sorghum and next 2 ingredients to a boil in a 3-qt. saucepan over medium-high heat, stirring occasionally; reduce heat to medium, and cook, stirring occasionally, 6 to 7 minutes or until mixture is reduced by half. Cool completely (about 30 minutes).

4. Preheat oven to 275°. Place lightly greased wire racks in 2 aluminum foil-lined 15- x 10-inch jelly-roll pans. Remove plastic wrap from ribs, and place ribs on wire racks. Cover with aluminum foil to seal. Bake 2 hours. Remove foil, and bake 3 more hours or until meat begins to pull away from bones, basting with sorghum mixture every 30 minutes. Increase oven temperature to 400°, and bake 10 more minutes or until ribs are browned.

BRAISED BEEF SHORT RIBS

Braising these ribs makes them so fork-tender, and they're perfect paired with mashed potatoes or polenta. Look for short ribs that are all about the same size so they'll cook evenly.

YIELD: 6 SERVINGS   TOTAL: 10 HOURS, INCLUDING MARINADE TIME

2¼ cups dry red wine, divided
2¼ cups beef broth, divided
2 garlic cloves, chopped
1 tsp. ground allspice
½ tsp. ground ginger
4 lb. beef short ribs, trimmed and cut in half
1 tsp. table salt

1 tsp. freshly ground black pepper
½ cup all-purpose flour
3 Tbsp. olive oil
1 carrot, chopped
½ onion, chopped
1 celery rib, chopped
2 Tbsp. tomato paste

1. Combine ¼ cup wine, ¼ cup broth, garlic, allspice, and ginger in a shallow dish; add ribs, turning to coat. Cover and chill ribs for 4 to 6 hours, turning occasionally.

2. Remove ribs from marinade, reserving marinade. Sprinkle ribs with salt and pepper; dredge in flour.

3. Cook ribs, in batches, in hot oil in a Dutch oven over medium-high heat 15 minutes or until browned. Remove ribs, and set aside.

4. Reduce heat to medium; add carrot, onion, and celery, and sauté 7 minutes or until browned. Add tomato paste; cook, stirring constantly, 3 minutes.

5. Preheat oven to 300°. Return ribs to pan. Stir in reserved marinade and remaining 2 cups wine and 2 cups broth; bring mixture to a boil, and cover tightly.

6. Bake at 300° for 3 hours. Remove ribs.

7. Skim fat from sauce and discard; simmer sauce for 12 to 15 minutes or until reduced by half. Serve sauce with ribs.

tip from the **PITS**

I like spareribs—especially St. Louis cut—because they are big and fatty and more forgiving during cooking. Buy the biggest ones you can find. When you turn the rack over, you don't want to see bone.

HARRISON SAPP, SOUTHERN SOUL BARBEQUE, ST. SIMONS ISLAND, GEORGIA

WEEKEND BRISKET

The trick to perfect brisket is to avoid overcooking it. This method of braising it in the oven gives you a leg up and helps keep the meat moist. When choosing a brisket, try to buy one with an even thickness throughout.

YIELD: 6 TO 8 SERVINGS
TOTAL: 6 HOURS, 15 MINUTES, INCLUDING HORSERADISH CREAM

2	garlic cloves, minced	1	(4- to 5-lb.) brisket flat, trimmed
1	Tbsp. kosher salt	1	yellow onion, halved and thinly sliced
1	Tbsp. freshly ground black pepper	1	Tbsp. vegetable oil
2	Tbsp. light molasses, honey, or sorghum	6	garlic cloves, chopped
2	Tbsp. yellow mustard	1	cup beef broth
¼	tsp. ground red pepper		Horseradish Cream

1. Stir together first 6 ingredients in a small bowl to form a paste. Rub on brisket, and let stand at room temperature 1 hour.

2. Preheat oven to 250°. Cook onion in hot oil in a large Dutch oven over medium-high heat, stirring occasionally, 5 minutes or until tender. Add 6 garlic cloves, and sauté 30 seconds. Remove from heat, and add beef broth, stirring to loosen browned bits from bottom of skillet. Place brisket in Dutch oven, fat side up. Spoon onion mixture over brisket.

3. Bake, covered, at 250° for 4 to 5 hours or until fork-tender. Let stand 30 minutes. Thinly slice brisket across the grain. Serve with Horseradish Cream.

HORSERADISH CREAM

This versatile and creamy sauce is delicious on just about any beef dish. Serve it with brisket, roast beef sandwiches, or steaks.

YIELD: ABOUT 1¼ CUPS   TOTAL: 10 MINUTES

1	cup sour cream	1	pickled jalapeño pepper, stemmed, seeded, and minced (optional)
1	tsp. prepared horseradish		
1	garlic clove, minced		

Stir together sour cream, horseradish, minced garlic, and, if desired, pickled jalapeño pepper in a small bowl. Add salt to taste. Refrigerate in an airtight container for up to 1 week.

TEXAS-STYLE BARBECUE BEEF BRISKET

The best part about this brisket recipe is the slow cooker does most of the work for you. Serve it up with a side of slaw and Texas toast for a complete meal.

YIELD: MAKES 4 TO 6 SERVINGS
TOTAL: 7 HOURS, 40 MINUTES

1	large sweet onion, sliced
3	garlic cloves, chopped
1	Tbsp. chili powder
1	Tbsp. jarred beef soup base
1	Tbsp. Worcestershire sauce
1	tsp. ground cumin
½	tsp. freshly ground black pepper
1½	tsp. hickory liquid smoke
1	(2- to 3-lb.) beef brisket flat, trimmed
¼	cup beer
3	Tbsp. bottled chili sauce

1. Lightly grease a 6-qt. slow cooker; add onion and garlic. Stir together chili powder and next 5 ingredients. Rub chili powder mixture over brisket; place brisket over onion mixture in slow cooker.

2. Whisk together beer and chili sauce. Slowly pour mixture around brisket (to avoid removing spices from brisket).

3. Cover and cook on LOW 7 to 8 hours (or on HIGH 4 to 5 hours) or until fork-tender. Uncover and let stand in slow cooker 20 minutes.

4. Remove brisket from slow cooker; cut brisket across the grain into thin slices. Return brisket to slow cooker, and spoon pan juices over meat.

Note: We tested with Heinz Chili Sauce.

BBQ&A

WITH ELIZABETH KARMEL, CAROLINACUETOGO.COM

What do you look for when selecting a brisket?

Buy the whole brisket instead of the just the flat or point (deckle). You almost never see the deckle being sold at the grocery store. Butchers often call the individual muscles they sell the "first cut," but I call it the second cut.

SMOKED GOUDA-STUFFED BURGERS WITH ROSEMARY KETCHUP

Homemade rosemary-infused ketchup makes these burgers bistro-worthy. Store any leftover ketchup in an airtight container in the refrigerator for up to one month.

YIELD: 8 SERVINGS   TOTAL: 1 HOUR, 5 MINUTES

Rosemary Ketchup
1   (28-oz.) can whole tomatoes in puree
½   cup dry red wine
½   cup firmly packed brown sugar
¼   cup red wine vinegar
3   sprigs fresh rosemary
1   tsp. table salt
1   tsp. freshly ground black pepper

Burgers
2   lb. ground beef
1   tsp. table salt
1   tsp. freshly ground black pepper
8   oz. smoked Gouda cheese, cut into 1-inch cubes
2   red onions, cut into ¼-inch-thick slices
8   hamburger buns, split
2   cups baby arugula

1. Prepare Rosemary Ketchup: Process canned tomatoes in a food processor or blender until smooth. Combine pureed tomatoes, and next 5 ingredients in a medium saucepan.

2. Bring to a boil. Reduce heat, and simmer 30 minutes or until mixture is reduced to 2 cups. Remove rosemary stems. Let cool.

3. Prepare Burgers: Preheat grill pan or cast-iron skillet to medium-high heat. Gently combine ground beef, salt, and pepper. Shape into 8 balls. Place 1 cheese cube into each ball, shaping beef to enclose cheese and molding to ¾-inch patties.

4. Grill burgers 6 minutes on each side or until done. At the same time, grill onion slices 3 to 4 minutes on each side, and grill buns 1 minute or until toasted. Top each bun bottom evenly with Rosemary Ketchup, followed by a burger, onion slices, arugula, and bun top.

SKILLET BARBECUE CHICKEN *(pictured)*

Get the flavor of barbecue without ever firing up the grill. The prepared barbecue sauce makes prep time super fast, but you can always substitute with your favorite homemade sauce instead.

YIELD: 4 SERVINGS   TOTAL: 15 MINUTES

4   (6-oz.) skinned and boned chicken breasts
3   garlic cloves, minced
1   Tbsp. Southwest chipotle seasoning blend
¼   tsp. kosher salt
1   Tbsp. olive oil
½   cup honey-roasted garlic barbecue sauce

1. Place chicken between 2 sheets of plastic wrap; pound to ½-inch thickness using a meat mallet. Rub garlic over chicken, and sprinkle evenly with seasoning blend and salt.

2. Heat oil in a large nonstick skillet over medium-high heat. Add chicken; cook 3 to 4 minutes on each side. Add barbecue sauce and ¼ cup water, scraping pan to loosen browned bits; cook 1 to 2 minutes or until chicken is done.

SPATCHCOCK SMOKED CHICKEN

When the weather outside is dreadful, it is still possible to smoke indoors. The trick is to wrap the pan with aluminum foil and leave enough room for smoke to circulate. This is delicious served with White Barbecue Sauce (page 323).

YIELD: 4 SERVINGS   TOTAL: 3 HOURS, 40 MINUTES

4   cups hickory, apple, or mesquite wood chips
1   (4-lb.) whole chicken
1   Tbsp. smoked paprika
1   Tbsp. chili powder
2   tsp. garlic powder
1   tsp. dried tarragon
1   tsp. table salt
1   tsp. freshly ground black pepper
½   tsp. ground red pepper
2   Tbsp. melted butter

1. Soak wood chips in water for 1 hour. Drain and place in the bottom of a deep roasting pan. Place a rack over the chips.

2. Preheat oven to 250°. Remove backbone from chicken. Carefully loosen skin from breasts and thighs of chicken without removing it.

3. Combine paprika, and next 6 ingredients. Rub mixture underneath skin of chicken.

4. Place chicken on rack in roasting pan. Cover pan with aluminum foil, leaving a "tent" to allow smoke to circulate. Bake 2 hours or until a meat thermometer inserted into thigh registers 155°.

5. Uncover chicken. Brush with butter. Increase oven temperature to 400°. Bake 20 minutes longer or until skin is browned and a meat thermometer inserted into the thigh registers 170°.

SLOW-COOKED BARBECUE CHICKEN

Find chicken already cut up in the meat department at your grocery store. You can also ask the butcher to cut it up for you.

YIELD: 6 SERVINGS   TOTAL: 5 HOURS, 20 MINUTES

2   tsp. table salt
1½ tsp. paprika
½   tsp. garlic powder
½   tsp. freshly ground black pepper
1   (3- to 3½-lb.) cut-up whole chicken
½   cup cola soft drink

⅓   cup ketchup
¼   cup firmly packed light brown sugar
2   Tbsp. apple cider vinegar
2   Tbsp. bourbon
1   lemon, sliced

1. Stir together first 4 ingredients in a small bowl. Sprinkle over chicken. Place chicken in a single layer in a lightly greased 6-qt. slow cooker.

2. Whisk together cola soft drink and next 4 ingredients in a small bowl. Slowly pour mixture between chicken pieces (to avoid removing spices from chicken). Place lemon slices in a single layer on top of chicken.

3. Cover and cook on HIGH 5 hours (or on LOW 6½ to 7½ hours) or until done.

4. Transfer chicken pieces to a serving platter; discard lemon slices. Skim fat from pan juices in slow cooker. Pour pan juices over chicken; serve immediately.

— TRY THIS —

SLOW-COOKED BARBECUE CHICKEN SANDWICHES:

Prepare recipe as directed through Step 3. Remove chicken from slow cooker, and let cool slightly (about 10 to 15 minutes). Discard lemons. Skin, bone, and shred chicken. Skim fat from pan juices, and pour over chicken. Serve chicken over sliced Sweet Potato Cornbread (page 314). Top with Easy Pickled Sweet Onions & Peppers (page 339) and your choice of slaw (starting on page 268).

BARBECUE SHRIMP

This New Orleans favorite is simple to prepare, and you'll want to soak up every last bit of the spicy butter sauce with a crusty baguette.

YIELD: 4 SERVINGS   TOTAL: 2 HOURS, 50 MINUTES

- 1 cup butter, divided
- 6 garlic cloves, pressed
- ½ cup Worcestershire sauce
- ¼ cup fresh lemon juice
- ¼ cup bottled chili sauce
- 2 tsp. freshly ground black pepper
- 1½ Tbsp. Old Bay seasoning
- 1 tsp. paprika
- 1 tsp. dried Italian seasoning
- 1 lemon, sliced
- 2 lb. unpeeled, large raw shrimp
- Hot sauce (optional)
- Lemon wedges
- 2 French bread baguettes, sliced

1. Melt ¼ cup butter in a skillet over medium-high heat 2 minutes; add garlic, and sauté until fragrant and lightly browned. Remove from heat; spoon into a 6-qt. oval-shaped slow cooker. Add remaining ¾ cup butter, Worcestershire sauce, and next 7 ingredients. Cover and cook on LOW 2 hours.

2. Add shrimp to slow cooker. Cover and cook on HIGH 45 minutes or until shrimp turn pink, stirring once after 30 minutes. Add hot sauce, if desired. Serve with lemon wedges and French bread.

CHEF'S SIDE

JIMMY HAGOOD, FOOD FOR THE SOUTHERN SOUL, CHARLESTON

LOWCOUNTRY RED RICE

YIELD: 20 SERVINGS   TOTAL: 1 HOUR

- 3 center-cut bacon slices
- 8 oz. sliced and quartered smoked kielbasa
- ½ yellow onion, chopped
- 1 red bell pepper, chopped
- 1 green bell pepper, chopped
- 1 Tbsp. tomato paste
- 6 cups uncooked rice
- 1 cup tomato juice
- 1 (20-oz.) can whole tomatoes, undrained
- 1 tsp. hot sauce
- 6 cups chicken broth

1. Preheat oven to 300°. Cook bacon in Dutch oven over medium-high heat until crisp. Remove bacon, and drain on paper towels, reserving 2 Tbsp. drippings in pan. Crumble bacon. Add sausage and cook 5 minutes, stirring occasionally. Remove from pan. Add onions and peppers, and sauté until tender (about 5 minutes). Stir in tomato paste, stirring occasionally, 3 minutes. Add rice, tomato juice, tomatoes with juice, and hot sauce. Stir in broth and add back in kielbasa and crumbled bacon.

2. Spoon into a 3-qt. baking dish coated with cooking spray. Bake, covered, at 300° for 45 minutes or until rice is tender.

FIERY SIDES

What's a barbecue without a slew of sides?
These salads, slaws, baked beans, greens,
and other dishes are just what you need
to round out your best barbecue meal.

WATERMELON, ARUGULA & PECAN SALAD

Arugula is a peppery, tender green that pairs perfectly with juicy summer watermelon, sharp Gorgonzola cheese, and a spicy-sweet vinaigrette. Baby spinach and mâche are great alternatives to arugula.

YIELD: 6 TO 8 SERVINGS   TOTAL: 30 MINUTES, INCLUDING PEPPER JELLY VINAIGRETTE

½ baby watermelon, cut into thin
    wedge slices
½ (6-oz.) package arugula

Pepper Jelly Vinaigrette
1   cup crumbled Gorgonzola cheese
¾   cup chopped pecans, toasted

Combine watermelon and arugula in a large bowl; add vinaigrette, tossing gently to coat. Transfer watermelon mixture to a serving platter, and sprinkle evenly with cheese and pecans.

PEPPER JELLY VINAIGRETTE

Pepper jelly is a perfect condiment served with cream cheese or roasted meat. Here it is the secret ingredient in this tangy-hot dressing. Red and green pepper jellies are equally delicious.

YIELD: ¾ CUP   TOTAL: 5 MINUTES

¼ cup rice wine vinegar
¼ cup pepper jelly
1   Tbsp. fresh lime juice
1   Tbsp. grated onion

1   tsp. table salt
¼ tsp. freshly ground black pepper
¼ cup vegetable oil

Whisk together first 6 ingredients. Gradually add oil in a slow, steady stream, whisking until blended. Store in airtight container in refrigerator for up to 1 week.

HOT BACON CAPRESE SALAD *(pictured)*

This classic Italian salad takes a trip to the South, where everything tastes better with bacon. Thick slices of bacon are the secret to the delicious vinaigrette that's drizzled over ripe summer tomatoes and creamy mozzarella cheese.

YIELD: 6 TO 8 SERVINGS   TOTAL: 25 MINUTES

2½ lb. heirloom tomatoes, cut into ½-inch slices
1 (16-oz.) package fresh mozzarella cheese, cut into ½-inch slices
½ cup fresh basil leaves

6 center-cut bacon slices, coarsely chopped
3 to 4 Tbsp. red wine vinegar
2 Tbsp. olive oil
½ tsp. kosher salt
½ tsp. freshly ground black pepper

1. Arrange tomatoes and cheese on a serving platter, placing basil leaves between slices. Sprinkle with desired amount of salt and pepper.

2. Sauté chopped bacon in a large skillet over medium heat 6 to 8 minutes or until crisp. Remove from heat, reserving bacon and 2 Tbsp. drippings in skillet. Let stand 1 minute. Add vinegar and oil, stirring to loosen browned bits from bottom of skillet. Sprinkle with ½ tsp. kosher salt and ½ tsp. black pepper. Drizzle warm bacon mixture over tomatoes and cheese. Serve immediately.

GRILLED WATERMELON WITH BLUE CHEESE & PROSCIUTTO

Grilling watermelon may seem a little out of the ordinary, but it is an ideal way to enjoy one of summer's favorite fruits. Grilling intensifies the sweetness and lends a smoky flavor to the melon.

YIELD: 4 SERVINGS   TOTAL: 20 MINUTES

3 (½-inch-thick) watermelon rounds, quartered
1 Tbsp. olive oil
4 oz. thinly sliced prosciutto

4 oz. blue cheese, crumbled
Fresh basil leaves
2 tsp. bottled balsamic glaze

1. Preheat grill to 350° to 400° (medium-high) heat. Brush both sides of each watermelon quarter with olive oil, and season with desired amount of kosher salt and pepper. Cut prosciutto into thin strips.

2. Grill watermelon quarters, without grill lid, 1 minute on each side or until grill marks appear.

3. Transfer watermelon to a serving plate; top with blue cheese, prosciutto strips, and fresh basil. Drizzle watermelon with balsamic glaze. Serve immediately.

ARUGULA WITH WARM BACON VINAIGRETTE

YIELD: 4 SERVINGS   TOTAL: 10 MINUTES

4	center-cut bacon slices	¼	tsp. kosher salt
1	shallot, minced	¼	tsp. freshly ground black pepper
4	Tbsp. extra virgin olive oil	1	(5-oz.) package arugula or mixed greens
2	Tbsp. red wine vinegar	⅓	cup crumbled goat cheese

1. Cook bacon in a 10-inch nonstick skillet over medium heat 6 minutes or until crisp. Remove bacon, reserving drippings in skillet. Crumble bacon. Sauté shallot in drippings 2 minutes or just until tender.

2. Transfer shallot and drippings to a small bowl. Whisk in oil and next 3 ingredients. Toss arugula with vinaigrette on a platter. Top with goat cheese and bacon. Serve immediately.

CHEF'S SIDE

ELIZABETH KARMEL, CAROLINACUETOGO.COM

COOL AS A CUCUMBER SALAD

This salad beats coleslaw hands down as a simple side to grilled seafood and barbecue. The vinegar dressing and the fresh cucumbers will cut through the richness of any meat it's served with.

YIELD: 4 SERVINGS   TOTAL: 3 HOURS, 30 MINUTES, INCLUDING CHILL TIME

2	English cucumbers	½	Tbsp. kosher or sea salt
4	shallots	1	cup unseasoned rice vinegar
½	cup sugar		

1. Wash and dry cucumbers. Peel alternating strips of green skin off cucumber with vegetable peeler. Using a mandoline, slice cucumber very thin. Set aside.

2. Peel shallots. Using a mandoline, slice shallots very thin. Mix cucumber and shallots. Set aside.

3. Whisk together sugar, salt, and vinegar until completely dissolved. Pour over cucumber and shallot slices, and mix well.

4. Pour vegetable mixture in a nonreactive (plastic or glass) container with a tight lid and refrigerate, turning occasionally, for at least 3 hours or overnight before serving. Taste and adjust seasonings as desired. Store in an airtight container in refrigerator for up to 5 days.

GRILLED PEACH & AVOCADO SALAD

This recipe calls for firm avocados so that they can stand up to the grill. When choosing avocados at the store, look for those that are almost ripe. Check under the "button" on the stem end. If it's green, it's the one you want; if it's brown, it's overripe.

YIELD: 6 SERVINGS   TOTAL: 20 MINUTES

- 4   large peaches, peeled, divided
- 7   Tbsp. canola oil, divided
- 2   Tbsp. Champagne vinegar or white wine vinegar
- ½   tsp. honey
- ¼   tsp. kosher salt
- ⅛   tsp. freshly ground black pepper
- 2   firm avocados, peeled and quartered
- 6   cups loosely packed arugula
- ½   cup freshly grated Manchego or Parmesan cheese

1. Preheat grill to 350° to 400° (medium-high) heat.

2. Chop 1 peach, and place in a blender; process peach, 6 Tbsp. canola oil, vinegar, and honey until smooth. Add kosher salt and freshly ground pepper.

3. Halve remaining 3 peaches. Gently toss peaches and avocados in remaining 1 Tbsp. canola oil; add salt and pepper to taste.

4. Grill peach halves and avocado quarters, covered with grill lid, 2 minutes on each side or until charred. Slice and serve over arugula. Top with peach vinaigrette and cheese.

tip from the PITS

Summertime and grilling go hand in hand because of the abundance of great veggies. Corn, potatoes, tomatoes, peppers, squash, and zucchini are great veggies to grill. You can even get into fruit. A fresh, sweet peach charred on the grill is great as an appetizer or in a salad.

JUSTIN & JONATHAN FOX, FOX BROS. BAR-B-Q, ATLANTA

HEIRLOOM TOMATO SALAD WITH LADY PEAS

An ode to summer, this colorful heirloom tomato salad comes together quickly. It features small, sweet lady peas, but you can substitute another fresh field pea if you prefer.

YIELD: 6 SERVINGS   TOTAL: 10 MINUTES, INCLUDING DRESSING

1   cup fresh lady peas
Lemon-Herb Dressing with Basil, divided
2   lb. assorted heirloom tomatoes, cut
    into ¼-inch-thick slices

4   fresh basil leaves
1   (4-oz.) package crumbled
    goat cheese (optional)

1. Cook peas in boiling salted water to cover in a large saucepan 8 to 10 minutes or just until tender. Drain and rinse until completely cool. Drizzle ¼ cup Lemon-Herb Dressing with Basil over peas, and toss to coat.

2. Arrange tomato slices on a platter or individual serving plates. Spoon peas over tomatoes; sprinkle with basil, goat cheese, and salt and pepper to taste. Serve with remaining dressing.

LEMON-HERB DRESSING WITH BASIL

This fresh dressing has a slight kick from the crushed red pepper. If you're sensitive to spice, you can reduce it to ¼ teaspoon.

YIELD: ¾ CUP   TOTAL: 5 MINUTES

⅓   cup canola oil
⅓   cup chopped fresh basil
1   Tbsp. honey mustard
1   tsp. lemon zest

¼   cup fresh lemon juice
1   tsp. table salt
½   tsp. dried crushed red pepper

Whisk together all ingredients until blended. Season with salt to taste. Store in an airtight container in refrigerator for up to 5 days.

ZUCCHINI-CARROT SALAD

A mandoline is a handy tool for cutting the zucchini into equal lengths for this salad. For best results, make the matchstick carrots yourself, keeping them the same size as the zucchini. Store-bought matchstick carrots are often dried out.

YIELD: 4 SERVINGS   TOTAL: 40 MINUTES, INCLUDING DRESSING

1 lb. zucchini	¼ cup firmly packed fresh mint leaves, coarsely chopped
2 cups matchstick carrots	2 Tbsp. thinly sliced fresh chives
½ cup Catalina Dressing	½ cup French fried onions

1. Cut zucchini lengthwise into ⅛- to ¼-inch-thick slices. Stack 2 or 3 slices on a cutting board, and cut lengthwise into thin strips. Repeat with remaining zucchini.

2. Toss together zucchini, carrots, and desired amount of dressing; let stand 20 minutes, tossing occasionally.

3. Sprinkle mint and chives over zucchini mixture, and add salt and pepper to taste. Top with French fried onions.

CATALINA DRESSING

This tangy dressing is so easy to make, you may never buy bottled again. Make extra to have on hand, and store it in the refrigerator for up to two weeks.

YIELD: 1½ CUPS   TOTAL: 5 MINUTES

½ cup olive oil	¼ cup grated sweet onion
¼ cup sugar	½ tsp. paprika
¼ cup ketchup	½ tsp. Worcestershire sauce
¼ cup red wine vinegar	½ tsp. hot sauce

Whisk together olive oil, sugar, ketchup, vinegar, onion, paprika, Worcestershire sauce, hot sauce, and salt and pepper to taste. Store in an airtight container in refrigerator for up to 2 weeks.

SOUTH CAROLINA SLAW

It's not South Carolina slaw if the recipe doesn't have mustard—in this case it's both Dijon and dry mustards. And the thinner the cabbage, the better.

YIELD: 6 CUPS   TOTAL: 15 MINUTES

½ head thinly sliced cabbage (about 1 lb.)
1 cup shredded carrot
½ cup apple cider vinegar
¼ cup sugar
¼ cup vegetable oil

2 Tbsp. Dijon mustard
2 tsp. dry mustard
1 tsp. celery seeds
1 tsp. kosher salt
½ tsp. freshly ground black pepper

1. Place cabbage and carrot in a bowl. Whisk together vinegar and next 7 ingredients in a saucepan until sugar dissolves; bring to a boil over medium-high heat.

2. Pour over cabbage mixture; toss to coat. Serve immediately.

MEMPHIS SLAW

The cabbage is always coarsely chopped in Memphis slaw, and the flavors are big and bold—it has to stand up to the standout pulled pork and ribs it's typically served with.

YIELD: 8 CUPS   TOTAL: 1 HOUR, 15 MINUTES

1 Tbsp. firmly packed light brown sugar
2 tsp. kosher salt
1 tsp. paprika
½ tsp. dry mustard
½ tsp. dried oregano
½ tsp. freshly ground black pepper
¼ tsp. granulated garlic

¼ tsp. ground coriander
¼ tsp. onion powder
½ cup mayonnaise
¼ cup apple cider vinegar
½ head cabbage (about 1 lb.)
1 cup diced green bell pepper
1 cup diced red onion

1. Whisk together brown sugar and next 8 ingredients in a bowl. Whisk in mayonnaise and vinegar until sugar dissolves.

2. Cut cabbage into thick slices; cut slices crosswise. Fold cabbage, bell pepper, and red onion into mayonnaise mixture until coated.

3. Let stand 1 hour before serving, tossing occasionally.

South Carolina Slaw

Central Texas Slaw
(page 271)

Western North Carolina Slaw
(page 270)

Eastern North Carolina Slaw
(page 270)

Memphis Slaw

WESTERN NORTH CAROLINA SLAW

(pictured on page 269)

Ketchup is the key ingredient in western North Carolina coleslaws. It gives the chopped slaw an interesting color and signature tangy flavor.

YIELD: ABOUT 4 CUPS   TOTAL: 1 HOUR, 15 MINUTES

⅓ cup ketchup
⅓ cup apple cider vinegar
2 Tbsp. sugar
½ tsp. kosher salt

½ tsp. freshly ground black pepper
¼ tsp. hot sauce
½ head cabbage (about 1 lb.), grated
¼ large sweet onion, grated

1. Whisk together ketchup, and next 5 ingredients in a bowl. Add cabbage and onion; toss to coat.

2. Let stand 1 hour before serving, tossing occasionally.

EASTERN NORTH CAROLINA SLAW

(pictured on page 269)

One of the finest chopped slaws, eastern North Carolina coleslaws are typically extra tart in flavor and are always served with hot sauce and chopped whole hog.

YIELD: 4 CUPS   TOTAL: 1 HOUR, 15 MINUTES

½ cup white vinegar
¼ cup sugar
1 tsp. kosher salt
¼ tsp. freshly ground black pepper

½ head cabbage (about 1 lb.), grated
½ cup chopped celery
Hot sauce

1. Whisk together vinegar, and next 3 ingredients. Add cabbage and celery; toss to coat.

2. Let stand 1 hour before serving, tossing occasionally. Serve with hot sauce.

CENTRAL TEXAS SLAW *(pictured on page 269)*

In true Texas style, this slaw gets its Southwestern flavor from the jalapeño pepper and cilantro. Omit the jalapeño seeds to tone down the heat.

YIELD: ABOUT 4 CUPS   TOTAL: 1 HOUR, 15 MINUTES

¼ cup white vinegar
¼ cup extra virgin olive oil
2 Tbsp. sugar
3 to 4 Tbsp. fresh lime juice
1½ tsp. kosher salt
½ tsp. ground coriander
¼ tsp. ground cumin
¼ tsp. ground red pepper
¼ tsp. freshly ground black pepper

2 cups thinly sliced red cabbage
2 cups thinly sliced white cabbage
½ cup shredded carrot
1 medium jalapeño pepper (with seeds), thinly sliced
½ red bell pepper, thinly sliced
½ yellow bell pepper, thinly sliced
½ cup chopped fresh cilantro

1. Whisk together vinegar, and next 8 ingredients in a large bowl.

2. Add cabbages, carrot, jalapeño pepper, and bell peppers. Toss to coat.

3. Chill 1 hour before serving, tossing occasionally. Stir in cilantro just before serving.

GRILLED CONFETTI COLESLAW

(pictured on page 287)

Grilling cabbage gives it a smoky flavor that pairs well with pulled pork or burgers. Using it in this rainbow-colored slaw makes it a welcome addition to any backyard cookout.

YIELD: 6 TO 8 SERVINGS   TOTAL: 1 HOUR, 25 MINUTES

1 small head red cabbage, cut into ¼-inch-thick slices
1 small head green cabbage, cut into ¼-inch-thick slices
3 Tbsp. olive oil
2 carrots, peeled and shredded
1 yellow bell pepper, thinly sliced

2 green onions, chopped
¼ cup loosely packed fresh flat-leaf parsley, chopped
½ cup mayonnaise
3 Tbsp. apple cider vinegar
2 Tbsp. honey

1. Preheat grill to 350° to 400° (medium-high) heat.

2. Brush cabbage slices with olive oil. Grill 2 to 3 minutes on each side or until slightly charred. Let cool, and thinly slice.

3. Combine sliced cabbage, carrots, bell pepper, green onions, and parsley in a serving bowl.

4. Whisk together mayonnaise, vinegar, honey, and table salt and black pepper to taste. Pour dressing over cabbage mixture, tossing well to coat. Cover and refrigerate at least 1 hour before serving.

BARBECUE DEVILED EGGS

Take this traditional picnic favorite to a whole new level with smoked pork butt. You can make your own (page 84), or swing by your favorite barbecue joint and pick up a half pound to go.

YIELD: 2 DOZEN   TOTAL: 1 HOUR, 30 MINUTES

- 1 · dozen hard-cooked eggs, peeled
- ¼ cup mayonnaise
- ⅓ cup finely chopped Smoked Pork Butt (page 84)
- 1 Tbsp. Dijon mustard
- ¼ tsp. table salt
- ½ tsp. freshly ground black pepper
- ⅛ tsp. hot sauce
- Paprika (optional)

1. Slice eggs in half lengthwise, and carefully remove yolks, keeping egg whites intact.

2. Mash together yolks and mayonnaise, and stir in pork and next 4 ingredients; blend well.

3. Spoon yolk mixture evenly into egg white halves, and let chill for 1 hour before serving. Garnish with paprika, if desired.

— TRY THIS —

SMOKY PIMIENTO CHEESE DEVILED EGGS: Prepare recipe as directed in Step 1. Mash together yolks with ½ cup mayonnaise, 1½ cups freshly grated smoked or sharp Cheddar cheese, ½ cup finely chopped jarred roasted red bell pepper, 2 Tbsp. Dijon mustard, and a pinch of ground red pepper. Season with table salt and black pepper to taste. Spoon yolk mixture into egg white halves. Garnish with chopped chives, diced country ham, or sliced pickled okra. Cover and chill 1 hour before serving.

PIG SKIN DEVILED EGGS: Prepare recipe as directed in Step 1. Mash together yolks, ½ cup mayonnaise, 1 Tbsp. chopped fresh flat-leaf parsley, 1 Tbsp. finely chopped chives, 3 Tbsp. sweet pickle relish, 2 Tbsp. sour cream, 1 tsp. spicy brown mustard, 1 tsp. Asian hot chili sauce (such as Sriracha), and ⅛ tsp. table salt; blend well. Spoon yolk mixture into egg white halves. Garnish with pickled okra slices and chopped pork crackling strips. Cover and chill 1 hour before serving.

Hot Potato Salad

Bacon Potato Salad

BACON POTATO SALAD

Smoky bacon infuses traditional, creamy potato salad. Allow the boiled potatoes to cool slightly, and mix gently with the dressing to avoid ending up with mashed potatoes.

YIELD: 6 SERVINGS   TOTAL: 1 HOUR, 45 MINUTES

- 6 to 8 medium potatoes (about 3 lb.), peeled and cut into 1-inch cubes
- ½ lb. cooked and crumbled bacon slices
- 6 green onions, chopped
- 2 celery ribs, finely chopped
- 2 Tbsp. diced pimiento, drained
- ¾ tsp. table salt
- ¼ tsp. freshly ground black pepper
- ½ cup mayonnaise
- ½ cup sour cream

1. Bring potatoes and water to cover to a boil in a Dutch oven over medium-high heat, and cook 15 to 18 minutes or until tender; drain and let cool slightly.

2. Place cooked potatoes in a large bowl. Add bacon, chopped green onions, and next 4 ingredients. Stir together mayonnaise and sour cream until blended. Pour over potato mixture, tossing gently to coat.

3. Cover and chill at least 1 hour.

HOT POTATO SALAD

This potato salad is a new take on twice-baked potatoes and is the perfect accompaniment with burgers and barbecue. Freezing the cheese makes it much easier to grate.

YIELD: 6 TO 8 SERVINGS   TOTAL: 2 HOURS

- 1 lb. processed cheese (such as Velveeta)
- 8 russet potatoes (about 4 lb.)
- 1½ cups mayonnaise
- 1 cup half-and-half
- ½ cup chopped yellow onion
- 1 cup sliced pimiento-stuffed Spanish olives
- Vegetable cooking spray
- 6 center-cut bacon slices, cut into 2-inch pieces

1. Freeze cheese 45 minutes to 1 hour. Meanwhile, cook potatoes in boiling water to cover 25 to 30 minutes or until tender; drain and cool completely.

2. Peel potatoes, and cut into 1-inch cubes. Grate frozen cheese, using large holes of a box grater.

3. Preheat oven to 325°. Whisk together mayonnaise and half-and-half in a large bowl. Stir in onion, olives, potatoes, and cheese until blended. Add table salt and black pepper to taste. Spoon into a 13- x 9-inch baking dish coated with cooking spray. Top with bacon pieces.

4. Bake at 325° for 55 minutes. Increase oven temperature to broil, and broil 5 minutes or until bacon is crisp. Let stand 5 minutes before serving.

GRILLED FINGERLING POTATO SALAD

This grilled potato salad is definitely worth the effort. Smoke from the grill infuses the sweet fingerlings accented with crumbled bacon, tangy vinaigrette, and tart shallot pickles.

YIELD: 8 SERVINGS   TOTAL: 3 HOURS, INCLUDING VINAIGRETTE AND PICKLES

6 cups fingerling potatoes (about 3 lb.), halved lengthwise	3 Tbsp. Pickled Shallots
2 Tbsp. extra virgin olive oil	2 Tbsp. chopped fresh chives
1 tsp. kosher salt	2 Tbsp. chopped fresh flat-leaf parsley
½ tsp. freshly ground black pepper	1 tsp. chopped fresh thyme
3 Tbsp. Whole Grain Mustard Vinaigrette	3 Tbsp. cooked and crumbled bacon slices (optional)

1. Preheat grill to 350° to 400° (medium-high) heat. Toss potatoes in olive oil; sprinkle with 1 tsp. salt and ½ tsp. black pepper. Place, cut sides down, on cooking grate; grill, covered with grill lid, 2 minutes or until grill marks appear.

2. Remove from grill. Place potatoes in a single layer in center of a large piece of heavy-duty aluminum foil. Bring up foil sides over potatoes; double-fold top and side edges to seal, making a packet. Grill potatoes, in foil packet, covered with grill lid, 15 minutes on each side.

3. Remove packet from grill. Carefully open packet, using tongs. Cool 5 minutes. Toss together potatoes, vinaigrette, next 4 ingredients, and, if desired, bacon.

WHOLE GRAIN MUSTARD VINAIGRETTE

YIELD: ⅔ CUP   TOTAL: 5 MINUTES

¼ cup white wine vinegar	½ tsp. freshly ground black pepper
1 Tbsp. firmly packed light brown sugar	⅛ tsp. table salt
3 Tbsp. whole grain mustard	⅓ cup olive oil

Whisk together vinegar, and next 4 ingredients. Add olive oil in a slow, steady stream, whisking constantly until smooth. Store in an airtight container in refrigerator for up to a week.

PICKLED SHALLOTS

YIELD: 1½ CUPS   TOTAL: 1 HOUR, 20 MINUTES, INCLUDING CHILL TIME

¾ cup red wine vinegar	½ tsp. dried crushed red pepper
⅓ cup sugar	1½ cups thinly sliced shallots
2 Tbsp. kosher salt	

Bring ¾ cup water, vinegar, sugar, kosher salt, and dried crushed red pepper to a boil, whisking until sugar and salt are dissolved. Pour over shallots in a sterilized canning jar. Cool to room temperature. Cover and chill 1 hour. Store in an airtight container in refrigerator for up to a week.

SMOKY MASHED SWEET POTATO BAKE

Heating the buttermilk and milk before adding them to the cooked sweet potatoes ensures a velvety texture.

YIELD: 6 TO 8 SERVINGS   TOTAL: 1 HOUR

4   lb. russet potatoes
3   tsp. table salt, divided
1¼ cups warm buttermilk
½   cup warm milk
¼   cup melted butter

½   tsp. freshly ground black pepper
1   cup mashed baked sweet potatoes
1½ Tbsp. chopped canned chipotle
    peppers in adobo sauce

1. Preheat oven to 350°. Peel baking potatoes; cut into 2-inch pieces. Bring potatoes, 2 tsp. salt, and water to cover to a boil in a large Dutch oven over medium-high heat; boil 20 minutes or until tender. Drain. Return potatoes to Dutch oven, reduce heat to low, and cook, stirring occasionally, 3 to 5 minutes or until potatoes are dry.

2. Mash potatoes with a potato masher to desired consistency. Stir in warm buttermilk, warm milk, melted butter, pepper, and remaining 1 tsp. salt, stirring just until blended.

3. Stir in sweet potatoes and chopped chipotle peppers, and spoon mixture into a lightly greased 2½-qt. baking dish or 8 (10-oz.) ramekins. Bake at 350° for 35 minutes.

CHEF'S SIDE

PITMASTER TROY BLACK

GRILLED SWEET POTATO PLANKS

YIELD: 6 SERVINGS   TOTAL: 20 MINUTES

⅓   cup olive oil
1   Tbsp. minced shallot
1   Tbsp. chopped fresh rosemary
1   tsp. kosher salt

1   tsp. coarsely ground black pepper
3   large sweet potatoes, peeled
    and cut into ¼-inch-thick slices
½   cup crumbled blue cheese

1. Preheat grill to 350° to 400° (medium-high) heat. Stir together first 5 ingredients in a small bowl. Brush olive oil mixture over sweet potato slices.

2. Grill, covered with grill lid, 3 to 4 minutes on each side or until tender. Place potatoes on a serving platter; sprinkle with blue cheese.

GARLIC-PARSLEY STEAK FRIES

A garlic press is an inexpensive tool that makes easy work of preparing the garlic in this recipe. If you don't have a garlic press, use the flat side of a chef's knife to press and mince the garlic into a paste.

YIELD: 6 SERVINGS   **TOTAL: 1 HOUR**

2   Tbsp. olive oil
1   large garlic clove, pressed
8   russet potatoes (about 3 lb.)
½   tsp. kosher salt

Vegetable cooking spray
2   Tbsp. chopped fresh parsley
Ketchup (optional)

1. Preheat oven to 425°.

2. Combine oil and garlic in a large bowl. Scrub potatoes; pat dry. Cut each potato lengthwise into 6 (1-inch-thick) wedges; add to oil mixture. Toss wedges until thoroughly coated. Sprinkle wedges with salt; toss well. Place wedges on a large baking sheet coated with cooking spray.

3. Bake at 425° for 50 minutes or until wedges are tender and golden. Remove from pan; sprinkle with parsley. Serve with ketchup, if desired.

SWEET POTATO CHIPS

A candy thermometer is an essential tool for this recipe to maintain the oil at the correct temperature for frying. Cooking the potatoes in small batches also helps to fry them evenly.

YIELD: 6 TO 8 SERVINGS   **TOTAL: 40 MINUTES**

2   sweet potatoes, peeled (about 2 lb.)
Peanut oil

1. Cut sweet potatoes into 1/16-inch-thick slices, using a mandoline.

2. Pour peanut oil to depth of 3 inches into a Dutch oven; heat over medium-high heat to 300°.

3. Fry potato slices, in small batches, stirring often, 4 to 4½ minutes or until crisp.

4. Drain on a wire rack over paper towels.

5. Immediately sprinkle with desired amount of kosher salt. Cool completely, and store in an airtight container at room temperature up to 2 days.

MACARONI SALAD *(pictured)*

This creamy, confetti-colored salad is a great side dish for all types of barbecue.

YIELD: 6 SERVINGS   TOTAL: 14 MINUTES

- 1 cup (4 oz.) uncooked elbow macaroni
- ½ cup mayonnaise
- 1 Tbsp. apple cider vinegar
- 1½ tsp. sugar
- ¾ tsp. dry mustard
- ½ tsp. freshly ground black pepper
- ¼ tsp. table salt
- ⅓ cup thinly sliced celery
- ⅓ cup finely chopped red bell pepper
- ¼ cup finely chopped red onion
- ¼ cup shredded carrot
- 1 Tbsp. chopped fresh chives

1. Cook pasta according to package directions. Combine mayonnaise and next 5 ingredients, stirring with a whisk.

2. Stir in cooked pasta, celery, and remaining ingredients. Refrigerate in an airtight container up to 3 days.

TOMATO & GORGONZOLA PASTA SALAD

Beefsteak tomatoes work best here because of their sweet and intense flavor, but other small tomatoes work well, too.

YIELD: 8 SERVINGS   TOTAL: 1 HOUR, 10 MINUTES

- 1 (16-oz.) package rigatoni pasta
- ½ cup Lemon-Shallot Vinaigrette
- 1¼ lb. beefsteak tomatoes, seeded and chopped
- 4 oz. Gorgonzola cheese, crumbled
- ½ (5-oz.) package arugula

1. Prepare pasta according to package directions. Toss together hot pasta and vinaigrette in a large bowl. Cool completely (about 30 minutes).

2. Stir tomatoes and cheese into pasta mixture. Just before serving, stir in arugula; add table salt and black pepper to taste.

LEMON-SHALLOT VINAIGRETTE

YIELD: 1 CUP   TOTAL: 10 MINUTES

- ½ cup fresh lemon juice
- 1 shallot, minced
- 1 cup olive oil
- ¼ cup minced fresh flat-leaf parsley
- 1 Tbsp. honey
- 1 Tbsp. coarse-grained Dijon mustard

Stir together lemon juice and shallot; let stand 5 minutes. Whisk in olive oil and next 3 ingredients. Add salt and pepper to taste. Refrigerate in an airtight container up to 1 week.

BAKED SMOKIN' MAC & CHEESE

This macaroni and cheese gets its flavor from smoked Gouda and smoked ham. The crunchy cornflake topping is the ideal counterpoint to the creamy noodles.

YIELD: 8 SERVINGS   TOTAL: 1 HOUR

1   lb. uncooked cellentani (corkscrew) pasta
3   Tbsp. butter, divided
¼   cup all-purpose flour
3   cups milk
1   (12-oz.) can evaporated milk
1   cup (4 oz.) shredded smoked Gouda cheese
½   cup (2 oz.) shredded sharp Cheddar cheese

3   oz. cream cheese, softened
½   tsp. table salt
¼   tsp. ground red pepper, divided
1   (8-oz.) package chopped smoked ham
Vegetable cooking spray
1¼ cups cornflakes cereal, crushed
1   Tbsp. butter, melted

1. Preheat oven to 350°. Prepare pasta according to package directions.

2. Meanwhile, melt 2 Tbsp. butter in a Dutch oven over medium heat. Gradually whisk in flour; cook, whisking constantly, 1 minute. Gradually whisk in milk and evaporated milk until smooth; cook, whisking constantly, 8 to 10 minutes or until slightly thickened. Whisk in Gouda cheese, next 3 ingredients, and ⅛ tsp. ground red pepper until smooth. Remove from heat, and stir in ham and pasta.

3. Pour pasta mixture into a 13- x 9-inch baking dish coated with cooking spray. Stir together crushed cereal, remaining 1 Tbsp. melted butter, and remaining ⅛ tsp. ground red pepper; sprinkle over pasta mixture.

4. Bake at 350° for 30 minutes or until golden and bubbly. Let stand 5 minutes before serving.

tip from the PITS

All veggies are ideal for grilling. My philosophy is that if you can eat it, you can grill it. To prevent them from burning, I use the rule of thumb direct versus indirect cooking. If something takes longer than 20 minutes to cook, you should use indirect heat; if it's less than 20 minutes, you should use direct. Vegetables usually fall in the direct cooking category.

ELIZABETH KARMEL, CAROLINACUETOGO.COM

Classic Baked
Macaroni & Cheese
(page 288)

Tangy Baked Beans
(page 289)

Old-Fashioned
Collard Greens
(page 294)

Grilled Confetti
Coleslaw
(page 271)

CLASSIC BAKED MACARONI & CHEESE *(pictured on page 286)*

Everyone will love this extra-cheesy mac and cheese. You can substitute cavatappi or corkscrew pasta for the elbow macaroni if you want to switch up the classic look.

YIELD: 8 SERVINGS   TOTAL: 1 HOUR, 15 MINUTES

1 (8-oz.) package elbow macaroni	½ tsp. freshly ground black pepper
2 Tbsp. butter	¼ tsp. ground red pepper
2 Tbsp. all-purpose flour	1 (8-oz.) block sharp Cheddar cheese,
2 cups milk	shredded and divided
½ tsp. table salt	

1. Preheat oven to 400°. Prepare pasta according to package directions. Keep warm.

2. Melt butter in a large saucepan or Dutch oven over medium-low heat; whisk in flour until smooth. Cook, whisking constantly, 2 minutes. Gradually whisk in milk, and cook, whisking constantly, 5 minutes or until thickened. Remove from heat. Stir in salt, black and red pepper, 1 cup shredded cheese, and cooked pasta.

3. Spoon pasta mixture into a lightly greased 2-qt. baking dish; top with remaining 1 cup cheese.

4. Bake at 400° for 20 minutes or until bubbly. Let stand 10 minutes before serving.

— TRY THIS —

ONE-POT MACARONI AND CHEESE: Prepare recipe as directed stirring all grated Cheddar cheese into thickened milk mixture until melted. Add cooked pasta, and serve immediately.

TANGY BAKED BEANS

(pictured on page 286)

The best thing about this recipe is that the dried beans don't require soaking. The slow cooker does all the work for you.

YIELD: 8 TO 10 SERVINGS   TOTAL: 13 HOURS, 45 MINUTES

1	(16-oz.) package dried navy beans	2	Tbsp. yellow mustard
1	cup ketchup	1	tsp. table salt
½	cup chopped onion	1	tsp. Worcestershire sauce
½	cup firmly packed light brown sugar	½	tsp. garlic powder
3	Tbsp. apple cider vinegar	2	center-cut bacon slices, diced
3	Tbsp. cane syrup		

1. Combine beans and 6 cups water in a 6-qt. slow cooker. Cover and cook on LOW 8 hours.

2. Stir together ketchup and next 8 ingredients; stir into beans. Sprinkle bacon over top. Cover and cook on LOW 5 hours. Uncover and cook on LOW 30 minutes or until slightly thickened.

BBQ&A

WITH SKIP STEELE, BOGART'S SMOKEHOUSE, ST. LOUIS

What are your favorite foods to serve with barbecue?

I have German roots—and St. Louis is a historically German town, too—so I like to serve a German-style slaw with my pulled pork. I also love to serve baked beans. At Bogart's, our baked beans are cooked in the pit underneath the brisket so they get flavored from the brisket drippings.

APPALACHIAN CIDER BAKED BEANS

Two iconic Appalachian flavors, sorghum syrup and salt pork, are highlighted in this delicious baked beans dish. Look for sorghum syrup with the pancake syrups and salt pork in the bacon or meat department at your grocery store.

YIELD: 8 SERVINGS   TOTAL: 17 HOURS, INCLUDING SOAK TIME

3 cups dried pinto beans
3 cups apple cider
8 oz. thinly sliced salt pork, divided
2 small yellow onions, peeled

1 Tbsp. dry mustard
6 Tbsp. sorghum syrup
1 tsp. table salt
Hot water

1. Place pinto beans in a large bowl. Cover with cold water 3 inches above beans; cover and let soak 12 hours.

2. Drain beans, reserving liquid; transfer to a Dutch oven. Add apple cider; bring to a boil over medium heat. Gently boil, uncovered and stirring occasionally, 30 minutes.

3. Remove from heat; drain, reserving liquid. Layer 4 oz. sliced salt pork in a 2-qt. Dutch oven. Spoon beans over salt pork; combine onions and beans.

4. Preheat oven to 300°. Combine dry mustard, sorghum syrup, and salt in a small saucepan; cook over medium heat, stirring often, 3 minutes or until mustard and salt dissolve. Pour mixture over beans; top with remaining 4 oz. sliced salt pork. Add reserved bean liquid and, if necessary, hot water to cover. Bake, covered, at 300° for 3 hours, adding hot water as needed. Bake 2 more hours or until beans are tender.

LUCKY BLACK-EYED PEAS

Have good luck year-round with this tasty black-eyed pea dish scattered with salt pork and spicy jalapeño pepper.

YIELD: 4 TO 6 SERVINGS   TOTAL: 8 HOURS, INCLUDING SOAK TIME

- 1 (16-oz.) package dried black-eyed peas
- 2 oz. salt pork
- 1 large onion, chopped
- 1 tsp. bacon drippings
- ½ tsp. freshly ground black pepper
- Garnishes: sliced jalapeño pepper, fresh parsley

1. Rinse and sort peas according to package directions. Place peas in a large Dutch oven; cover with cold water 2 inches above peas, and let soak 6 to 8 hours (or see the quick-soak method below). Drain peas, and rinse thoroughly.

2. Bring salt pork and 1 qt. water to a boil in Dutch oven over medium-high heat; reduce heat to medium-low, and simmer 30 minutes. Add peas, onion, next 2 ingredients, water to cover, and, if desired, jalapeño pepper.

3. Bring to a boil over medium-high heat. Cover, reduce heat, and cook, stirring occasionally, 1 hour to 1 hour and 30 minutes or until peas are tender and liquid thickens slightly. (Uncover after 1 hour to allow liquid to evaporate, if necessary.)

4. Season with salt and pepper to taste. Sprinkle with parsley.

— TRY THIS —

QUICK-SOAK BLACK-EYED PEAS: Place peas in a Dutch oven; cover with cold water 2 inches above peas. Bring to a boil; boil 1 minute. Cover, remove from heat, and let stand 1 hour. Drain peas, and rinse thoroughly. Proceed as directed in Step 2.

COLLARD GREENS GRATIN *(pictured)*

Prechopped collard greens are convenient in this comfort-food dish. If you prefer, you can use fresh bunches. Just be sure to remove the tough stems and ribs before chopping.

YIELD: 6 TO 8 SERVINGS   TOTAL: 2 HOURS, 30 MINUTES

5   cups heavy cream
3   garlic cloves, minced
2   cups freshly grated Parmigiano-Reggiano cheese, divided
1   tsp. cornstarch

2   (1-lb.) packages chopped collard greens
8   center-cut bacon slices, diced
2   cups chopped yellow onion
½   cup panko (Japanese breadcrumbs)
1   Tbsp. olive oil

1. Preheat oven to 350°. Bring first 2 ingredients to a boil over medium-high heat. Reduce heat to low, and simmer 30 minutes or until reduced by half. Stir in 1 cup cheese.

2. Stir together cornstarch and 1 Tbsp. water. Whisk into cream mixture until thickened.

3. Cook collards in boiling salted water to cover 5 to 7 minutes or until tender; drain and pat dry with paper towels. Cool 10 minutes; coarsely chop.

4. Cook bacon in a large skillet over medium-high heat, stirring often, 8 to 10 minutes or until crisp. Add onion, and cook 5 minutes or until tender. Stir in collard greens, and cook, stirring constantly, 3 minutes. Stir in cream mixture. Add table salt and black pepper to taste.

5. Pour mixture into a lightly greased 11- x 7-inch baking dish. Stir together panko, olive oil, and remaining 1 cup cheese; sprinkle over collard mixture.

6. Bake at 350° for 35 to 40 minutes or until panko is golden brown. Let stand 5 minutes before serving.

OLD-FASHIONED COLLARD GREENS

(pictured on page 287)

Potlikker is the flavorful juice left over after cooking greens. Dunk cornbread in it, or serve it with the greens over hot rice.

YIELD: 6 SERVINGS   TOTAL: 3 HOURS

1½ lb. smoked ham hocks
1   Tbsp. hot sauce (such as Tabasco)
1   tsp. celery salt

3   bunches fresh collard greens (about 2¾ lb.)
Hot pepper vinegar

1. Place first 3 ingredients and 1 qt. water in a large Dutch oven. Bring to a boil; simmer, uncovered, 1 hour.

2. Trim and discard thick stems from collard green leaves. Tear leaves into 2-inch pieces.

3. Place leaves in a large bowl of water. Swish leaves around to remove any dirt. Remove leaves from bowl, and discard water. Add leaves to Dutch oven; stir. (The pot will be full, but the leaves will cook down.) Cover and simmer, stirring every 30 minutes, for 1½ hours.

4. Remove ham hocks; remove meat from hocks, and chop. Discard any fat. Return meat to Dutch oven. Serve greens with hot pepper vinegar and potlikker.

GREEN BEANS WITH CHARRED ONIONS

Get a jump start on this recipe and cook the green beans ahead of time. Store them in the refrigerator the day before, and proceed with step two.

YIELD: 4 SERVINGS   TOTAL: 30 MINUTES

1   lb. fresh green beans, trimmed
1   large red onion, cut into 4 wedges
2   Tbsp. olive oil, divided
1   garlic clove, minced
6   fresh thyme sprigs

2   Tbsp. red wine vinegar
1   Tbsp. butter
¼   cup loosely packed fresh flat-leaf parsley, chopped
2   Tbsp. thinly sliced fresh chives

1. Cook beans in boiling salted water to cover in a Dutch oven over medium-high heat 4 minutes or until crisp-tender. Plunge beans into ice water to stop the cooking process. Drain; pat dry.

2. Sprinkle onion wedges with table salt and black pepper to taste, and cook in 1 Tbsp. hot olive oil in a large cast-iron skillet over medium-high heat 3 minutes on each side or until charred and tender. Remove onions from skillet; wipe skillet clean.

3. Cook garlic in remaining 1 Tbsp. oil in skillet over medium heat 30 seconds or until fragrant. Add beans and thyme, and cook, stirring occasionally, 3 minutes or until beans are slightly charred. Stir in vinegar, next 3 ingredients, and onion wedges; toss to coat. Remove from heat; sprinkle with salt and pepper to taste. Serve hot.

FRIED GREEN TOMATOES

YIELD: 20 SLICES   TOTAL: 40 MINUTES

4   medium-size green tomatoes cut into
    ½ inch slices
1   cup self-rising white cornmeal mix
½   cup panko (Japanese breadcrumbs)

½   cup all-purpose flour
4   large egg whites
3   Tbsp. olive oil

1. Sprinkle tomatoes with table salt and black pepper. Let stand 10 minutes. Meanwhile, combine cornmeal and panko in a shallow dish. Place flour in a second shallow dish. Whisk egg whites in a medium bowl until foamy. Dredge tomato slices in flour, shaking off excess. Dip in egg whites, and dredge in cornmeal mixture.

2. Cook half of tomatoes in 1½ Tbsp. hot oil in a nonstick skillet over medium heat 4 to 5 minutes each side or until golden brown. Season with table salt to taste. Place on wire rack in a jelly-roll pan, and keep warm in 225° oven. Repeat with remaining oil and tomatoes.

PEPPER JELLY SAUCE

⅔   cup red pepper jelly
2   Tbsp. spicy brown mustard

1   tsp. prepared horseradish
1   tsp. orange zest

Stir together all ingredients. Refrigerate in an airtight container for up to a week.

BLUE CHEESE-DILL SAUCE

½   cup sour cream
½   cup 2% low-fat plain yogurt
2   tsp. chopped fresh dill

2   oz. crumbled blue cheese
1   tsp. fresh lemon juice
¼   tsp. table salt

Stir together all ingredients. Refrigerate in an airtight container for up to 3 days.

CITRUS-GINGER AÏOLI

1   cup mayonnaise
1   tsp. lime zest
1   tsp. orange zest
4   tsp. fresh lime juice

1   Tbsp. fresh orange juice
2   tsp. finely grated fresh ginger
1   garlic clove, minced

Stir together all ingredients. Refrigerate in an airtight container for up to 3 days.

SRIRACHA RÉMOULADE

1½ cups mayonnaise
4   green onions, sliced
2   Tbsp. chopped fresh parsley

2   to 3 Tbsp. Asian hot chili sauce (such
    as Sriracha)
1   garlic clove, pressed

Stir together all ingredients. Refrigerate in an airtight container for up to 3 days.

NUTTY OKRA

Salting the okra and letting it stand before dredging releases the natural moisture and helps the coating stick.

YIELD: 4 SERVINGS   TOTAL: 42 MINUTES

1   lb. fresh okra, cut into ½-inch pieces*
1   tsp. table salt
1   large egg white, lightly beaten
1   cup all-purpose baking mix

½   cup finely chopped salted dry-roasted peanuts
½   tsp. freshly ground black pepper
    Peanut oil

1. Toss okra with salt, and let stand 20 minutes. Add egg white, stirring to coat. Stir together baking mix and next 2 ingredients in a large bowl. Add okra, tossing to coat; gently press peanut mixture onto okra, shaking off excess.

2. Pour oil to depth of 2 inches into a Dutch oven or cast-iron skillet; heat to 375°. Fry okra, in batches, 2 to 4 minutes or until golden; drain on paper towels.

* 1 (16-oz.) package frozen cut okra, thawed, may be substituted.

WITH JUSTIN & JONATHAN FOX, FOX BROS. BAR-B-Q, ATLANTA

What are your favorite foods to serve with barbecue?

It depends on the season. You can go traditional with sides like stew, potato salad, and beans, or very Southern with collards and mac 'n' cheese. Cold salads are great in the summertime. But, don't be afraid to cross cultures and serve Asian or Mexican flavors with your barbecue. Have fun with it and keep it fresh.

SMASHED FRIED OKRA *(pictured)*

A fun, new way to enjoy a Southern favorite—smashing okra into these "fritters" before you fry them creates more surface area for the perfect amount of crisp and crunch.

YIELD: 4 TO 6 SERVINGS   TOTAL: 40 MINUTES

1 lb. fresh okra	2 cups fine yellow cornmeal
1½ cups buttermilk	Canola oil

1. Use a meat mallet to smash okra, starting at tip of pod and working toward stem end. Place buttermilk in a shallow dish, and place cornmeal in another shallow dish. Stir desired amount of table salt and black pepper into buttermilk and cornmeal. Dip okra in buttermilk; dredge in cornmeal, shaking off excess.

2. Pour oil to depth of 2 inches into a large Dutch oven; heat to 350°. Fry okra, in batches, 2 to 3 minutes or until browned and crisp, turning once. Remove okra, using a slotted spoon; drain on paper towels. Add salt and pepper to taste.

SIMPLE STIR-FRIED OKRA

Prepare this easy stir-fry dish with frozen whole okra. The results will be just as tender, delicious, and full of flavor as fresh.

YIELD: 4 TO 6 SERVINGS   TOTAL: 40 MINUTES

1 medium-size sweet onion, chopped	2 Tbsp. vegetable oil
1 tsp. mustard seeds*	1 (16-oz.) package frozen okra, thawed, or 1 lb. fresh okra
½ tsp. ground cumin	
¼ tsp. dried crushed red pepper	¾ tsp. table salt

1. Sauté first 4 ingredients in hot oil in a large skillet over medium-high heat 5 minutes or until onion is tender.

2. Add okra; sauté 15 minutes or until okra is lightly browned. Stir in salt. Drain on paper towels. Add salt and pepper to taste.

* ½ tsp. dry mustard may be substituted for 1 tsp. mustard seeds.

GRILLED ROMAINE CAESAR SALAD

Grilling the romaine for this traditional Caesar salad infuses it with smoke to make it a flavor-packed match with the creamy dressing. Romaine hearts typically come in a package of three. You can also use one large head of romaine cut into six wedges.

YIELD: 6 SERVINGS   TOTAL: 20 MINUTES

Garlic-Thyme Croutons
1/4 cup olive oil
2 garlic cloves, pressed
8 oz. crusty French bread, cut into
   1/2-inch cubes
2 tsp. chopped fresh thyme
Salad
1/2 cup freshly grated Parmesan cheese

1/4 cup fresh lemon juice
2 Tbsp. mayonnaise
1 tsp. Dijon mustard
4 garlic cloves
1/2 cup olive oil, divided
3 romaine lettuce hearts, halved
   lengthwise
Shaved Parmesan cheese

1. Prepare croutons: Heat oil in a large skillet over medium heat. Add garlic; cook 30 seconds. Add bread cubes, thyme, and table salt and black pepper to taste, tossing well to coat. Cook 5 minutes, stirring constantly, until bread is toasted. Remove croutons from pan to cool.

2. Prepare salad: Preheat grill to 350° to 400° (medium-high) heat.

3. Combine cheese, lemon juice, mayonnaise, Dijon mustard, and garlic in a food processor. Pulse until combined. With food processor running, slowly add 1/3 cup oil and process until smooth. Set aside.

4. Brush romaine hearts with remaining oil. Grill romaine hearts, cut sides down, 2 to 3 minutes or until charred.

5. Place 1 romaine heart onto each plate. Drizzle with dressing, and sprinkle with croutons and shaved Parmesan.

GRILLED CORN & BUTTER BEAN SALAD

When in season, fresh butter beans from the farmers' market or grocery store make this summer-fresh salad even better.

YIELD: 8 TO 10 SERVINGS   TOTAL: 3 HOURS, 20 MINUTES

1   (16-oz.) package frozen butter beans*
4   ears fresh corn, husks removed
1   large red onion, cut into thick slices
1   large red bell pepper, cut into thick rings
¾   cup mayonnaise
3   Tbsp. chopped fresh basil

1   garlic clove, pressed
1   tsp. table salt
1   tsp. Worcestershire sauce
½   tsp. freshly ground black pepper
1   cup halved grape tomatoes

1. Cook butter beans according to package directions; drain and cool completely (about 20 minutes).

2. Meanwhile, preheat grill to 350° to 400° (medium-high) heat. Grill corn, covered with grill lid, 15 minutes or until done, turning every 4 to 5 minutes. (Some kernels will begin to char and pop.) At the same time, grill onion and bell pepper, covered with grill lid, 5 minutes on each side or until tender. Cool all vegetables completely (about 20 minutes).

3. Cut kernels from cobs. Discard cobs. Chop onion and bell pepper into ½-inch pieces.

4. Stir together mayonnaise and next 5 ingredients. Stir in tomatoes, corn kernels, and onion and pepper pieces. Add salt to taste. Cover and chill 2 to 8 hours before serving. Store in refrigerator up to 3 days.

* Fresh butter beans may be substituted.

CREAMED CORN

A corn cutter and creamer is a great tool to extract all of the sweet juices from the fresh corn. The corn "milk" also acts as a natural thickener. If you don't have a corn cutter, you can just as easily use a chef's knife. Scrape the corn cobs with the side of the knife to make sure you extract all of the liquid.

YIELD: 6 TO 8 SERVINGS   TOTAL: 30 MINUTES

13 ears fresh corn, husks removed
1   cup milk
1   Tbsp. unsalted butter
½   tsp. table salt
⅛   tsp. freshly ground black pepper
Chopped green onions

1. Remove silks from corn. Use a corn cutter and creamer set over a bowl to cut and cream the kernels from the cobs.

2. Transfer creamed corn to a large skillet. Add milk and next 2 ingredients.

3. Cook over low heat, stirring often, 30 minutes. (If corn becomes too thick, add more milk to desired consistency.) Sprinkle with pepper and green onions.

CHEF'S SIDE

SKIP STEELE, PAPPY'S SMOKEHOUSE, ST. LOUIS

PAPPY'S COLESLAW

YIELD: 8 TO 10 SERVINGS   TOTAL: 8 HOURS, INCLUDING CHILL TIME

1   head green cabbage, finely shredded
1   large white onion, finely sliced
Dressing
1   cup sugar
1   cup white vinegar
¾   cup vegetable oil
2   tsp. table salt
1   tsp. celery seed
1   tsp. dry mustard

1. Layer cabbage and onion in a nonreactive bowl or pan, ending with top layer of cabbage.

2. Prepare Dressing: Combine sugar and next 5 ingredients in a medium saucepan. Bring to a boil and pour over cabbage and onion mixture. Do not stir.

3. Cover and refrigerate overnight. Mix well before serving. Refrigerate in an airtight container for up to 1 week.

HUSH PUPPIES *(also pictured on page 254)*

Whether served at a barbecue or alongside your favorite grilled dishes, these traditional fried cornbread bites are even better with the new flavor twists added below.

YIELD: ABOUT 2 DOZEN   TOTAL: 35 MINUTES

Vegetable oil

1½ cups self-rising white cornmeal mix

¾ cup self-rising flour

¾ cup diced sweet onion

1½ Tbsp. sugar

1   large egg, lightly beaten

1¼ cups buttermilk

1. Pour oil to depth of 3 inches into a Dutch oven; heat to 375°. Combine cornmeal mix and next 3 ingredients. Add egg and buttermilk; stir just until moistened. Let stand 10 minutes.

2. Drop batter by rounded tablespoonfuls into hot oil, and fry, in 3 batches, 2 to 3 minutes on each side or until golden. Keep warm in a 200° oven.

TRY THIS

BACON-AND-CARAMELIZED-ONION HUSH PUPPIES:

Increase onion to 1½ cups. Cook 5 center-cut bacon slices in a medium skillet over medium heat 5 to 6 minutes or until crisp; drain bacon on paper towels, reserving 2 Tbsp. drippings in skillet. Crumble bacon. Sauté onion in hot drippings over medium-low heat 12 to 15 minutes or until golden brown. Proceed with recipe as directed, stirring in onion and bacon with cornmeal mix in Step 1.

JALAPEÑO-PINEAPPLE HUSH PUPPIES: Prepare recipe

as directed, stirring in ½ cup canned pineapple tidbits and 2 to 3 Tbsp. seeded and diced jalapeño pepper with cornmeal mix in Step 1.

SKILLET CORNBREAD

A well-seasoned cast-iron skillet is essential to a golden crust on cornbread. For even more flavor, coat the sides and bottom of your skillet with two to three tablespoons of bacon drippings.

YIELD: 8 TO 10 SERVINGS   TOTAL: 55 MINUTES

1 cup plain yellow cornmeal	1/4 tsp. baking soda
1 cup all-purpose flour	2 cups buttermilk
1 Tbsp. baking powder	2 large eggs
1 tsp. kosher salt	1/2 cup butter

1. Preheat oven to 425°. Whisk together first 5 ingredients in a large bowl. Whisk together buttermilk and eggs; stir into cornmeal mixture just until combined. Heat a 10-inch cast-iron skillet over medium-high heat until it just begins to smoke. Add butter, and stir until butter is melted. Stir melted butter into cornbread batter. Pour batter into hot skillet.

2. Bake at 425° for 25 to 30 minutes or until golden and cornbread pulls away from sides of skillet. Invert cornbread onto a wire rack; serve warm.

CORNBREAD MUFFINS

Heating the muffin pans before filling them with batter results in a delicious crispy crust for these muffins.

YIELD: 2 DOZEN   TOTAL: 25 MINUTES

1/4 cup vegetable oil	1/2 cup butter, melted
3 cups self-rising white cornmeal mix	1 Tbsp. mayonnaise
1/4 cup sugar	3 large eggs, lightly beaten
2 cups buttermilk	

1. Preheat oven to 425°. Spoon 1/2 tsp. vegetable oil into each of 24 standard muffin cups. Heat muffin pans in oven 5 minutes.

2. Combine cornmeal mix and sugar in a large bowl; make a well in center of mixture. Stir together buttermilk and remaining ingredients; add to cornmeal mixture, stirring just until dry ingredients are moistened. Spoon batter into hot muffin pans, filling two-thirds full.

3. Bake at 425° for 15 minutes or until golden brown. Serve warm.

SWEET POTATO CORNBREAD *(pictured)*

If you're among those who love sweet cornbread, this recipe is sure to become your new favorite. To get 2 cups of mashed sweet potatoes, bake 1½ lb. of sweet potatoes at 425° for about 40 minutes.

YIELD: 6 SERVINGS   TOTAL: 50 MINUTES

2	cups self-rising white cornmeal mix	2	cups mashed cooked sweet potatoes (about 1½ lb. sweet potatoes)
3	Tbsp. sugar		
¼	tsp. pumpkin pie spice	1	(8-oz.) container sour cream
5	large eggs	½	cup butter, melted

1. Preheat oven to 425°. Stir together first 3 ingredients in a large bowl; make a well in center of mixture. Whisk together eggs and next 3 ingredients; add to cornmeal mixture, stirring just until moistened. Spoon batter into a lightly greased 9-inch square pan.

2. Bake at 425° for 35 minutes or until golden brown.

CHEESY CORNBREAD

Serve this Cheddar-buttermilk cornbread hot from the cast-iron skillet with a generous pat of butter.

YIELD: 8 SERVINGS   TOTAL: 35 MINUTES

1	Tbsp. vegetable oil	2	cups shredded sharp Cheddar cheese
2	cups buttermilk	1¾	cups self-rising yellow cornmeal mix
1	large egg		

1. Preheat oven to 450°. Coat bottom and sides of an 8-inch cast-iron skillet with vegetable oil; heat in oven 5 minutes.

2. Whisk together buttermilk, egg, cheese, and cornmeal. Pour into hot skillet.

3. Bake 25 minutes or until a wooden pick inserted into the center comes out clean.

— TRY THIS —

CHEESY CORNBREAD MUFFINS: Omit vegetable oil and prepare recipe as directed, spooning batter into a lightly greased 12-cup muffin pan, filling three-fourths full. Decrease bake time to 15 to 17 minutes or until tops are golden brown.

SPICE IT UP

Pair these marinades, rubs, sauces, pickles, and more with your favorite smoky barbecue dishes.

NORTH CACKALACKY BARBECUE SAUCE *(pictured)*

Vinegar-based sauces, like this slightly spicy sauce, are traditional in eastern North Carolina and don't require refrigeration.

YIELD: ABOUT 1⅔ CUPS   TOTAL: 30 MINUTES

2   cups apple cider vinegar
¼   cup ketchup
2   Tbsp. firmly packed brown sugar
2   Tbsp. hot sauce
1½ tsp. dried crushed red pepper

½   tsp. coarse black pepper
⅛   tsp. ground red pepper
2   tsp. table salt
1   Tbsp. fresh squeezed lemon juice
½   cup apple juice

Stir together all ingredients in a medium saucepan over medium heat; bring to a boil. Reduce heat; simmer, stirring occasionally, until reduced to 1⅔ cups, about 25 minutes.

EL SANCHO BARBECUE SAUCE

This Texas-style barbecue sauce is sweet and spicy and ideal with smoked brisket, pulled pork, or even beef ribs.

YIELD: ABOUT 3 CUPS   TOTAL: 35 MINUTES

⅓   cup tomato paste
½   cup ketchup
1   cup apple cider vinegar
¼   cup yellow mustard
¼   cup Worcestershire sauce
1   Tbsp. hot sauce
1   Tbsp. granulated onion

1   Tbsp. granulated garlic
1   Tbsp. kosher salt
2   tsp. hickory liquid smoke
1   tsp. coarse tellicherry black pepper
1   cup sugar
⅓   cup honey

Stir together tomato paste and next 10 ingredients in a medium saucepan over medium heat. Add sugar and honey, and bring to a boil. Reduce heat; simmer, stirring occasionally, for about 30 minutes. Refrigerate in an airtight container up to 1 week.

RIB APPLE GLAZE

YIELD: ABOUT 1 CUP   TOTAL: 5 MINUTES

½   cup applesauce
½   cup smoky barbecue sauce
½   cup honey

¼   tsp. kosher salt
¼   tsp. coarse black tellicherry pepper
1   tsp. hot sauce

Stir together all ingredients until well blended. Refrigerate in an airtight container up to 5 days.

LEXINGTON BARBECUE SAUCE _(pictured at top)_

Lexington, North Carolina, is known for this tart tomato-and-vinegar-based barbecue sauce. It also serves as the base for chopped pork shoulder and Lexington "red slaw."

YIELD: ABOUT 2 CUPS   TOTAL: 10 MINUTES

1½ cups apple cider vinegar
⅓ cup firmly packed brown sugar
¼ cup ketchup
1 Tbsp. hot sauce
1 tsp. browning and seasoning sauce
½ tsp. table salt
½ tsp. onion powder
½ tsp. freshly ground black pepper
½ tsp. Worcestershire sauce

Stir together all ingredients in a medium saucepan; cook over medium heat, stirring constantly, 7 minutes or until sugar dissolves. Cover and chill until ready to serve.

Note: We tested with Kitchen Bouquet Browning & Seasoning Sauce.

SWEET MUSTARD BARBECUE SAUCE _(pictured second from top)_

A tangy take on South Carolina barbecue sauce, this is great served with pork or chicken and can be stored in the refrigerator for up to one month.

YIELD: ABOUT 2 CUPS   TOTAL: 15 MINUTES

1 cup apple cider vinegar
⅔ cup yellow mustard
½ cup sugar
2 Tbsp. chili powder
1 tsp. white pepper
1 tsp. freshly ground black pepper
¼ tsp. ground red pepper
½ tsp. hot sauce
2 Tbsp. butter
½ tsp. soy sauce

1. Stir together first 8 ingredients in a saucepan over medium heat; bring to a boil, reduce heat, and simmer 10 minutes.

2. Remove from heat, and stir in butter and soy sauce.

TOMATILLO BARBECUE SAUCE

(pictured on page 320, third from top)

Often used for salsa verde, tomatillos add a bright flavor to this green barbecue sauce. Look for tomatillos with tightly fitting husks; shriveled husks mean they are past their prime.

YIELD: 3 CUPS   TOTAL: 2 HOURS, 10 MINUTES

2½ lb. green tomatoes, coarsely chopped
1½ lb. tomatillos, husked and coarsely
    chopped
2 garlic cloves, pressed
½ to 1 cup sugar
1 cup white vinegar

1 large sweet onion, coarsely chopped
    (about 1½ cups)
1 Tbsp. dry mustard
1 tsp. table salt
½ tsp. dried crushed red pepper

1. Cook all ingredients in a large Dutch oven over medium-low heat 2 hours or until green tomatoes and tomatillos are tender. Cool.

2. Process mixture, in batches, in a food processor or blender until smooth, stopping to scrape down sides. Serve over grilled chicken, fish, or shrimp.

SWEET-&-SPICY BARBECUE SAUCE *(pictured on page 320, third from bottom)*

Perfect for both heat lovers and those sensitive to spice. If you like things hot, increase the heat by leaving the seeds in the jalapeño. If you are a member of the not-so-hot team, omit the dried crushed red pepper.

YIELD: 5 CUPS   TOTAL: 45 MINUTES

½ cup chopped sweet onion
2 garlic cloves, minced
1 jalapeño pepper, seeded and minced
1 Tbsp. olive oil
1 (32-oz.) bottle ketchup
1 cup firmly packed dark brown sugar
1 cup apple cider vinegar

½ cup apple juice
½ cup honey
1 Tbsp. Worcestershire sauce
1 tsp. kosher salt
1 tsp. freshly ground black pepper
1 tsp. celery seeds
½ tsp. dried crushed red pepper

Sauté onion, minced garlic, and jalapeño pepper in hot olive oil in a large saucepan over medium-high heat 4 to 5 minutes or until tender. Stir in ketchup and remaining 9 ingredients. Bring to a boil, stirring occasionally. Reduce heat to low; simmer, stirring occasionally, 30 minutes. Use immediately, or refrigerate in an airtight container up to 1 month.

WHITE BARBECUE SAUCE

(pictured on page 320, second from bottom)

The famous creamy and tangy sauce from Big Bob Gibson's barbecue restaurant in North Alabama is the best way to spice up smoked chicken.

YIELD: 1½ CUPS   TOTAL: 5 MINUTES

1 cup mayonnaise	½ tsp. garlic powder
⅓ cup apple cider vinegar	½ tsp. onion powder
1 tsp. Worcestershire sauce	½ tsp. freshly ground black pepper
½ tsp. kosher salt	¼ tsp. hot sauce

Stir together mayonnaise, vinegar, and 3 tsp. water and next 6 ingredients in a small bowl. Serve immediately, or refrigerate in an airtight container for up to 3 days.

THICK & ROBUST BARBECUE SAUCE *(pictured on page 320, at bottom)*

This sauce is best for basting steak, pork, and chicken while grilling, and should be brushed on about 10 minutes before the meat is done. Before grilling, set aside some sauce for serving at the table.

YIELD: 1¼ CUPS   TOTAL: 45 MINUTES

¾ cup apple cider vinegar	2 Tbsp. chopped onion
½ cup ketchup	1 Tbsp. firmly packed brown sugar
¼ cup Worcestershire sauce	1 tsp. fresh lemon juice
1 garlic clove, minced	½ tsp. dry mustard
¼ cup chili sauce	Dash of ground red pepper

1. Stir together all ingredients in a medium saucepan over medium heat; bring to a boil. Reduce heat; simmer, stirring occasionally, 40 minutes.

2. Divide sauce into separate containers for basting and serving at the table. (Basting brushes used on raw food should not be dipped into table sauce.)

3. Discard any remaining basting sauce, and refrigerate leftover table sauce in an airtight container for up to 5 days.

SMOKY DRY RUB *(pictured far left)*

Smoked paprika is the hero of this rub. It can be found in the spice aisle of your grocery store and is made by drying smoked sweet peppers for a distinctive flavor.

YIELD: ½ CUP   TOTAL: 5 MINUTES

¼ cup firmly packed dark brown sugar
2 Tbsp. smoked paprika
1 Tbsp. kosher salt
2 tsp. garlic salt
2 tsp. chili powder

2 tsp. freshly ground black pepper
1 tsp. onion salt
1 tsp. celery salt
1 tsp. ground red pepper
1 tsp. ground cumin

Stir together ingredients until well blended. Store in an airtight container up to 1 month.

HILL COUNTRY RUB *(pictured second from left)*

This pantry-friendly seasoning blend from Elizabeth Karmel of CarolinaCueToGo.com pays homage to the barbecue traditions of Texas Hill Country. It's her go-to spice mixture for just about everything.

YIELD: 1¾ CUPS   TOTAL: 5 MINUTES

1½ cups kosher salt
¼ cup coarsely ground black pepper

2 Tbsp. ground red pepper

Stir together ingredients until well blended. Store in an airtight container up to 1 month.

PORK BUTT DRY RUB

(pictured on page 324, second from right)

For the best flavor, allow pork butt rubbed with this sweet spiced mixture from Christopher Prieto to stand for about at least an hour before cooking.

YIELD: ABOUT 3½ TBSP.   TOTAL: 5 MINUTES

4   tsp. seasoned salt
2   tsp. firmly packed dark brown sugar
1½ tsp. granulated sugar
1½ tsp. paprika
¼   tsp. garlic powder

¼   tsp. freshly ground black pepper
⅛   tsp. dry mustard
⅛   tsp. ground cumin
1/16 tsp. ground ginger

Stir together ingredients until well blended. Store in an airtight container up to 1 month.

PRIZE-WINNING BARBECUE RUB *(pictured on page 324, far right)*

You probably already have the ingredients for this easy seasoning mix in your pantry.

YIELD: 2 CUPS   TOTAL: 5 MINUTES

¾   cup firmly packed light brown sugar
½   cup paprika
2½ Tbsp. coarse sea salt
1½ Tbsp. freshly ground black pepper
1   Tbsp. garlic powder

1   Tbsp. onion powder
2   tsp. ground ginger
1   tsp. ground cumin
½   tsp. ground red pepper

Stir together ingredients until well blended. Store in an airtight container up to 1 month.

BEEF RUB

The secret to Christopher Prieto's beef rub is the tellicherry peppercorns, which are black peppercorns that have been left on the vine longer for a richer flavor.

YIELD: ABOUT 2¼ CUPS   TOTAL: 5 MINUTES

1   cup kosher salt
1   cup coarse tellicherry black pepper

3   Tbsp. granulated garlic
2   tsp. ground red pepper

Stir together all ingredients until well blended. Store in an airtight container up 1 month.

SEASON ALL RUB *(pictured)*

Use Christopher Prieto's signature rub on anything you want to throw on the grill or smoker: fish, steaks, pork, or chicken.

YIELD: ABOUT 2 CUPS   TOTAL: 5 MINUTES

¾ cup paprika
½ cup turbinado sugar
¼ cup seasoned salt
¼ cup coarse black pepper

2 Tbsp. granulated garlic
1 Tbsp. granulated onion
1 Tbsp. dried oregano
2 tsp. chipotle powder

Stir together all ingredients until well blended. Store in an airtight container up to 1 month.

SPICY HOT VINEGAR MARINADE

Whether used as a marinade or as a mop sauce during grilling, this tangy mixture will boost the flavor of anything you grill.

YIELD: 1½ CUPS   TOTAL: 5 MINUTES

1 cup apple cider vinegar
¼ cup firmly packed dark brown sugar
¼ cup vegetable oil

3 Tbsp. dried crushed red pepper
4 tsp. table salt
2 tsp. freshly ground black pepper

Stir together ingredients until well blended. Refrigerate in an airtight container up to 1 week.

RIB BRAISING LIQUID

This mixture is just the ticket for spritzing on ribs as they cook. It will soak into the meat to produce the ultimate tangy and sweet flavor.

YIELD: 1 CUP   TOTAL: 5 MINUTES

1 cup apple juice
1 Tbsp. Smoky Dry Rub (page 325)

2 tsp. balsamic vinegar
1 garlic clove, minced

Stir together all ingredients until well blended. Refrigerate in an airtight container up to 1 week.

PORK BRINE INJECTION *(pictured)*

This brine injection is ideal for adding moisture to a large cut of meat like a pork butt. It helps prevent the meat from drying out while on the smoker and helps intensify the flavor during the cooking process.

YIELD: ABOUT 2½ CUPS   TOTAL: 5 MINUTES

2 cups apple juice	1 tsp. hot sauce
¼ cup white vinegar	1 Tbsp. Worcestershire sauce
1⅛ cups sugar	2 Tbsp. Season All Rub (page 329)
¼ cup kosher salt	

Stir together all ingredients until sugar dissolves. Refrigerate in an airtight container up to 1 week.

ALL-PURPOSE PORK BRINE

From ribs to chops and even roasts, this brine is a great vehicle for pumping up flavor. Be sure to let the mixture cool before adding any meat. Otherwise you may inadvertently "boil" it.

YIELD: 1½ QT.   TOTAL: 1 HOUR, 10 MINUTES

1½ qt. hot water	2 tsp. coarsely ground black pepper
3 Tbsp. kosher salt	4 garlic cloves, crushed
2 Tbsp. chopped fresh thyme	2 bay leaves
2 Tbsp. firmly packed brown sugar	½ large lemon, sliced

Stir together all ingredients in a large Dutch oven until salt and sugar dissolve. Let stand 1 hour. Refrigerate in an airtight container up to 1 week.

CHICKEN SLATHER

Coat your chicken liberally with Christopher Prieto's sweet and savory slather before the bird goes on the smoker. It will help give the skin a deep color and help provide the meat with an intense flavor.

YIELD: 1½ CUPS   TOTAL: 5 MINUTES

1½ cups applesauce
⅓ cup Season All Rub (page 329)
⅓ cup melted butter

Stir together all ingredients until well blended. Refrigerate in an airtight container up to 1 week.

CHICKEN BRINE

Soaking your chicken in this sweet-and-salty brine will add instant flavor while helping keep the bird moist and juicy during the cooking process.

YIELD: 8 CUPS   TOTAL: 5 MINUTES

½ cup kosher salt
2⅔ Tbsp. firmly packed brown sugar
1 Tbsp. fresh chopped thyme
2 garlic cloves, minced
2⅔ Tbsp. freshly ground black pepper

Stir together 8 cups water and remaining ingredients until sugar dissolves. Refrigerate in an airtight container up to 1 week.

I always try to brine my poultry. Brine provides an amazing layer of moisture and flavor that is unmatched, but you have to make it properly, apply it properly, and wash it off before you season the meat. Two of my favorite brining liquids are Cane Patch syrup and Dr. Pepper. I only inject poultry when it is a larger bird like a turkey or a whole chicken that I wasn't able to brine. And I always coat the skin with salted butter before cooking to add more moisture and color during cooking.

**CHRISTOPHER PRIETO,
PRIME BARBECUE,
WENDELL, NORTH CAROLINA**

BEEF INJECTION (pictured)

Injecting large cuts of beef—such as the Beef Chuck Roll on page 64—with a basic injection helps ensure they stay moist during the long cooking process.

YIELD: ABOUT 2½ CUPS   TOTAL: 5 MINUTES

2   cups beef stock
1   Tbsp. Worcestershire sauce

1   Tbsp. soy sauce
1   Tbsp. jarred beef soup base

Combine first 4 ingredients and ½ cup water. Refrigerate in an airtight container for up to 1 week.

BEEF MARINADE

This simple marinade of balsamic vinegar and soy sauce adds a ton of flavor and can help tenderize tough cuts of meat like flank steak.

YIELD: ABOUT 1 CUP   TOTAL: 8 MINUTES

1   cup balsamic vinegar
2   Tbsp. soy sauce
2   Tbsp. honey

2   green onions, thinly sliced
2   tsp. chopped fresh rosemary
2   tsp. dried crushed red pepper

Combine all ingredients in a saucepan. Bring to a boil, and cook, whisking occasionally, for 5 minutes. Cool completely before using as a marinade. Refrigerate in an airtight container for up to 1 week.

BBQ&A

WITH TIM BYRES, SMOKE, DALLAS

What are 5 must-have barbecue tools?

1. A charcoal chimney is a must even if you're cooking over a wood fire. It helps preheat the grill and get a solid base-fire going.
2. Insulated gloves, like welder's gloves
3. A small shovel, like a camping shovel, for moving coals
4. A cleaver
5. A butcher's knife

Peppery Texas Pickles
(page 338)

Zucchini & Squash Pickles
(page 338)

Sweet-Hot Cukes & Peppers
(page 339)

Easy Pickled Sweet Onions
& Peppers (page 339)

ZUCCHINI & SQUASH PICKLES

(pictured on page 337)

Salting the zucchini, squash, and onion not only enhances flavor, but it also removes excess water and allows the pickling liquid to soak into the veggies.

YIELD: 1 QT.   TOTAL: 2 HOURS, 40 MINUTES, PLUS 3 DAYS CHILL TIME

2   medium zucchini (about 12 oz.)
2   medium-size yellow squash (about 12 oz.)
1   red onion, halved and cut into
     ⅛-inch-thick slices
Parchment paper
2½ Tbsp. kosher salt

½   cup apple cider vinegar
½   cup rice vinegar
¾   cup sugar
1   tsp. celery seeds
1   tsp. mustard seeds
¼   tsp. dry mustard

1. Cut zucchini and yellow squash lengthwise into ⅛-inch-thick slices, using a mandoline or sharp knife. Spread zucchini, yellow squash, and onion in a single layer on 2 parchment paper-lined baking sheets. Sprinkle with salt. Let stand 1 hour. Transfer to a colander, rinse, and drain. Place in a wide-mouthed 1-qt. jar, filling to ½ inch from top.

2. Bring vinegars to a boil in a medium saucepan over medium heat. Add sugar; cook, stirring constantly, 3 to 5 minutes or until dissolved. Stir in next 3 ingredients. Bring to a boil, immediately remove from heat, and pour over vegetables. Cool 1 hour. Cover and chill 3 days before serving. Refrigerate up to 2 months.

PEPPERY TEXAS PICKLES *(pictured on page 336)*

Kirby cucumbers, also known as pickling cucumbers, are a great choice for these spicy pickles. You can store these pickles in either the refrigerator or the freezer, keep them to enjoy yourself or share them as gifts during the holidays.

YIELD: 3 QT.   TOTAL: 15 MINUTES, PLUS 2 DAYS CHILL TIME AND 8 HOURS FREEZE TIME

2   lb. pickling cucumbers, sliced
1   cup chopped fresh cilantro
6   small dried red chile peppers
4   garlic cloves, thinly sliced
1   large sweet onion, sliced

3   cups white vinegar (5% acidity)
⅓   cup sugar
2   Tbsp. canning-and-pickling salt
1   Tbsp. pickling spice

1. Place first 5 ingredients in a large plastic bowl (do not use glass).

2. Combine vinegar, 1 cup water, and next 3 ingredients in a 4-cup glass measuring cup. Microwave at HIGH 3 minutes; remove from microwave, and stir until sugar dissolves. Pour hot mixture evenly over cucumber mixture. Cover and chill 48 hours.

3. Spoon evenly into quart canning jars or freezer containers, leaving ½ inch of room at the top; seal, label, and freeze pickles 8 hours or up to 6 months. Thaw in refrigerator before serving; use thawed pickles within 1 week.

SWEET-HOT CUKES & PEPPERS

(pictured on page 337)

English cucumbers offer the same crisp, fresh flavor as regular cucumbers without the seeds. Paired with sweet bell peppers, vibrant red onion, and slightly hot serrano peppers, this combo is great served as a salad or a condiment.

YIELD: 1 QT.   TOTAL: 3 HOURS, 30 MINUTES, INCLUDING CHILL TIME

1½ large English cucumbers, thinly sliced (about 1 lb.)

1 (8-oz.) package mini bell peppers, thinly sliced

½ medium-size red onion, sliced

1 or 2 serrano peppers, seeded and thinly sliced

2 garlic cloves, minced

2 tsp. kosher salt

⅓ cup Champagne vinegar

¼ cup sugar

1 Tbsp. toasted sesame seeds

½ tsp. mustard seeds

¼ tsp. celery seeds

1. Stir together cucumbers, and next 5 ingredients in a large bowl. Stir together vinegar, and remaining 4 ingredients in a small bowl. Let both mixtures stand, stirring occasionally, 1 hour.

2. Drain cucumber mixture. (Do not rinse.) Pour vinegar mixture over cucumber mixture; stir to coat. Chill 2 to 24 hours. Serve with a slotted spoon. Refrigerate up to 2 months.

EASY PICKLED SWEET ONIONS & PEPPERS *(pictured on page 337)*

Serve this simple-to-prepare relish atop chicken, cornbread, or on the side. Sweet onions, such as Vidalia, Texas 1015, or Walla Walla, are all great options and can be found year-round.

YIELD: 1 QT.   TOTAL: 8 HOURS, 20 MINUTES, INCLUDING CHILL TIME

1 (12-oz.) bottle rice vinegar

1 cup apple cider vinegar

½ cup sugar

½ tsp. dried crushed red pepper

2 sweet onions, sliced

6 mini bell peppers, sliced

2 garlic cloves

6 fresh thyme sprigs (optional)

1. Bring rice vinegar, and next 3 ingredients to a boil in a medium saucepan.

2. Toss together onion slices, bell pepper slices, garlic cloves, hot vinegar mixture, and, if desired, thyme sprigs in a large bowl. Let stand 2 hours. Cover and chill 6 hours. Refrigerate in an airtight container up to 1 week.

PICKLED JALAPEÑO SLICES *(pictured)*

Red jalapeño peppers are just green jalapeños that stayed on the vine longer. You can often find them with green jalapeños in the produce department, but feel free to substitute them with other small red peppers if you can't find them.

YIELD: 4 (½-PT.) JARS   TOTAL: 45 MINUTES, PLUS 1 DAY STANDING TIME

¾ lb. green jalapeño peppers	1 tsp. canning-and-pickling salt
¼ lb. red jalapeño peppers	4 large garlic cloves, halved
1½ cups white vinegar (5% acidity)	4 bay leaves

1. Sterilize 4 jars, and prepare lids.

2. While jars are boiling, put on gloves, and cut jalapeño peppers into ¼-inch slices, discarding stem ends. Combine vinegar, salt, and 1½ cups water in a medium stainless steel saucepan; bring to a boil.

3. Place 2 garlic halves and 1 bay leaf in each hot jar. Pack jars tightly with peppers, leaving ½-inch headspace. Cover peppers with hot pickling liquid, leaving ½-inch headspace. Seal and process jars, processing 10 minutes.

4. Remove jars from water, and let stand, undisturbed, at room temperature 24 hours. To check seals, remove the bands, and press down on the center of each lid. If the lid doesn't move, the jar is sealed. If the lid depresses and pops up again, the jar is not sealed. Store properly sealed jars in a cool, dark place up to 1 year. Refrigerate after opening.

CANDIED JALAPEÑOS

This spicy condiment is easy to prepare. Just be sure to chill at least 48 hours ahead of time so the jalapeños have time to take on a fiery-sweet crunch.

YIELD: 1⅓ CUPS   TOTAL: 15 MINUTES, PLUS 2 DAYS CHILL TIME

1 (12-oz.) jar pickled jalapeño pepper slices	¾ cup sugar
4 red chile peppers, sliced	1 tsp. lime zest

Drain pickled jalapeño pepper slices, discarding liquid and reserving jar and lid. Toss together jalapeño slices, red chile pepper slices, sugar, and lime zest. Let stand 5 minutes, stirring occasionally. Spoon into reserved jar, scraping any remaining sugar mixture from bowl into jar. Cover with lid, and chill 48 hours to 1 week, shaking jar several times a day to dissolve any sugar that settles.

PICKLED ASPARAGUS

When spring asparagus is plentiful, pickling is the perfect way to preserve its flavor. Look for thick spears with an even thickness.

YIELD: 3 (1-PT.) WIDE-MOUTHED JARS   **TOTAL: 45 MINUTES, PLUS 1 DAY STANDING TIME**

2½ cups white vinegar (5% acidity)
⅓ cup sugar
¼ cup canning-and-pickling salt
2 tsp. dried crushed red pepper
1 tsp. pickling spice

3¼ lb. fresh asparagus (about 3 large bunches)
6 dill sprigs
3 garlic cloves

1. Sterilize 3 wide-mouthed jars, and prepare lids.

2. While jars are boiling, bring 2 cups water, vinegar, and next 4 ingredients to a boil in a 3-qt. stainless steel saucepan over medium-high heat, stirring until sugar and salt dissolve.

3. Rinse asparagus; snap off and discard tough ends. Trim spears to 4-inch lengths. Place 2 dill sprigs and 1 garlic clove in each hot jar. Tightly pack asparagus, cut ends down, in jars, leaving ½-inch headspace. Cover with hot pickling liquid, leaving ½-inch headspace.

4. Seal and process jars, processing 10 minutes.

5. Remove jars from water, and let stand, undisturbed, at room temperature 24 hours. To check seals, remove the bands, and press down on the center of each lid. If the lid doesn't move, the jar is sealed. If the lid depresses and pops up again, the jar is not sealed. Store properly sealed jars in a cool, dark place up to 1 year. Refrigerate after opening.

SQUASH PICKLE MEDLEY

These impressive pickles are delicious served alongside your favorite barbecue as a condiment or on their own.

YIELD: 4 (1-PT.) WIDE-MOUTHED JARS
TOTAL: 4 HOURS, 10 MINUTES, PLUS 1 DAY STANDING TIME

4 large zucchini (2½ lb.)	Ice cubes
4 large yellow squash (1¼ lb.)	2 cups white vinegar (5% acidity)
1 (8-oz.) onion, halved vertically and cut crosswise into ¼-inch slices (curved strips)	2 cups sugar
	1 tsp. mustard seeds
	½ tsp. celery seeds
⅓ cup canning-and-pickling salt	¼ tsp. ground turmeric

1. Wash zucchini and yellow squash, and trim stem and blossom ends; cut squash crosswise into ¼-inch slices. Toss zucchini, yellow squash, and onion with salt in a very large bowl. Cover vegetables with ice cubes. Cover and let stand at room temperature 3 hours.

2. Sterilize 4 wide-mouthed jars, and prepare lids.

3. While jars are boiling, drain vegetables but do not rinse, discarding brine and any unmelted ice. Return drained vegetables to bowl. Combine vinegar and next 4 ingredients in a medium stainless steel saucepan. Bring to a boil over medium-high heat.

4. Pack squash and onion mixture tightly into hot jars, leaving ½-inch headspace. Cover vegetables with hot pickling liquid, leaving ½-inch headspace. Seal and process jars, processing 10 minutes.

5. Remove jars from water, and let stand, undisturbed, at room temperature 24 hours. To check seals, remove the bands, and press down on the center of each lid. If the lid doesn't move, the jar is sealed. If the lid depresses and pops up again, the jar is not sealed. Store properly sealed jars in a cool, dark place up to 1 year. Refrigerate after opening.

PICKLED OKRA

When selecting okra for pickling, look for smaller pods, which tend to be the most tender.

YIELD: 5 (1-PT.) WIDE-MOUTHED JARS **TOTAL: 50 MINUTES, PLUS 1 DAY STANDING TIME**

3 lb. (2½- to 3-inch) fresh okra
3 cups white vinegar (5% acidity)
⅓ cup canning-and-pickling salt
2 tsp. dill seeds

5 garlic cloves, peeled
3 small fresh hot red peppers, halved (optional)

1. Sterilize 5 wide-mouthed jars, and prepare lids.

2. While jars are boiling, wash okra and trim stems, leaving caps intact. Combine vinegar, salt, dill seeds, and 3 cups water in large stainless steel saucepan. Bring to a boil.

3. Place 1 garlic clove and, if desired, 1 hot pepper half in each hot jar. Pack okra pods tightly in jars, placing some stem end down and some stem end up and leaving ½-inch headspace. Cover okra with hot pickling liquid, leaving ½-inch headspace.

4. Seal and process jars, processing 10 minutes.

5. Remove jars from water, and let stand, undisturbed, at room temperature 24 hours. To check seals, remove the bands, and press down on the center of each lid. If the lid doesn't move, the jar is sealed. If the lid depresses and pops up again, the jar is not sealed. Store properly sealed jars in a cool, dark place up to 1 year. Refrigerate after opening.

BREAD-&-BUTTER PICKLES

Don't skip the step of scrubbing the wax off commercial cucumbers. You can avoid the wax altogether by buying organic cucumbers or those from a local farmers' market.

YIELD: 7 (1-PT.) JARS   TOTAL: 4 HOURS, 10 MINUTES, PLUS 1 DAY STANDING TIME

4¾ lb. medium cucumbers
4   large onions
1   large green bell pepper, chopped
¼   cup canning-and-pickling salt
2½ cups white vinegar (5% acidity)

2   cups sugar
2   Tbsp. mustard seeds
¾   tsp. ground turmeric
5   whole cloves

1. Scrub cucumbers thoroughly to remove any wax; trim stem and blossom ends, and cut cucumbers crosswise into ¼-inch-thick slices. Cut onions in half, and slice crosswise into ⅛-inch-thick slices. Place cucumber, onion, and bell pepper in a bowl; toss with salt. Cover and let stand 3 hours at room temperature; drain.

2. Sterilize 7 jars, and prepare lids. While jars are boiling, bring vinegar and next 4 ingredients to a boil in an 8-qt. stainless steel or enameled stockpot, stirring just until sugar dissolves. Add drained cucumber mixture, and cook, stirring often, 7 to 10 minutes or until mixture is thoroughly heated and cucumber peels turn dark green.

3. Pack vegetables into hot jars. Cover vegetables with hot pickling liquid, leaving ½-inch headspace. Seal and process jars, processing 10 minutes.

4. Remove jars from water, and let stand, undisturbed, at room temperature 24 hours. To check seals, remove the bands, and press down on the center of each lid. If the lid doesn't move, the jar is sealed. If the lid depresses and pops up again, the jar is not sealed. Store properly sealed jars in a cool, dark place up to 1 year. Refrigerate after opening.

QUICK CONFETTI PICKLES

Find gorgeous jewel-toned radishes at your grocery store during their peak season, April through September. Their peppery flavor is a great complement to the sweet pickling spice blend.

YIELD: 2 (1-PT.) JARS   TOTAL: 1 HOUR, PLUS 1 DAY CHILL TIME

1	English cucumber
1	medium-size yellow squash
4	Tbsp. canning-and-pickling salt, divided
1	medium carrot
2	pink, purple, or red icicle radishes or 10 standard-size radishes
4	dill sprigs
1	cup apple cider vinegar
1/4	cup sugar
2	Tbsp. fresh lemon juice
1	tsp. dill seeds

1. Wash vegetables. Score cucumber and squash lengthwise with a fork, leaving furrows in the peel on all sides. (This makes scalloped edges when vegetables are sliced.) Trim stem and blossom ends of cucumber and squash; cut into 1/8-inch slices. Place in a colander in sink; sprinkle with 2 Tbsp. salt, and toss gently. Let drain 30 minutes.

2. Meanwhile, peel carrot, and cut carrot and radishes into 1/8-inch-thick slices. Toss with drained cucumber and squash.

3. Place 2 dill sprigs in each of 2 sterilized jars or nonreactive containers with lids. Pack vegetables in jars, leaving 1/2-inch headspace.

4. Bring vinegar, next 3 ingredients, remaining 2 Tbsp. salt, and 2 cups water to a boil in a 1 1/2-qt. stainless steel saucepan over medium-high heat, stirring until sugar and salt dissolve. Pour hot vinegar mixture over vegetables to cover. Apply lids. Chill 24 hours before serving. Store in refrigerator up to 3 weeks.

CHOWCHOW

Enjoy this traditional relish any time of year by canning it. For an even more vibrant condiment, use red cabbage.

YIELD: 5 (1-PT.) WIDE-MOUTHED JARS TOTAL: 1 HOUR, PLUS 1 DAY STANDING TIME

5   green bell peppers, chopped
5   red bell peppers, chopped
2   large green tomatoes, chopped
2   large onions, chopped
½   small cabbage, chopped
¼   cup canning-and-pickling salt

3   cups sugar
2   cups white vinegar (5% acidity)
1   Tbsp. mustard seeds
1½ tsp. celery seeds
¾   tsp. turmeric

1. Stir together first 5 ingredients and salt in a large Dutch oven. Cover and chill 8 hours. Rinse and drain; return mixture to Dutch oven. Stir in sugar and remaining ingredients. Bring to a boil; reduce heat, and simmer 3 minutes.

2. Sterilize 5 jars, and prepare lids. Ladle hot mixture evenly into each hot sterilized jar, leaving ½-inch headspace. Seal and process jars, processing 10 minutes.

3. Remove jars from water, and let stand, undisturbed, at room temperature 24 hours. To check seals, remove the bands, and press down on the center of each lid. If the lid doesn't move, the jar is sealed. If the lid depresses and pops up again, the jar is not sealed. Store properly sealed jars in a cool, dark place up to 1 year. Refrigerate after opening.

GREEN TOMATO CHOWCHOW

A meat grinder makes easy work of processing the tomatoes in this recipe. You can find relatively inexpensive handheld models and even meat grinder attachments for your stand mixer.

YIELD: 4 (1-PT.) WIDE-MOUTHED JARS   **TOTAL: 1 HOUR, PLUS OVERNIGHT STANDING TIME**

4	qt. (about 24 large) sliced green tomatoes
½	cup table salt
1	large head cabbage, cored and shredded
1	lb. red bell peppers, seeded and finely chopped
1	lb. onions, finely chopped
1	hot red pepper, finely chopped

1	cup firmly packed brown sugar
2	Tbsp. mustard seeds
1	Tbsp. celery seeds
1	Tbsp. whole cloves
1	Tbsp. ground allspice
2	tsp. dry mustard
3	pt. white vinegar (5% acidity)

1. Combine tomatoes and salt in a large glass, ceramic, or stainless steel container. Cover and let stand overnight; drain. Rinse and drain in 2 baths of cold water. Soak tomatoes in cold water to cover 30 minutes; drain.

2. Sterilize 4 wide-mouthed jars, and prepare lids.

3. While jars are boiling, grind tomatoes into a stainless steel stockpot, using coarse blade of a meat grinder, or food processor. Stir in remaining ingredients, and cook, uncovered, over medium-high heat 1 hour, stirring occasionally to prevent sticking.

4. Quickly ladle chowchow into hot jars, leaving ½-inch headspace. Seal and process jars, processing 10 minutes.

5. Remove jars from water, and let stand, undisturbed, at room temperature 24 hours. To check seals, remove the bands, and press down on the center of each lid. If the lid doesn't move, the jar is sealed. If the lid depresses and pops up again, the jar is not sealed. Store properly sealed jars in a cool, dark place up to 1 year. Refrigerate after opening.

GRILLED SWEET ONION-&-MANGO CHUTNEY

This smoky and sweet chutney is the perfect topping for pork or chicken. You can make it ahead and store in the refrigerator for up to one week.

YIELD: 6 TO 8 SERVINGS   TOTAL: 50 MINUTES

2   large sweet onions, cut into ½-inch slices
2   mangoes, peeled and cut into ½-inch slices
2   Tbsp. olive oil
½   cup white wine vinegar
⅓   cup firmly packed light brown sugar

2   Tbsp. minced fresh ginger
1   tsp. lime zest
½   tsp. table salt
1   jalapeño pepper, seeded and minced
⅓   cup chopped fresh cilantro
2   Tbsp. fresh lime juice

1. Preheat grill to 300° to 350° (medium) heat. Brush both sides of onions and mangoes with olive oil. Grill onions, covered with grill lid, 5 to 6 minutes on each side until softened and grill marks appear. At the same time, grill mangoes 2 to 3 minutes on each side or until softened and grill marks appear. Remove from grill; cover and let stand 15 minutes.

2. Meanwhile, bring vinegar and next 4 ingredients to a boil in a small saucepan over medium-high heat. Reduce heat to low, and simmer 5 minutes. Add jalapeño, and simmer 5 minutes. Remove from heat; transfer to a bowl.

3. Chop onion and mangoes, and stir into vinegar mixture. Stir in cilantro and lime juice. Serve chutney warm or at room temperature.

METRIC EQUIVALENTS

The information in the following charts is provided to help cooks outside the United States successfully use the recipes in this book. All equivalents are approximate.

EQUIVALENTS FOR DIFFERENT TYPES OF INGREDIENTS

Standard Cup	Fine Powder (ex. flour)	Grain (ex. rice)	Granular (ex. sugar)	Liquid Solids (ex. butter)	Liquid (ex. milk)
1	140 g	150 g	190 g	200 g	240 ml
¾	105 g	113 g	143 g	150 g	180 ml
⅔	93 g	100 g	125 g	133 g	160 ml
½	70 g	75 g	95 g	100 g	120 ml
⅓	47 g	50 g	63 g	67 g	80 ml
¼	35 g	38 g	48 g	50 g	60 ml
⅛	18 g	19 g	24 g	25 g	30 ml

DRY INGREDIENTS BY WEIGHT

(To convert ounces to grams, multiply the number of ounces by 30.)

1 oz	=	¹⁄₁₆ lb	=	30 g
4 oz	=	¼ lb	=	120 g
8 oz	=	½ lb	=	240 g
12 oz	=	¾ lb	=	360 g
16 oz	=	1 lb	=	480 g

LENGTH

(To convert inches to centimeters, multiply the number of inches by 2.5.)

1 in	=	2.5 cm				
6 in	=	½ ft	=	15 cm		
12 in	=	1 ft	=	30 cm		
36 in	=	3 ft	=	1 yd	=	90 cm
40 in	=	100 cm	=	1 m		

LIQUID INGREDIENTS BY VOLUME

¼ tsp	=						1 ml
½ tsp	=						2 ml
1 tsp	=						5 ml
3 tsp	=	1 Tbsp	=		½ fl oz	=	15 ml
		2 Tbsp	=	⅛ cup	1 fl oz	=	30 ml
		4 Tbsp	=	¼ cup	2 fl oz	=	60 ml
		5⅓ Tbsp	=	⅓ cup	3 fl oz	=	80 ml
		8 Tbsp	=	½ cup	4 fl oz	=	120 ml
		10⅔ Tbsp	=	⅔ cup	5 fl oz	=	160 ml
		12 Tbsp	=	¾ cup	6 fl oz	=	180 ml
		16 Tbsp	=	1 cup	8 fl oz	=	240 ml
		1 pt	=	2 cups	16 fl oz	=	480 ml
		1 qt	=	4 cups	32 fl oz	=	960 ml
					33 fl oz	=	1000 ml = 1 l

COOKING/OVEN TEMPERATURES

	Fahrenheit	Celsius	Gas Mark
Freeze Water	32° F	0° C	
Room Temperature	68° F	20° C	
Boil Water	212° F	100° C	
Bake	325° F	160° C	3
	350° F	180° C	4
	375° F	190° C	5
	400° F	200° C	6
	425° F	220° C	7
	450° F	230° C	8
Broil			Grill

INDEX

SUBJECT INDEX

ISBN-13: 978-0-8487-4480-9
ISBN-10: 0-8487-4480-2
Library of Congress Control Number: 2015930570

Printed in the United States of America
First Printing 2015

OXMOOR HOUSE

Creative Director: Felicity Keane
Art Director: Christopher Rhoads
Executive Photography Director: Iain Bagwell
Executive Food Director: Grace Parisi
Managing Editor: Elizabeth Tyler Austin
Assistant Managing Editor: Jeanne de Lathouder

ULTIMATE BOOK OF BBQ

Editor: Sarah A. Gleim
Editorial Assistant: April Smitherman
Senior Designer: Melissa Clark
Assistant Test Kitchen Manager: Alyson Moreland Haynes
Recipe Developers and Testers: Stefanie Maloney, Callie Nash, Karen Rankin
Food Stylists: Nathan Carrabba, Victoria E. Cox, Margaret Monroe Dickey,
    Catherine Crowell Steele
Photo Editor: Kellie Lindsey
Senior Photographer: Hélène Dujardin
Senior Photo Stylists: Kay E. Clarke, Mindi Shapiro Levine
Senior Production Managers: Greg A. Amason, Sue Chodakiewicz

CONTRIBUTORS

Pitmaster: Christopher Prieto
Writer: Ashley Strickland Freeman
Executive Editor: Katherine Cobbs
Assistant Project Editor: Melissa Brown
Compositors: AnnaMaria Jacob, Anna Ramia
Recipe Developers and Testers: Ashley Strickland Freeman; Tamara Goldis, R.D.;
    Christopher Prieto; Leah Van Deren
Recipe Editor: Julie Christopher
Copy Editors: Donna Baldone, Julie Bosche
Proofreader: Rebecca Henderson
Indexer: Mary Ann Laurens
Fellows: Laura Arnold, Kylie Dazzo, Nicole Fisher, Loren Lorenzo,
    Caroline Smith
Food Stylists: Ana Price Kelly, Katelyn Hardwick
Photographer: Greg DuPree
Photo Stylists: Mary Clayton Carl, Lydia DeGaris-Pursell, Katelyn Hardwick,
    Amanda Widis

TIME HOME ENTERTAINMENT INC.

Publisher: Margot Schupf
Vice President, Finance: Vandana Patel
Executive Director, Marketing Services: Carol Pittard
Publishing Director: Megan Pearlman
Assistant General Counsel: Simone Procas